CANADIAN ETHNOGRAPHY SERIES VOLUME 1

"Only God Can Own the Land"

THE ATTAWAPISKAT CREE

Series Editors:
Bryan D. Cummins
MCMASTER UNIVERSITY

John L. Steckley
HUMBER COLLEGE

BRYAN D. CUMMINS

PEARSON
Prentice
Hall

Toronto

National Library of Canada Cataloguing in Publication

Cummins, Bryan David, 1953–
    "Only God can own the land" : the Attawapiskat Cree / Bryan D. Cummins ;
edited by John L. Steckley.

(Canadian ethnography series : v. 1)
Includes bibliographical references and index.
ISBN 0-13-177065-9

1. Cree Indians—Land tenure—Ontario—Attawapiskat Region. 2. Cree Indians—Ontario—
Attawapiskat Region—Government relations. 3. Land use—Ontario—Attawapiskat Region.
I. Steckley, John, 1949– II. Title. III. Series.

E99.C88C85 2004   333.2'089'973   C2003-901699-4

ISBN 0-13-177065-9

Vice President, Editorial Director: Michael J. Young
Executive Acquisitions Editor: Jessica Mosher
Senior Marketing Manager: Judith Allen
Associate Editor: Patti Altridge
Production Editor: Cheryl Jackson/Martin Tooke
Copy Editor: Judy Eaton
Proofreader: Susan Adlam
Production Coordinator: Trish Ciardullo
Page Layout: Heidi Palfrey
Cover and Interior Design: Gillian Tsintziras
Cover Image: Digital Vision/Photodisc

1 2 3 4 5   08 07 06 05 04

Printed and bound in Canada.

To the late Ed Rogers, who was a major influence on my development as an anthropologist. I hope he would have liked *"Only God Can Own the Land."*

Contents

Preface

CANADIAN ETHNOGRAPHY SERIES

The Canadian Ethnography Series is intended to familiarize undergraduate students with the background and recent history of some of the diverse cultures that make up this country. While the series has as its primary audience students taking courses in anthropology, the monographs will be useful to students of Canadian studies, indigenous studies, sociology and history.

The series of monographs will examine the distinct histories and contemporary experiences of some of the diverse cultures that make up Canada. The ethnographies will look at a variety of themes, such as indigenous rights, multiculturalism and socioeconomic development. While some of the topics may resemble those covered by sociologists or historians, each book in our series will provide a firsthand, detailed description of a particular Canadian culture based on personal experience. It is our belief that good case studies are critical for a better understanding.

Through ethnographies, students get to know a people in greater depth. In order to enhance this experience, the ethnographies in our series will be supported with the use of some pedagogical features. Each book in the series will be short, averaging no more than 200 pages in length, and will include learning objectives, key terms with glossary and content questions. The series is intended to be accessible to today's post-secondary students.

Acknowledgments

Funding for this research was generously provided by The Presidents' Committee on Northern Studies (PCONS), Research Program for Technology Assessment in Subarctic Ontario (TASO), The School of Graduate Studies (McMaster University), The Phillips Fund for Native American Studies (The American Philosophical Society) and The Professional Development Fund of the Canadian Union of Public Employees (CUPE). The assistance was greatly appreciated.

Thanks to Drs. Richard Preston, David Damas, and Trudy Nicks for their guidance and suggestions.

Reg Louttit and Joseph Louttit were wonderfully supportive and helpful during my stay in Attawapiskat. This work could never have been completed without them.

Thank you to Daisy Njoku of the National Anthropological Archives (Smithsonian) for all her help.

Thanks to all the people of the Attawapiskat First Nation. May they prosper.

A special thank you to Trent University's Anthropology 100 class, Durham campus, Summer 2002 for their suggestions.

I am grateful to John Steckley for his comments and suggestions.

My appreciation to the editorial staff at Pearson Education for all their hard work.

Joanne Briggs drew the map of the Mushkegowuk region. I thank her.

Finally, a very special thank-you to Tricia for all her support.

Bryan D. Cummins, 2003

chapter one

Introduction

LEARNING OBJECTIVES

After reading this chapter, students should be able to:

1. Distinguish between land use and land tenure.

2. Outline various means through which encapsulation can be resisted.

3. Distinguish between encapsulation and assimilation.

4. State the fundamental hypothesis of this work (i.e., what viewpoint is being challenged?)

5. Outline the methodologies employed by the researcher.

The land is of fundamental importance to the First Nations of Canada. Nowhere is this more true than among the First Nations that are found throughout the northern reaches of the country. While decades of government policies have tried to impose **assimilation** on First Nations peoples, their relationships to the land have remained steadfast.

Without a doubt, **land use** and **land tenure** among the Attawapiskat Cree have changed in the last century. However, this is not to deny that there have been continuities as well. In order to understand the changes and continuities, it is essential to examine the role of the State as well as other non-Native incursions into Cree life. For example, what effect did Treaty 9 and the implementation of the **registered trapline system** have on traditional notions of tenure? Did hunting for trade take priority over hunting for subsistence? What changes have there been in the makeup of hunting groups and/or hunting partnerships?

This study challenges a belief that has been held both by some anthropologists (Turner and Wertman, 1977; Trudeau, 1966; Liebow and Trudeau, 1962; Rogers, 1972) and indeed some members of Attawapiskat itself, that Cree land use is non-existent or in an irreversible decline. The study examines land use activities and changing patterns of tenure in the context of Euro-Canadian encroachment. The analysis is both quantitative and qualitative. Harvest figures over the ninety-year span are analyzed as well as the nature of the relationships between the Cree and Euro-Canadians, especially those with the State.

LAND USE AND LAND TENURE

We must distinguish between *land use* and *land tenure*. Crocombe (in Lundsgaard, 1974:1) helps make this distinction. He notes first that "land" refers to space on, above and below the surface of the earth. "Rights to the land," that is, rights to land use, apply to things growing in, living on, attached to or contained in the land or water. He notes further that land use is the physical exploitation of land by humans, and that land use is conditioned by land tenure. "Land tenure" is used to refer to social, political and exploitative patterns of behaviour exhibited by a person or group of people with regard to land. Land use and land tenure are closely intertwined, for the latter is a system of behavioural patterns that serves to control a society's use of environmental resources, that is, a society's "land use." Land tenure, then, is best seen as a "system of interpersonal and intergroup relations through which [people's] relationship with part of [their] environment is mediated" (Lundsgaard, 1974:15).

ENCAPSULATION AND RESISTANCE

Framing the research is the notion of **encapsulation**. Bailey (1969:147–149) defines the notion of encapsulation as the process through which the dominant or encapsulating society or culture, through greater political resources, larger size and more specialized political roles, subsumes the subordinate group or society. In addition, there is an essential difference between the groups in values and ideas about human nature and the natural condition of human communities and the relation between humans and nature. These centre upon such notions as accumulation of wealth, personal prestige and honour, the common good and control of nature. These are, then, essential differences in world view.

Bailey's (1969) basic argument is that politics is essentially played out like a game and, as such, has rules. These rules determine who can (and will) play, and which moves are legitimate and which are not. In the case of indigenous peoples, however, the encapsulator has predetermined the game and the rules. Thus, much everyday political activity involves manipulating the rules of a given system to obtain whatever rewards are to be had. In Canada, a classic example of how the rules may be manipulated can be found in Aboriginal hunting rights. Although the right to hunt geese is included in the treaties, this right may be denied because of the law under the Migratory Birds Convention Act (MBCA). Natives, of course, recognize their right to hunt geese because of treaty provisions. The government, however, states that in the case of disputes federal legislation overrides any treaty right. Hence, the government contends that the MBCA takes precedence over treaty rights. How strongly this will be enforced is at the discretion of the government, which leaves open the opportunity for manipulating the rules.

Bailey (1969:149–151) sees a number of forms that encapsulation may take: 1) nominal, in which the dominant society cannot, or chooses not to, interfere with the subordinate society; 2) the predatory stance, in which the dominant society does not interfere with the subordinate society as long as tribute is paid; 3) integration, which Bailey defines as radical change, if not abolition. To this we may add 4) abolition as an alternative unto itself, independent of integration; and 5) indirect rule, in which the dominant society does not interfere with the subordinate society as long as the latter adheres to the former's normative pattern (Rodman, 1987:unpublished ms). Within the Canadian context, most of these approaches have been used in various places at different times.

A number of criteria determine the nature of encapsulation. These include resources, economic interest in the subordinate society, tolerance of the subordinate's cultural practices and distance from the encapsulator's core. These need to be borne in mind as we examine Attawapiskat land use and tenure.

There exist three basic responses to encapsulation (or *intended* encapsulation): acquiescence, **resistance** and compromise (Rodman, 1987: unpublished ms). Canadian First Nations have, at various times, attempted all of these responses. Today, though, there is a hybrid response: resistance through negotiated compromise, with the aim being self-government. Self-government, by virtue of its goal of disengagement, implies resistance, but its strategies are consistent with the larger political system of Euro-Canadian society.

Comaroff (1985) has examined patterns of resistance among the Tshidi—an African people—to European domination. She notes that frequently among the powerless, "the attempt to reassert control, to return to the world some form of coherence and tractability, continues" (1985:260). But it is misleading to seek such resistance solely in large-scale movements. As she observes, "if we confine our historical scrutiny to...revolution successfully achieved, we discount the vast proportion of human social action which is played out, perforce, on more humble scale" (1985:261). The point, then, is that we must also look for the subtle, the tactful, the diplomatic and the apparently apolitical for evidence of resistance. In addition, resistance can be evidenced in both continuity and change when those continuities and/or changes are in opposition to the dictates of the dominant society. In the Attawapiskat case, this contention is demonstrated repeatedly.

In a similar vein, Scott (1985) notes what he labels "everyday forms of resistance": foot dragging, dissimulation, false compliance and feigned ignorance. These are actions that may do little to alter a subjugated situation in the short run, but may be more effective than overt rebellion in undercutting repression over time. Thus, when the encapsulator and encapsulated manipulate the rules of the game, each is attempting to make a statement about the past, present and future. They are, according to Scott, offering "a critique of things as they are as well as a vision of things as they should be...[they are writing] a kind of social text..." (1985:23).

Azarya and Chazan (1987) state that one form of resistance open to the encapsulated is **self-enclosure**, which entails a reduced use of state channels, but does not involve deviance from state regulations. Examples of this include moving from urban to rural habitation, producing for subsistence rather than for trade or export and renouncing positions

. high visibility that may increase one's exposure to state pressures. Further, self-enclosure may involve "a retreat to traditional forms or to narrower bases of solidarity" (1987:126), for example, those that are regional or ethnic. These traditional structures are protected bases to which one returns when "more autarchic and familiar settings are sought against uncontrollable fluctuations in employment, cost of living, or arbitrary political rule" (1987:127). Examples of these are found repeatedly in Attawapiskat history since the turn of the century: deliberate returns to their own workable systems of land tenure, a return to hunting for food over hunting for trade and, in the modern era, adoption of a locally controlled school and locally maintained police force. In the 1980s, a regional council and regional harvesters association were created.

The State has pursued (consciously or not) the encapsulation of Native people in ' Canada through such measures as the Indian Act, the various treaties, a complex bureaucracy and various and sundry forms of legislation. The degree of encapsulation is reflected in the fact that there are fourteen federal ministries or departments alone dealing with Native people, in addition to (in some instances) provincial ministries and departments. This reflects Bailey's (1969) contention that encapsulation is a function of greater political/legal complexity of the encapsulator. The Attawapiskat First Nation also comes under the conditions of Treaty 9 (1905 and 1929), which further subjects them to Euro-Canadian control. And, as is well known, the conditions under which treaties were signed, and the obligations and responsibilities contained therein, are under considerable debate.

It is important to distinguish between *encapsulation* and *assimilation*. In assimilation the emphasis is on the cultural. In areas where there is cultural diversity, but with one group predominating, there will be pressure for the subordinate groups to alter their basic culture and assume a broad-based, homogeneous cultural solidarity: that is, the culture held by the dominant group. Assimilation may be a voluntary step, or it may be achieved through coercion. Encapsulation differs from assimilation in its emphases and goals. We might safely argue that a subordinate society never seeks encapsulation. Encapsulation implies loss of sovereignty, loss of power and often loss of economic self-sufficiency. The encapsulator cares less about cultural retention than it does about restricting the economic and political strength of the subordinate society. Encapsulation, then, implies wresting economic and political strength from the subordinate society. Assimilation does not necessarily have these objectives. Indeed, one might assimilate and thrive in the dominant society. If one is a member of the encapsulated society, these aspirations are greatly curtailed. Encapsulation, then, is ultimately *control.*

In this study, in addition to legal/political institutions (i.e., the "State" proper), I consider other forms of Euro-Canadian incursions such as the church(es) and the fur trading companies, principally the Hudson's Bay Company (HBC) and Revillon Freres. Insofar as these represent the interests of Euro-Canadians, they will be examined and analyzed as encapsulating factors. They both served to considerably alter the traditional culture of Native people in James Bay. It should also be noted that the fur trading companies linked the Cree with the world economic systems, in that the HBC was a company controlled from Britain and subject to fluctuating fur prices abroad. The effects of these ultimately trickled down to the Cree trapper in James Bay.

I am not going to argue, *a priori*, that such intrusions denied the Attawapiskat people their culture, or are inherently detrimental. Rather, I am contending that over time the various Euro-Canadian forms of incursion served to initiate a process of encapsulation upon the Attawapiskat First Nation. However, I am also suggesting that one cannot assume that this process is a *fait accompli*. The data reveal that while the process of encapsulation was underway, there was, as well, a concomitant Native effort at retaining their culture. Thus, while one might argue that Treaty 9, the Indian Act and other forms of legislation have politically and legally subjugated the Cree, the people have not acquiesced. In many fundamental ways they have retained their culture. In addition, there has been a simultaneous process of *resistance*, as evidenced by protests against restrictions on the goose hunt and fights over reserve land. Thus, it might be suggested that while the Attawapiskat Cree are linked to the State, they have not been totally dominated by it. As will be shown, these twin processes of encapsulation and resistance have resulted in new initiatives and patterns of land use and tenure on the part of the Attawapiskat Cree.

NATIVE AND NON-NATIVE PERCEPTIONS OF LAND USE IN THE SUBARCTIC

During my initial stay in Attawapiskat in 1988 it was suggested to me by a number of people that 10 per cent or less of the population was involved in any land use activities. This raised a number of immediate questions. Is this contention true? If so, why has land use dropped so dramatically? If it is not true, why do local people have this *perception*? What factors have shaped their view of themselves? These concerns remained with me as I conducted fieldwork.

The study challenges an intuitive understanding held by many non-Natives and Natives that land use activities are declining or have declined as Euro-Canadians move into the north. Among anthropologists, there is no consensus regarding the prevalence and future of subarctic land use. Rogers (1972:133) wrote that

> The environmental changes that have transpired have not been as forceful in altering the Mistassini's way of life as contact with Euro-Canadians. At first it was the fur trade, then the missionary, and, finally, the tourist and industrial personnel. During the present century, this contact with outsiders has increased tremendously, and soon the way of life of the Mistassini will be *totally* altered, becoming much closer to that of the West (emphasis added).

Presumably, this "total" alteration includes a decline in hunting, fishing and trapping. Henriksen (1973:115) acknowledges the incursion of Whites into Labrador but also recognizes the potential for Naskapi (Innu) co-existence with Euro-Canadians, with the former remaining on the land. He stresses the importance of protecting these cultures from disintegration and of helping them find an effective bargaining position with the outside world. His statements are forceful. He states that it is "our duty" to help other cultures "resist" the intrusion of our culture. The Innu would be able to exist without "relief" if they were given a little more assistance in the utilization of the resources of the Davis Inlet area.

In western Hudson Bay, Trudeau (1966) and Liebow and Trudeau (1962) considered the effects of non-Native incursion on the Winisk Cree. By 1955, Trudeau argues, the Winisk Cree had gone "[f]rom a trapping and hunting economy...to a wage-earning economy, and...year round residence at the post" (1966:ii). Liebow and Trudeau observed that people stated that they "lived better," "dressed better" and "nobody starved to death anymore" (1962:202). Perhaps most interesting is the observation that almost all men chose wage labour over trapping when confronted with an actual choice. This was in spite of contentions that neither activity was more desirable than the other. The reasons for ultimately choosing wage labour, they conclude, lie in the fact that wage labour provided security, and whether working or not, one could get emergency rations from the government, missionary, HBC or other Cree (1962:204). They further note that hunting for fresh food was perhaps the most important single activity displaced by wage labour (1962:201).

Brody (1983) most eloquently discusses the "sentence of death" he sees as having been imposed on hunting societies by "an accumulation of judgments" made by White society (1983:xi). In spite of this decree, he ponders how these same hunting cultures have "somehow repeatedly escaped their execution" (1983:xii). In his analysis of the Native economy (1983:190–215), Brody details the extensive use made of the land by the Beaver (a Dene people), and how this economy is "a hidden one." Most significant, however, is that in contrast to Attawapiskat seven years later, there was a declaration among the Beaver that "virtually everyone is a hunter and trapper" (1983:209). People wanted to believe that hunting was alive.

Elsewhere in the Western Subarctic, Asch (in Watkins, 1977:47–61) attests that despite conscious and unconscious efforts to pressure the Dene to abandon their traditional culture, it has not only survived, but "traditional economic, social, and political institutions and values persist, and in some cases flourish" (1977:60). Rushforth (in Watkins, 1977:39), in a brief but detailed analysis, finds that there has been neither a decrease nor an increase over the years in the numbers of Bear Lake Dene involved in land use activities. Like researchers such as Turner and Wertman (1977), he notes a restructuring of partnerships and scheduling (e.g., short hunting/trapping trips from the village as opposed to "wintering over"). In addition, he notes that in 1974/1975, 27 to 42 per cent of their food needs were met through traditional subsistence activities (1977:43).

In terms of perception of land use, there is an interesting comparison between the Bear Lake Dene and the Attawapiskat Cree. Rushforth (1977:44) notes that, despite permanent residence in Fort Franklin since the 1950s and the concomitant exposure to White culture, the Dene have retained much of their traditional culture and most of their traditional values. Part of this is due to the recognition of the value of a bush oriented life and the foods and materials it provides. This contrasts with Attawapiskat, where such recognition is not widespread. The findings of Asch and Rushforth are largely consistent with those of the Berger inquiry. Berger (1977:43) outlines in detail the production of fur and game for the Mackenzie valley populations and the need to retain a hunting culture, as well as noting the difficulties quantifying this production.

Turner and Wertman (1977) do not foresee the continuation of a bush oriented economy in Shamattawa. They note how "a return to pre-contact conditions or even the conditions of the fur trade traditional period is neither possible nor desired by the Shamattawa Cree" (1977:40). They conclude that "[t]he young must become more or less resigned to participation in the wider economic system *strictly in Euro-Canadian terms* unless they want a meaningless existence as wards of the state" (1977:95, emphasis added). Turner and Wertman note, however, that while there is widespread opposition to this both at Shamattawa and elsewhere, the impersonal welfare system and other forms of government control have wrested away any face-to-face contact and hence, interaction and grounds for compromise.

This study may be viewed, then, as a testing of the intuitive assumption (on some parts) of the demise of hunting economies. It examines in detail one community and its exploitation of its traditional lands. It is thus a retesting of the conclusions of Brody, Turner and Wertman, Asch, Rushforth, Rogers and Henricksen.

RESEARCH METHODOLOGIES

My research strategies for the study combined the methodologies of the ethnohistorian and the ethnographer. In order to document land use historically, I conducted archival and literature searches. In the field, I utilized interviews, participant observation and, to a limited extent, questionnaires. These methods were instrumental in determining both the extent and nature of land use today as well as changing forms and perceptions of land tenure.

Before departing for the field and archives, I engaged in a considerable amount of reading pertaining to the research topic. Broadly speaking, the literature consisted of three categories of reference: land use and tenure of contemporary hunters and gatherers in general, land use and tenure of Subarctic Canadian hunters, and that literature pertaining specifically to Attawapiskat.

Archival material was chiefly maintained by three institutions: Indian and Northern Affairs Canada (INAC, formerly Department of Indian and Northern Affairs), the Hudson's Bay Company, and the Ministry of Natural Resources. Lesser amounts of material were found at the Ontario Native Affairs Directorate.

I made an initial trip to Attawapiskat in the fall of 1988, funded by the Presidents Committee on Northern Studies, before the fieldwork was undertaken. My actual fieldwork took place between January and May of 1990. Thus, I was not unfamiliar with the community when fieldwork began. The literature review was also invaluable to me insofar as it placed the community in both ethnographic and historical context.

Participant observation is the *sine qua non* of ethnography. During the period of fieldwork, I lived with a very capable research assistant and interpreter who happened to be the son of the chief. I was able to engage in a certain amount of informal participant observation simply due to the fact that I lived with a local person, as opposed to residing in one of the teachers' residences or other government building. The everyday realities of cutting and hauling firewood, fetching water, listening to conversations in Cree and witnessing the skinning of animals were instructive. Among these and other activities, I participated in ice fishing, the spring goose hunt, public meetings (regarding local takeover of education as well as the James Bay Trappers Council) and the winter carnival events. These were all undertaken in the company of local people familiar with the activities and eager to share them with me. These experiences were educational in ways that significantly transcend interviews or library research. Furthermore, they provided a basis for elaboration of certain principles and normative patterns of Cree life.

The goose hunt was an especially valuable experience. I made a number of trips with two different people who were eager to share with me, and teach me about, the science of the goose hunt. The goose hunt, I came to learn, is far more than simply the shooting of game or the semi-annual revival of a centuries old tradition. It could only be in the context of experiencing the hunt that I could come to appreciate the importance of this and other events.

It has almost become an unwritten rule that ethnographers recount in print some pivotal or defining moment in their fieldwork. Sometimes, these are moments of profound insight. More often, they are incidents of crisis that reflect the ineptitude or naivete of the ethnographer. In my case, it is the latter. I was not unfamiliar with the north, as I had grown up in northern Quebec. As well, I had spent a year on reserve in a northern part of that province before going to Attawapiskat. However, in 1990, my northern days were long past. Early one morning in February, my host informed me that we were going to travel for about an hour to visit some men who were going to check their fishing nets that had been set under the ice. He was always very careful to make sure that I was properly dressed before embarking on any snowmobile journey. We went through my wardrobe: T-shirt, heavy cotton shirt, sweater, two pairs of socks, long johns, snowmobile suit, caribou hide mitts, snowmobile boots, hat, helmet with visor. We started off. Within a half-hour, snow had entered my boots and my feet were nearly frozen. I tapped my friend on the shoulder and explained the situation. He stopped the snowmobile and within a matter of minutes had cut some branches from a tree for me to recline on, started a fire and had removed my socks and boots and put them over the fire to dry. Turning to me, he told me to get as close to the fire as I could to warm up. He then firmly but gently chastised me with words that ring as loud today as they did on that cripplingly cold day in 1990: "Didn't your mother ever tell you to do up your Ski-doo boots?" I survived (obviously), and we journeyed on after my feet thawed, my socks and boots dried and we had a couple of cups of tea. I took pictures that day of the men checking their nets. Very clearly visible on their beards and mustaches is frost that was caused by their breath. The next day, I checked with the local priest and was informed that the temperature that morning had hovered around the minus 30 degrees Celsius range. It was one of those moments when I was most grateful that I was in the company of somebody knowledgeable, intelligent and quick thinking. There was no doubt that he saved my feet, if not my life. I thanked him then and I thank him now.

Fieldwork is not always dangerous, of course. Many times, I sat for long hours in goose blinds with my companion, chatting about the matters that concern us all: family, friends, health, peace. At moments like these, we come to realize that the so-called "other" is really very much like us. There are universal concerns that affect all of humanity.

There can be moments of peaceful tranquility as well. In September 1993, I returned to Attawapiskat to make a film about the goose hunt. On the evening of our last day of shooting, our host—the same person with whom I stayed in 1990—wanted to show us an old moose hunting camp where he had been the previous year. As we sat in the waning sunlight, waiting for the tides to be right for travelling, the world was never more peaceful. Behind us, a snowy owl voiced his objection to our presence while we listened to the belugas offshore as they came to the surface to breathe. At that moment, I didn't want to be anywhere else in the world.

THE STUDY

The study is essentially in two parts. After an examination of the community of Attawapiskat, Chapters 3 through 5 examine Attawapiskat Cree land tenure. Chapter 3 examines what is known about "traditional" patterns of land tenure in western James Bay. Early ethnographic studies as well as analyses of archival materials by contemporary Subarctic scholars provide the basis for this chapter. Chapter 4 documents and analyzes non-Native incursions into the region and their subsequent impact upon traditional patterns. Again, the bulk of the data is archival, primarily from the Hudson's Bay Company archives, Indian and Northern Affairs and the National Archives of Canada. Chapter 5 examines contemporary notions of land tenure. These data were gathered during my fieldwork in Attawapiskat.

The second half of the study (Chapters 6 through 8) examines changing patterns of land use, specifically within the context of Euro-Canadian encroachment. The period from 1901 to 1952 is addressed in Chapter 6. This is the period of initial Euro-Canadian movement into Attawapiskat, including the establishment of fur trading posts, missions, Treaty 9 and the registered trap line system. Archival material, particularly from the Hudson's Bay Company archives, as well as John Honigmann's ethnographic studies, provide much of the data for this chapter. Chapter 7 examines the period from 1953 to 1985, when transportation and communication opened up Attawapiskat to the world. During this period, Cree resistance to Euro-Canadian incursions and intended encapsulation became more formalized. Again, archival material, especially from Indian and Northern Affairs and the National Archives of Canada, provide the raw data for the chapter. In addition, wildlife harvest studies, in particular those by Prevett *et al.* and Thompson and Hutchison, were used. Chapter 8 examines land use from 1985 to 1990, characterized by increasing diversification and specialization. This chapter relies on data gathered during my fieldwork. Chapter 9 contains a discussion and conclusions.

CONCLUSIONS AND DISCUSSION

Despite the fact that the land is of crucial importance to Canadian First Nations (especially those in the north), there is a perception among some people that land use by Canadian Native peoples is non-existent or in decline. This is a view held by some anthropologists and some Native people. In Attawapiskat in northern Ontario, there is no doubt that there have been changes in both land use and land tenure during the 20th century. These changes reflect, in part, the incursions of the State and other non-Native incursions in the north.

It is important to recognize that the State, the fur trading companies and the Church initiated a process of encapsulation; that is, they attempted to subsume First Nations, bringing them under political and economic control. However, it would be naive to believe that this intended encapsulation went unchallenged for, as documented throughout the colonized world, encapsulation is met with resistance. As will be shown, this is no less true with the Cree in James Bay. An important component of this study, then, is encapsulation and resistance.

Given the history of Natives and non-Natives in Canada, it is not surprising to find that there is disagreement among scholars regarding land use. While some see it as being as important as it ever was, others perceive a decline in land use among some First Nations. These differing views reflect, to some extent, the perceptions that the people hold of themselves. This raises an additional question: Why do some First Nations people see themselves as being less dependent or less attached to the land?

Only God Can Own The Land is a qualitative and quantitative study that tests the assumption, held by some people, that hunting economies are in demise. It examines Attawapiskat Cree land use and land tenure during the 20th century and how these were affected by non-Native encroachment. The study utilized the methodologies of the ethnohistorian and the ethnographer, using both archival material from a number of institutions and two periods of fieldwork (in 1988 and 1990).

CONTENT QUESTIONS

1. Distinguish between land use and land tenure.
2. What forms can encapsulation take?
3. How can resistance to encapsulation be expressed?
4. Distinguish between encapsulation and assimilation.
5. What assumption is being tested or challenged by this study?

chapter two

Attawapiskat: The Ethnohistorical Context

LEARNING OBJECTIVES

After reading this chapter, students should be able to:

1. Distinguish between a microband and a macroband.

2. Briefly describe the physical environment in which the Attawapiskat Cree live.

3. Distinguish between acculturation and assimilation.

4. Briefly describe the fundamental social/cultural characteristics (e.g., population, age, language, employment and resource use) of the Attawapiskat Cree in 1990.

5. Explain why employment statistics are misleading for Native communities such as Attawapiskat.

The community of Attawapiskat lies 1000 kilometres by air north of Toronto, to the immediate west of Akimiski Island on James Bay. It is one of seven communities (Winisk/Peawanuck, Attawapiskat, Kashechewan, (Fort) Albany, Moose Factory, New Post and MoCreebec) that make up the region known to the indigenous Cree as **Mushkegowuk askii**. In 1990, these communities had a total population of about 7000 people. Attawapiskat itself had an estimated population of 1100, with 240 residential houses in the community.

The original reserve (as determined by the 1929 adhesion to Treaty 9) is 160 kilometres inland on the Ekwan River, and was hardly, if ever, used for any prolonged period of time.

It would be hard for southern Canadians to describe what Attawapiskat is like physically without explaining it in terms of what it lacks by their standards. Nonas (1963) conducted fieldwork in Attawapiskat and in his thesis opened with a description of the community and *environs*:

> The land of the Attawapiskat Cree is **muskeg** country, swamp country; a country of flat clay bogs cut by rivers, crossed by creeks and lakes and fields of mud, and deep forest stretches; of empty coastal mud-flats and the darkness of the bush; a land of shallow, slow tidal rivers come suddenly alive with cold winds off the bay; of narrow twisting creeks cut by low rapids; of deep, cold fish lakes and mud. It is a country of flat, wooded shoreline, as grey as they are green; of thick willow patches and rooted thickets; of small disappearing open spaces in tall spruce forests as dark as dusk, and mossy summer trails that sog a foot and a half at each step.

Attawapiskat is situated at 52 degrees 55' latitude and 82 degrees 25' longitude. It falls into that geographical area known as the Hudson Bay Lowlands (or Hudsonian Biotic Province), which characteristically is flat and poorly drained. Tree species are somewhat limited to black spruce and balsam, with occasional willow, poplar and tamarack. Yet, residents report picking nearly fifteen species of berries, with cranberries predominating. Climatically, Attawapiskat is similar to other Subarctic communities: long, cold winters with surprisingly warm summers, albeit with cool nights. The summer of 1989 was quite hot; local people point to the fact that on at least one day it was the hottest location in the country. This, of course, was an aberration. Temperatures recorded from July 21 to August 2, 1989 recorded a high of 34 degrees Celsius (taken at 4 pm on July 24) and a low of 11 degrees Celsius (taken at 4 am on July 27). The coldest temperature recorded for the period from January to the end of April 1990 was –34 degrees Celsius at 8 am on February 17. On April 2 it reached 12 degrees Celsius at 4 pm, the warmest it reached in that four-month period. This was considered a "typical" winter and early spring. Winds frequently contribute to a considerable wind chill factor. The breakup of ice is typically the first or second week of May, freeze up occurs in the middle of November.

HISTORICAL OVERVIEW OF THE ATTAWAPISKAT CREE

The name "Attawapiskat" can be interpreted as "the opening in the rocks" (Reg Louttit, pers. comm.). The local priest interprets it as "there is room to pass between the rocks" or "deep water between high rocks." According to the local priest, when the Cree first arrived by canoe, they saw the Attawapiskat River from James Bay. At the mouth of the river were two big rocks, which did not appear to leave room for a canoe to pass in between. As they approached closer, they exclaimed "Ka tawak piskaw" which in English means, "there is room to pass between the rocks."

The people of Attawapiskat traditionally occupied a large area that extended from Kapiskau (sometimes spelled "Kapiskow") River in the south to Hudson Bay (Cape Henrietta Maria) in the north, and from Akimiski Island in the east to Lake Mississa in the west. (See Fig 2-1 below.) The Kapiskau River flows northeastward, emptying into James Bay about 35 kilometres south of the community. The people, however, travelled (and continue to do so) considerably inland along the river, that is, southwestward, in search of moose and other game. Lake Mississa is about 200 kilometres inland from Attawapiskat,

FIGURE 2-1	Mushkegowuk Region Showing Attawapiskat Territory

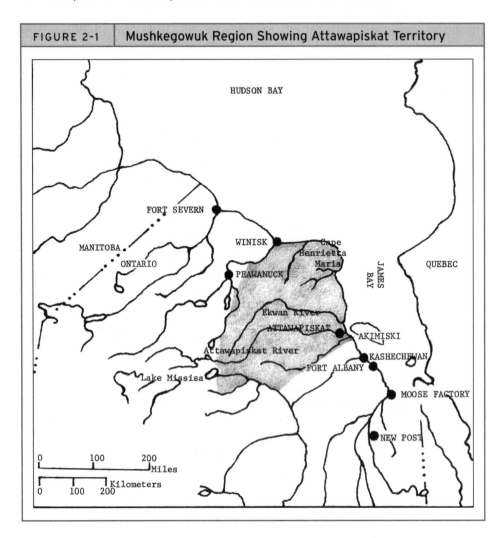

while the Hudson Bay coastline lies an equal distance to the north. Today, people from the community continue to exploit this vast region in pursuit of both food and furs.

The Attawapiskat Cree were not originally a coastal people but, rather, were widely distributed in the forest. The smallest social unit was the household, comprising two nuclear families, frequently headed by brothers or men who had married sisters. This might be extended to include a man doing **bride service**, that is, working to help the bride's family after marriage (Honigmann, 1981:221). Residence patterns were flexible, being bilocal (i.e., having a choice whether to live with or near either set of parents or families) or neolocal (i.e., setting up residence apart from both sets of parents or families). However, Honigmann (1953:811) suggests that prior to contact (in 1850), marriage was associated with patrilocal residence, after matrilocal bride service that normally lasted a year or two. There is reason to believe that in the pre-contact period **cross-cousin marriage** (i.e., marrying mother's brother's or father's sister's children) was preferred.

Two to five families represented a **microband**, which often travelled together. These bands were held together by kin bonds, and recognized an informal leader. His status was based upon age and wisdom. Constituent microbands, linked through affinal ties (related by marriage), created the **macroband**, which represented fifteen or so families. While no specific term was applied to these units, each occupied a particular river drainage, aware that other people occupied adjacent drainages.

The annual cycle, as practised by the majority of the people until the mid 20th century, was centred on the migratory patterns of waterfowl and caribou. Spring saw the movement of people from the inland areas to the coast to hunt molting ducks and to await the geese flying north. In the extreme north, the tundra of Cape Henrietta Maria and adjacent barren grounds accommodated caribou throughout the summer, and families went there to hunt. The arrival of the cold saw people move back inland to hunt caribou and moose. Rabbits as well were more accessible to snaring during the winter. The arrival of Europeans enhanced this pattern, as waterfowl were easier to procure with shotguns.

"Contact" in reality did not occur until the mid 19th century, although material culture had been altered by goods received through trade at Fort Albany beginning in the 1700s. The degree to which material culture was altered is open to debate. Father Vezina of the Oblates contends that, in 1978, older people still remembered using bows and arrows to kill small game, while Honigmann (1981:219) contends that informants in 1947 scarcely knew that the region's Natives formerly made stone axes and knives. However, Mary Spence, an Attawapiskat elder, recalls the making of bone needles and awls, as well as the construction of birch bark canoes. In 1990, the Attawapiskat Cree still made snowshoes (including the lacing, webbing, harness and frame), as well as boots, moccasins, and mitts from bush materials. Perhaps Honigmann overstated the degree of assimilation.

Acculturation, as opposed to assimilation (the former term suggesting culture *change*; the latter total or near total culture *loss*), was quite rapid when it reached Attawapiskat. Two fur trading companies—the Hudson's Bay Company (HBC) and Revillon Freres (RF) (bought out by the HBC within three decades)—quickly followed the Roman Catholic Church to the area. Treaty 9 was signed in 1905, and Attawapiskat received its reserve on the Ekwan River in 1930, although life continued around the post. Disease, starvation and further White incursions followed over the years. A hospital opened in 1951. The first airplane service began with weekly flights, operated by Austin Airways, in 1957. It was not until 1974, with the construction of an airstrip, that daily air service was offered.

A number of changes brought mixed blessings. In 1976, Special Constables (Native police officers under the direction of the Ontario Provincial Police) began working in Attawapiskat. That same year the John R. Nakogee School opened in the community, which accelerated the settlement of families in the village on a year-round basis. In 1979, television arrived in Attawapiskat, and a year later the first direct-dial phones appeared.

ATTAWAPISKAT IN 1990

There were about 1100 people in Attawapiskat in 1990, the year of the study. The population was a young one—fully 75 per cent of residents were under the age of 30. There were about 300 students enrolled in the elementary school (community-controlled since April 1990), with approximately 70 more travelling to Timmins, North Bay and Moosonee for secondary school. Twenty-seven college and university students attended schools outside the community. In addition, approximately 15 mature students were doing academic upgrading in preparation for academic or vocational training.

The daily language of conversation was Cree; however, only the older generation (those aged 50 or older) were unilingual. Most of those under the age of 50 had some White schooling and thus spoke some English. The Euro-Canadian influence was felt through the presence of the Hudson's Bay Company (now Northern Stores), the hospital, the school and the airport, which brought itinerant White professionals of various persuasions into the community on an almost daily basis. Two airlines serviced the community daily. The Church, of course, was omnipresent, as it had been for a century. The main denomination was Roman Catholicism; the priest was an Oblate and conducted services in both English and Cree. In 1990, the priest was quadrilingual, speaking Cree, Ojibwa, French and English, and had been in the north for decades.

Unemployment is high in Attawapiskat, as it is in most northern Native communities. One estimate in 1990 put it at approximately 75 per cent. This is misleading, however, because it ignores the numbers of full- and part-time trappers, as well as those who procure subsistence from the land. In addition, there were seasonal goose hunting guides, firewood vendors, artists, interpreters, self-employed hoteliers, sled makers and other "unclassified" employed people.

Not surprisingly, the White institutions and the band office offered the most opportunity for full-time, remunerative employment. The HBC employed approximately 13 local people; the hospital, about 50. The school, prior to the community assuming control, employed 21 local people. It would soon employ more people, in the form of teaching assistants and other para-professionals and professionals. The band office had a staff of about 30 people.

These opportunities for employment were not sufficient, however, given the population. During 1989/90 there were 217 people (between the ages of 21 and 64) on welfare, unemployment insurance or other forms of financial aid. Additionally, there were 13 people collecting old age security (pension), and 43 single mothers collecting family benefits. Government policy does not allow the release of community-specific social assistance payments; however, Indian and Northern Affairs Canada does provide provincial averages. In 1989/90, the average Ontario on-reserve family received $10,052 annually in social assistance payments. The average family consisted of four people. With this meagre amount, harvesting for products of domestic consumption becomes critically important.

In 1990, the community had 27 business/service organizations, including Gabe's Goose Camp, Bell Canada, the radio/television station and the Roman Catholic Mission. The volunteer fire department had a full-time chief, and 15 volunteers. There was also an emergency response team, which included 12 primary members and 12 alternates. There were close to 40 commercial buildings in the community.

Birds traditionally played a fundamental role in subsistence and continued to do so in 1990. Canada geese and "wavies" (the local term for blue geese and snow geese collectively) were shot and eaten in large numbers during both the spring and fall. In 1990, almost all adult males participated in goose hunting. Other avian species of importance were the willow ptarmigan, the sharp-tailed grouse and various shorebirds.In the last decade of the 20th century, moose and caribou continued to play an important role in subsistence, although Honigmann (1961:i) contends that the country is "chronically poor in such valuable large game animals as caribou, moose, and beaver." A significant number of men hunted moose, while the relative inaccessibility of caribou rendered their hunting more expensive and problematic. Nonetheless, caribou were still taken in considerable numbers, and their meat was shared throughout the community. Marten, muskrat, fox (both red and arctic, but mainly the former), weasel, otter and rabbits are all found in the region. This last species was, and continues to be, frequently snared for food purposes.

In 1990, fishing provided both recreation and subsistence. Available fish included white-fish, pike, suckers, speckled and other trout and pickerel, although historically whitefish might have played a more important role in subsistence than it did at the time of the study.

CONCLUSIONS AND DISCUSSION

Attawapiskat is located about 1000 kilometres by air north of Toronto. Located on the western shores of James Bay, it is a Cree community that had a population of approximately 1100 in 1990. Throughout the 20th century, the Attawapiskat First Nation underwent a number of profound changes but nevertheless retained its cultural integrity.

In many respects, the Attawapiskat Cree were, and are, typical Eastern Subarctic hunters. Historically, the people hunted throughout a large area, pursuing moose, geese and caribou. The smallest social unit was the household, consisting of two nuclear families, oftentimes headed by two brothers who had married sisters. Two to five families constituted a microband that often travelled under the informal leadership of a headman. A number of microbands, representing fifteen or so families, constituted a macroband, which occupied a river drainage. Up until the mid 20th century, a seasonal subsistence round, based on the movement and availability of game, was practised.

While the Attawapiskat Cree had been exposed to European trade goods in the 1700s, the people remained relatively unaffected by contact until much later. As the 20th century dawned, however, contact became much more intense as the fur trading companies, the Church and the government moved onto the land of the Attawapiskat Cree. Disease and starvation followed.

As the 20th century drew to a close, the community was still distinctly Cree, although it had a number of modern amenities including a school, a hospital, telephones, television and an airport. Cree was still the daily language of conversation, hunting and fishing were fundamentally important and essential Native values, including the sharing of meat, prevailed.

CONTENT QUESTIONS

1. Distinguish between a macroband and a microband.
2. Distinguish between acculturation and assimilation.
3. What are the main sources of Euro-Canadian influence on Attawapiskat?
4. What are the main bird, mammal and fish species relied on for subsistence?

chapter three

Traditional Land Tenure
of the Attawapiskat Cree

LEARNING OBJECTIVES

After reading this chapter, students should be able to:

1. Identify the three traditional units of social organization of the Mushkegowuk Cree.

2. State the two forms of ownership of land put forward by academic authors concerning aboriginal or traditional land tenure.

3. Outline Cree conservation practices and state their implications for discussion of territoriality and land tenure.

4. Discuss how Cree notions of ownership differ with various species being harvested.

5. Distinguish between physical and social boundaries.

It is essential to define our terms when dealing with such contentious issues as land tenure. There were traditionally three units of social organization among the Mushkegowuk Cree. The **nuclear family** rarely occupied a dwelling alone; rather, two brothers-in-law frequently lived together, aligned by the attachment of the sisters. To this unit might be added an aged parent or parents. Variations might include two brothers forming a household, and perhaps a son-in-law performing bride service.

The microband represents two to five (and perhaps as many as eight to ten) families who might aggregate around a good fishing site, such as an inland lake or present day Attawapiskat. These represent fluid bands, the members of which were often kin and who recognized a leader of limited authority. He was leader by virtue of age, wisdom, knowledge, ability, shamanistic powers and oratory skills.

The macroband consisted of 10 to 15 families and occupied a particular river drainage. Both Cooper (1933) and Flannery and Chambers (1986) have documented the traditional occupancies of these drainages in the Mushkegowuk region, listing family groups and drainages with which they were associated. No particular name existed in the dialect for this particular social unit. Affinal ties among the constituent microbands presumably held the unit together. Macrobands were restricted to their particular river drainage (hence, territory) by knowledge of an adjacent band's occupation of neighbouring drainages.

The ancestors of today's Attawapiskat band occupied all the territory from the Kapiskau River in the south to Hudson Bay (Cape Henrietta Maria) in the north, and from Akimiski Island in the east to Lake Mississa (about 200 kilometres inland) to the west. This has been contended by the current chief and council, and is supported by documentation in the archives of the Hudson's Bay Company (HBC) and documentation by Honigmann. Today's Attawapiskat band includes those people who occupied the Lake River, Opinaga, Attawapiskat proper, Lawachi and Kapiskau River drainages (hence, these people were in and of themselves macrobands). Thus, the term "Attawapiskat" does not only apply to those people who occupy(ied) the Attawapiskat drainage system, but also to all the people falling within the boundaries specified above. The numerous bands never constituted a formally recognized group. However, the HBC journals indicate that there was a recognition, by both traders and Natives, of family groups associated with certain territories who traded in Attawapiskat. Hence, there was a recognition of "Lake River" or "Opinaga" or "Lawachie" Indians who were all associated with the Attawapiskat Post. The "Attawapiskat Band" as such, however, is a formal recognition bestowed by the Canadian government via Indian Affairs.

ACADEMIC UNDERSTANDINGS OF CREE LAND TENURE: QUESTIONS OF WHO OWNS WHAT

Cooper (1933:1) argues that aboriginally in the eastern Subarctic the "hereditary individual or family hunting territory system prevail[ed];" this being a system whereby "all the land within the tribal [sic] limits is owned and occupied by individual Indians or by individual families." Under this system "every foot of the land...is owned by somebody." Cooper emphatically states that this was the system operating among the Moose, Albany, Kapiskau, Attawapiskat and Winisk Cree during the 1930s.

According to Cooper (1933), this system is hereditary in nature, passing from father to son(s), or to son-in-law, or, in rare instances, through the widow to a new husband if she remarries. Ordinarily then, the family hunting ground is owned by the father or by the family as such and is inherited by the man's sons when he dies. Morantz (1986), referring to the east side of James Bay, contends that nephews also inherited territories, and even non-relatives could claim unoccupied lands (although this would certainly be the exception, not a general rule). It is therefore not surprising to find that where this system is still found, the individual hunting territories have been in the family for generations.

The question of "individual" versus "family" ownership is an issue of debate. While Speck (1927, 1931) referred to the *family* hunting territories, Morantz (1986) contends that "Speck was wrong. Rights to the animals were clearly vested in individuals." She further notes that, in the HBC journals of the mid 19th century, references to hunting territories are always in terms of the individual, rather than the winter hunting group.

There is a danger involved in doing comparative studies of even very similar groups. Speck's (1927, 1931) contentions were based on fieldwork among the Montagnais (Innu) of Lac St. Jean, and the Montagnais-Naskapi (Innu) of the Labrador Peninsula and Nouveau Quebec, as well as the Ojibwa and Mi'kmaq. Morantz's (1986) work is based on archival data pertaining largely to East Main Cree. Can we extrapolate from one group to another? Did Speck expect his arguments regarding the Innu to apply to East Main Cree? In addition, HBC journals were written by Europeans with European biases (i.e., toward single rather than group ownership) and, hence, must be treated with certain circumspection.

The HBC journals for Attawapiskat cover only the period from 1919 to 1931. If we are to accept the observations of the traders as accurate reflections of the *Natives' understanding* of their concept of land tenure and territoriality, then there is a basis for the argument that rights were vested in the individual. We have, for example, the following entries (all emphases added): "David Kenkay left for *his* lands today" (HBC B.243/a/1); "John Chakasim, having gone to Wm. Nakogee's hunting ground, returned today..." (HBC B.243/a/1); "Jos. Carpenter arrived at the post at noon and left for *his* hunting grounds two hours later" (HBC B.243/a/5).

Flannery and Chambers (1986:108–144) re-examined the work of Cooper (1933). They note, as Cooper did, that reference to hunting territories was as much to the oldest male of the group (e.g., "Old Abraham's land") as it was to a specific family (e.g., "Paulmartin's land"). However, the recognized "owner" was the oldest man of the family group. The preferred composition of the hunting group was that of a man and his sons, or a man and his brothers. They observe, as well, that hunting without a close relative was sometimes referred to as "hunting alone." This even referred to those who hunted with a brother-in-law. Flannery and Chambers refer to a case cited by Cooper of Thomas Noah, who was said to "hunt alone" although his partner was James Tumigatik, his wife's brother.

Cooper (1933) states that the family hunting ground is inherited in the male line, usually from father to son(s), sometimes from brother to brother, or from father-in-law to son-in-law. Further, under certain conditions it may be held in trust by a widow for her children who are not of hunting age, or it may pass through the widow to her new husband if she remarries (Cooper, 1933:2). It is also possible, according to Cooper, that a father may donate part of his hereditary hunting ground to a son who comes of age and marries. On this last point, Cooper fails to elaborate. What is meant by "donate"? What becomes of the land after the son dies?

Virtually all of these possible scenarios regarding the transmission of territory were still to be found in Attawapiskat in 1990. Father/son combinations, brother/brother alliances, and father-in-law/son-in-law partnerships were still in existence.

Historically, there was a recognition of ownership on the parts of both the individual or family owners and the rest of the band. The recognition of ownership implies that there were rights and privileges associated with this ownership. Berry picking, fishing and the shooting of large game for food while passing through another's land were not resented. What was resented, however, was the trapping of fur-bearers on another person's land. Such actions often led to quarrels, violence and the taking of life "in the olden days." Witchcraft was also used as a retaliatory measure (Cooper, 1933:2). Cooper contends that Natives could, and did, ask for permission to hunt on another's land if they were having particularly poor luck on their own territory. Permission was customarily given, and often voluntarily offered by the person who was better off. This practice was still found in Attawapiskat in 1990.

Cooper (1933) referred to the Cree conservation practice of leaving a breeding stock of fur-bearers (e.g., taking four beavers from a colony of seven) and of rotating the land to allow it to replenish. This practice has been well documented in the Eastern Subarctic. The concept of conservation also implies notions of ownership, boundaries and trespass, which are serious considerations for any discussion of territoriality and land tenure. Morantz (1986) noted that:

> To undertake conservation measures implies a fairly well developed notion of private ownership of non-migratory animals...Conservation practices suggest the planning of the utilization of resources and therefore the necessity of agreed upon boundaries within which certain designated individuals control the harvesting of the animals.

Honigmann (1956:64) noted that, traditionally, hunters "walked" anywhere or fished in any stream within the territory of the macroband. He contends that the notion of territorial ownership by families did not appear until after the arrival of the Hudson's Bay Company. Rather, somebody might indicate first "discovery," therefore a claim, upon a beaver lodge by notching a nearby tree. Similarly, fishing sites were not owned but open to common use.

Preston (n.d.:66) adds that, prior to 1937, families had hereditary fur (but not food) hunting areas with "fluid" boundaries. These were recognized, but not without dispute. As well, along the coast there was a strip frequented by foxes that was generally open to common use. Food could be hunted anywhere. Flannery and Chambers (1986:127) note, as does Cooper (1933), that fishing and berry picking were not restricted to family territories. They add that, in the southern part of the Bay, the coastal strip utilized for goose hunting was open to all. Waterfowl are important in the Attawapiskat diet. Although hunters today often utilize the same goose areas year after year, there is also the belief that one can change locations as circumstances demand. It is likely that the coastal goose hunting areas have always been open to all.

Honigmann's (1961) position on the ownership of territories contrasts somewhat with that of Cooper (1933) and Flannery and Chambers (1986). He contends that "prior to White contact, family-owned hunting territories were unknown in the country, a band of several related families generally occupying a large portion of a river drainage" (1961:119). He further notes that, within the band territory, families travelled freely and were unhindered if they wished to join other bands. What we appear to be dealing with here is semantics (i.e., the definition of "own" and "ownership"), insofar as Honigmann states that "one may speak of ownership in the sense that particular families enjoy the right to exploit (but not to alienate) the resources of such land." What is implied, then, is *exclusive use rights but not rights of disposal*.

Territories, such as they were, could not extend back far in time, according to Honigmann (1961:119). He states that:

Apportionment of the Attawapiskat area among families with a coastal strip free to everyone was introduced relatively recently under the direction of the Hudson's Bay Company post manager. Families were allocated territories where they and their parents were presumed to have traditionally trapped. Such traditions, however, cannot be assumed to extend far back in time.

What we are faced with when comparing the stances of Cooper (1933) and Honigmann (1961) are differences in conceptions of "ownership" and differences in perceptions of aboriginality of tenure. What also needs discussing is the definition of "traditional."

In terms of our first problem, we need to ask a number of questions: What do we mean by "own"? What is owned? Following this, we must ask what constitutes violation of "ownership" (i.e., what constitutes theft or trespass)?

There appears to be a degree of consensus upon what is owned, if not on what constitutes ownership. Cooper (1933:2) has stated that berry picking, fishing and killing of game while passing through another's land are all acceptable practices. However, poaching or trespass in the sense of trapping and hunting is strongly resented as an injustice, as an infringement on strict rights. Similarly, Honigmann (1956:64) noted that people "walked" anywhere or fished in any stream within the territory of the macroband, and that people set fish weirs as they pleased, never disputing rights to a particular site. Preston (n.d.:66) likewise noted that any person could hunt for food (game) anywhere.

Flannery and Chambers (1986:128,129) are more specific in terms of the killing of game. A hunter might take what he needed for food while passing through another's territory to reach his own. Among some Cree there was the expectation that the skin of a game species killed for food would be given to the owner of the territory in acknowledgment of his ownership of the animals. On this point they did not find unanimity. In 1990, this was still true, albeit the giving of the skins also had a more pragmatic aspect. The hides were made into mitts, gloves and boots. It should also be noted that the skins are sometimes given to anybody who might use them, not just owners of the land. In 1990, younger hunters were not always aware of whose land they were on when big game was killed.

Flannery and Chambers (1986:129) also observed that some people objected to the picking of berries, gathering of moss and killing of ptarmigan (a bird that is a northern variety of grouse), claiming that such behaviour disturbed the game. The simple act of being on another's land, without having requested permission, or if not simply passing through, might be grounds for suspicion of poaching.

It is the nature of big game that allows them to be hunted without punishment on another's land under certain conditions. Because they do not remain in one area, it may be necessary to encroach on another hunter's territory to complete a chase that was begun on one's own. Thus, the completion of a hunt on another person's land is allowable. However, deliberately trespassing to kill moose or caribou, in other words, hunting on another person's land without permission, is disallowed. Intent is the crucial issue. Or, perhaps, game is associated with the territory where it yards (i.e., forms groups in one place).

There does appear to be unanimous agreement that fur-bearers, especially beaver, were considered the "property" of the person (or family) who "owned" the land. As noted above, Cooper (1933) sees trapping on another's land as trespass and an "infringement of rights." Honigmann (1956:64), in addition to his observations regarding the demarcating of beaver lodges, also notes that "it was illegal for somebody to set one trap upriver from another when no stream entered between the two points.

Flannery and Chambers (1986:129) state that poaching relatively sedentary fur-bearers, especially beaver, was deemed the most serious breach of norms. This was especially true when it involved encroachment on another's land to take beaver, because this species provided both food and trade potential.

Hansen (1989:1), in reference to Subarctic Algonkians generally, distinguishes between the rights of the group and the rights of the individual. The resources that were taken by the group members for barter or sale to Euro-Canadians were generally considered to be the property of the group, although furs were considered to be the property of the individual trapper. Other resources that were used domestically were considered to be "free goods." Members of neighbouring trapping groups were usually free to enter the trapping territory of others in search of food. However, any outsider who trapped in the group's trapping territory was considered to be a trespasser.

Cooper (1933) argues that violation of the norms regarding poaching and theft of fur-bearers often led to retaliation in the form of serious quarrels and, in the old days, violence, the taking of life and witchcraft. These actions, he notes, were "for the purpose of revenge upon the trespasser." He further contends that the system of ownership and resentment at and punishment for trespass "is and has been thoroughly upheld by current public opinion and the recognized moral and economic code of the Indians themselves" (Cooper, 1933:2). Preston (n.d.:66) refers to "occasional disputes" over the "fluid" boundaries that were recognized. Honigmann (1961:119) suggested that "among Indians disputes regarding illegal trapping are rare." Flannery and Chambers (1986:128,129) note that many Cree indicated that trespass, in the sense of an unwarranted incursion on another's hunting grounds, was resented. In contrast to the contentions of Cooper, they argue that direct confrontation between the disputing parties seldom occurred. Rather, less direct measures, such as spoiling traps by various means, were generally undertaken. These actions ensured that the perpetrator knew that the property owner was aware of the tresspass. Flannery and Chambers also state that, in the past, conjuring (again, an indirect method) was also done to inflict serious harm on the poacher. Outright retaliatory killings were rare.

Morantz (1986) dates the earliest reference to trespass in the James Bay area to 1745. She notes correspondence from 1777 in which the chief trader at Moose Factory told his counterpart at Albany of the encroachment of five Albany Post families on a Moose Factory resident's land, obliging the latter to leave his own grounds. Thus, it appears that notions of trespass, poaching and encroachment existed in the 18th century, substantiating the notion of individual (or family) territories. Morantz finds further evidence in the continuity of such phenomena as hunting group size, trapping for exchange, private ownership and conservation. Evidence for these first appear in the eighteenth century and continue to appear in the historical and ethnographic literature for eastern James Bay.

BOUNDARIES

To discuss trespass and poaching, we must acknowledge boundaries. Boundaries can be of two kinds: physical and social. **Physical boundaries** may be designated by landmarks or, in the cases of European and Euro-Canadian cultures, by fences. **Social boundaries** are more subtle and are established and defined by relationships between individuals and among groups of individuals. For example, in the Cree case, the household, microbands and macrobands all establish various degrees of "social boundaries." Social boundaries do two things simultaneously: they include some and exclude others. In the case of ethnic groups, for example, social boundaries are created and maintained by such things as language, religion and endogamy. As well, among such peoples as the Hutterites there exist physical and geographical boundaries in that there are discernible physical settings in which a group may live to the exclusion, or virtual exclusion, of others (Hostetler and Huntington, 1967).

The family hunting/trapping territory normally occupied a river drainage. The degree of rigidity of boundaries is disputed. Flannery and Chambers (1986:127) question Tanner's (1979:185–186) contention that "[today] people do not carry around a firm and fixed idea of boundaries in their heads." They suggest that "the way territories were conceived in the late 19th century suggests more 'boundedness' and permanence than perhaps is true in the present." They state that on the west coast of the bay (i.e., the area including Attawapiskat), where "anyone could hunt where they pleased" [sic] following Treaty 9, both older and younger men could describe in detail the locations of individual holdings in the past and those still in use. Natural features of the terrain and sometimes distance from the trading post were used to demarcate the territories (1986:127). The "edges" of contiguous holdings were reckoned within several miles, with reference to landscape features and sometimes to lands "belonging" to someone else.

Cooper (1933:1) contends that all of the land within a "tribe's [sic] territory is owned," with heights of land, chains of lakes and other natural features functioning as boundaries. These were "fairly well known" to members of the given band. Hansen (1989:3) states that the territories were circumscribed by an unmarked, yet "understood," boundary. The fur resources within the territory were the property of those who usually trapped in that area.

These, then, are the various perceptions and interpretations of Attawapiskat Cree land tenure principles and practices at the time of Euro-Canadian incursion into the region at the turn of the century. It remains now to examine the non-Native encroachment into the area and its ramifications on the Cree relationship to the land.

CONCLUSIONS AND DISCUSSION

The territory of the Attawapiskat First Nation comprises all of the territory that extends from Akimiski Island westward to Lake Mississa and northward to Cape Henrietta Maria on Hudson Bay. The ancestors of today's Attawapiskat Cree hunted throughout this vast territory, recognizing lands that were traditionally used by different family groups. Exactly who owned what, when and how ownership originated and how this ownership was passed down from generation to generation are open to debate.

Some scholars believe that rights to the land were vested in individuals, while others maintain that they were essentially in the hands of families. We must question whether this recognition is the result of contact with Europeans or if it existed prior to the fur trade. In other words, did the introduction of hunting for trade, as opposed to hunting for subsistence, affect the traditional notions of land tenure? There was, and is, a variety of resources on the land, including game animals, fur-bearers, fish and berries. Again, there is debate about the nature of ownership of these resources. The evidence seems to suggest that there were different protocols with each.

If there were notions of territories (as there seem to have been), then there must also have existed some sense of trespass. In turn, notions of trespass imply an awareness of boundaries, which may be either social or physical. Social boundaries among the Cree were determined by kinship, while geographical features such as lakes, rivers and hills determined physical boundaries. With these boundaries established and known by the Cree, the harvesting of resources took place, following the seasons and availability of game.

CONTENT QUESTIONS

1. What are the three traditional units of social organization among the Mushkegowuk Cree?
2. What are the two main contesting answers to the question "Who owns hunting territories"?
3. What is considered "owned" in these territories and what is not considered "owned"?
4. Distinguish between physical and social boundaries.

chapter four

Euro-Canadian Incursions 1901–1952 and Changes in Land Tenure

LEARNING OBJECTIVES

After reading this chapter, students should be able to:

1. Compare how the Church and the fur trade companies acted to encapsulate the Attawapiskat Cree.

2. Critically assess how the Church and the HBC reacted to the crisis faced by the Cree brought about by the depletion of resources.

3. Consider how the Cree trapper and the White trader viewed their relationship.

4. Compare the State and the Cree perspectives on Treaty 9.

5. Explain the failure of the registered trapline system.

Cooper noted in 1933 that the "traditional" hunting territory system, as he interpreted it, was in decline and that there was "widespread demoralization and extreme poverty among most of the Indians throughout [the] very large territory in which the family hunting ground system...prevailed" (1933:5). This he attributed to a "series of linked causes and effects":

...the partial breakdown of the family hunting ground system has led to the breakdown of the conservation system; the breakdown of the conservation system to the stripping of the land and the enormous diminution or disappearance of the furbearing animals (and to...game animals); the diminution of the furbearing animals to the present very widespread pauperism and undernutrition, amounting to near starvation; pauperism leading to widespread demoralization and mendicancy as well as loss of self respect and self dependence.

Cooper's basic contention, then, is that the traditional system was in decline, bringing with it other changes. To what may this be attributed? He argued that in the more southerly areas a contributing factor was White encroachment in the forms of railroads, mines, farms and trapping. In the more northerly areas, including James Bay, he contended that the Natives themselves had the impression that they no longer had government recognition of their family hunting grounds. They were further under the impression that the government not only did not recognize their rights, but that it also actively denied such rights. Cooper believed that it would be "relatively easy to correct [these] impression[s]." His proposed solution was "clearly to be some form of recognition or guarantee, – perhaps by some form of leasing or land patent or by some form of recognition similar to that given for mining claims, – of the traditional individual and family hunting grounds..." (Cooper, 1933:Appendix A:1). This, he argued, would in turn lead to a relatively quick restocking of the land and to economic independence and self support for the Natives. It was a White solution, incorporating White notions of ownership and White values.

Cooper notes that the Natives themselves sought government recognition of their traditional territories. Further, he adds that "the Indians...have been drifting rapidly from private ownership of real property to a system of communism in property holding. The chief remedy seems to be a reversion, from the present drift towards communism, back to private land ownership" (Cooper, 1933:Appendix A:4).

Cooper's main informants for the Attawapiskat data were Willy Allen from Albany, Jimmy Acickic (Shisheesh) from Attawapiskat, Willy Ethrington from Opinaga and William Louttit. From these men Cooper was able to gather much of his information. Allen suggested that even though some groups of men in the early decades of the 20th century still exploited areas that their fathers had hunted, frequently other men of their families were said to be "hunting all over," a phrase still echoing in Attawapiskat in 1990. Flannery and Chambers (1986:118) note that few of the sons of the men listed as having hunting rights to territories near the shore of the Attawapiskat River still utilized these areas in the 1930s, and there were few claimants for about 50 miles up each of the Lawachie, Attawapiskat and lower Ekwan Rivers.

While Cooper's (1933) cited reasons for the "breakdown" of the old system may have some validity, it is important to look more closely at the nature of relations and the nature of the *process* of relations between the encroaching Euro-Canadian forces and the Attawapiskat people.

MISSIONARIES, FUR TRADERS AND THE ENCAPSULATION PROCESS

The period of acculturation on James Bay's west coast began in 1685, when Fort Albany succeeded the establishment of Rupert's House and Moose Factory further south. For the Attawapiskat Cree, though, intense contact did not begin until two centuries later.

In the 1850s, missionaries from the Oblates of Mary Immaculate (OMI) began travelling to the Attawapiskat region. The Oblates contend that the visits to the region were, in part, encouraged by the impressive turnouts of 200 to 300 people at their services. Probably of equal importance was the fact that in 1852 the Anglican minister from Moose Factory was visiting Fort Albany and was able to convert former Catholics as well as non-Christians to his faith. The rush to convert Cree souls had begun. A Roman Catholic mission was established in Attawapiskat in 1893–94, followed by a permanent church and residence in 1912. The process of encapsulation was initiated through competition for Cree souls.

The encapsulation of Native people, perhaps especially in the north, has been a process that feeds and nurtures the various agents of the encapsulating Euro-Canadian society. There is a note of irony here. The State mandated itself the guardian of the Aboriginal people, and created the Indian Act for the purpose of assimilation, implying that Natives were somewhat less civilized than Euro-Canadians, in a state somewhere between barbarism and savagery. Yet it was precisely those alleged traits of "savagery" that were needed by the Church and fur traders. The Church legitimized its being in James Bay by citing the need to convert the Cree to Christ and to educate them in fundamental White ways. However, without the Cree being engaged in trapping, there could be no fur trade. Both the Church and the traders were working for a perceived higher order; the former for the Christian God, the latter for Euro-Canadian business. Thus, while on the one hand there is condemnation of the Cree as the "other," this reviled "other" serves the fundamental purpose of legitimizing the actions of Euro-Canadian agents. It becomes not a process of encapsulation, but of elevation to an eventual state of sameness with the encapsulators (recognizing, of course, that Euro-Canadian society is *not* a classless, homogeneous society). Honigmann (1962:7) noted that in 1948 "the priests encouraged the Indians to idealize White customs and urged the people to show 'proper respect for Whites.'" Motivated by a sense of moral correctness, the process of encapsulation unfolds, with the various agents of the State (the ubiquitous White triumvirate of Church, fur trader and police officer) bringing White religion, White economics, and White justice to the hinterlands.

Factors such as resources, economic interest in the subordinate society, tolerance of the subordinate's cultural practices and distance from the encapsulator's core will determine the nature and speed of encapsulation. Though relatively unaffected by the fur trade for 200 years (the result of trade at a distance), the arrival of the HBC and the Church in Attawapiskat at the turn of the 20th century greatly accelerated the process of encapsulation.

The case of Attawapiskat, as is the case with all Natives involved in the fur trade, provides an intriguing context for encapsulation. The Cree were at once a resource in themselves, as well as being a tool for the resource extraction of furs. While providing a resource item for the Churches, in terms of being souls to convert, they were also the means of extracting wealth for the fur traders, having skills that few Whites could hope to acquire. While Cree culture might have been perceived as less than White in its qualities, it met the needs of those who needed it to legitimize their being in the north.

If anyone doubts the role of Natives as resources and tools of the State, we need only consider the Beothuk of Newfoundland. It may be argued that they disappeared as a result of the fact that they *did not* fulfill any function in the White interests in Newfoundland. Europeans there primarily sought fish, not furs—a form of resource extraction in which the Beothuk had no active role to play. With few fur traders or missionaries there to safeguard the Beothuks' (and therefore their own) interests, that isolated nation was doomed. Upton (1977) has made a similar argument. The agents of the State have reasons to keep Natives alive, albeit suppressed. These reasons may have more to do with self interest than philanthropy.

Having argued that the process of encapsulation is motivated as much by self interest as it is by concern for Native interests, it is not surprising to find the various State agents working in conjunction, however subtle or unintended. With the establishment of the mission in Attawapiskat, the fur traders quickly followed. C.C. Chipman, in his *Annual Report on the Fur Trade for 1901-1902*, notes their relationship. The following was written February 3, 1903:

> The section of country between Albany and Severn for many years, until quite recently, had not been much hunted, but the establishment by the Roman Catholic Church of Mission Stations at the mouth of the Weenusk and Attawapiscat has drawn Indians to the Coast and those points and *necessitated* the Company also establishing there (HBC A.14/11) (emphasis added).

In this way, the various agents of the Euro-Canadian state aided and abetted each other in the encapsulation process. With personal, albeit different, interests in the Cree, each sought to constrain and shape the behaviour and **ideology** of the subordinate society.

In 1906, Revillon Freres (referred to by the locals as the "French Store") also established a post in Attawapiskat. The combined influence of the Mission and the fur companies was to have profound effects upon the people and the resources of the area. These included changes in traditional patterns of land use and tenure.

A Roman Catholic boarding school run by the Brothers at Fort Albany had begun accepting Attawapiskat children in 1902. It was a mixed blessing. Today, almost every adult is literate in his or her mother tongue. However, with literacy came numerous shifts in traditional social structures and demographics, as the missions and newly arrived fur trading companies drew more and more people from the interior to the coast.

We can speculate that the residential school in Fort Albany had, to some degree, altered the basic family and social structure. With children in school for several months a year, the traditional patterns of social organization would have been altered and this may have had ramifications for the perpetuation of traditional skills. Undoubtedly, the demographics of the region were altered as people moved in greater numbers to the proximity of the posts and mission.

Dr. Orford, Indian Agent at Moose Factory, articulated some of the effects of the mission, schools and fur companies in a letter written in 1941 to the Secretary of the Department of Indian Affairs. These effects had undoubtedly been felt years earlier. He stated that he had received numerous complaints of trespassing, observing that trappers from Albany "were filtering into [the Moose Factory area] and assuming trapping and hunting grounds which the Moose Cree normally consider their own private domain" (cited in Hansen, 1989:28). Apparently, the Albany hunters were fully aware of their trespassing, but gave several reasons for doing so: they believed that they were better trappers and hunters than the Moose Cree; the Attawapiskat hunters were moving into Albany Cree territory; and the Albany hunters' children were going to school in Moose Factory, and they wanted their traplines to be close to their children.

It is important to realize that documentation of trespass by Albany Cree upon Moose Factory territory goes back two centuries. What is fundamental here, however, is that we might explain this change in behaviour by looking at changes wrought by White movement into the region, notably the residential school system. We must also note that trespass was creating a ripple effect down the coast, from Attawapiskat to Moose Factory. No longer was trespass restricted to neighbouring bands; rather, it had assumed region-wide proportions. However, there were a large number of changes occuring in the early 20th century. We must not look for mono-causal explanations for the "breakdown" of traditional patterns of tenure and its concomitants of trespass and poaching. Rather, close contact of Native and non-Native cultures brought rapid and radical changes that need to be examined.

It has been noted by Honigmann that with the mission and fur traders, the population of Attawapiskat increased dramatically. Honigmann (1961:16) has hypothesized that this increased population density followed a decimation of what little large game existed in the area. He further suggests (1981:224) that on the west coast of James Bay, this decimation sometimes obliged large winter bands to break up into one, two or three family units. Also, the increased population facilitated the spread of diseases, many of them fatal to the Cree. Thus, we find in the first half of the 20th century disease and starvation rampant. The years of 1902–03 saw some of the best hunters die from disease and starvation (HBC Arch. B.3/b/102), a pattern that was repeated in 1903–04. This pattern of disease and starvation would occur sporadically over several decades, most notably in 1901, 1928, 1930–31 and 1946–48. A number of explanatory points must be stressed here. Honigmann (1961:15,16) states that while starvation occurred, it was probably less often fatal after the arrival of the Church and the HBC, as these two institutions were able to provide foodstuffs and better nourishment. Better nourishment, he suggests, increased life expectancy. Also, he contends that the increasing population, which began in the late 19th century, is attributable to increasing immigration from inland and northern regions. Finally, Reg Louttit of Attawapiskat observes that every period of starvation has been preceded by severe flooding which has eradicated virtually all but avian species (pers. comm., 1991). Thus, the apparent contradiction between increased population and disease and starvation makes more sense when one factors in immigration, increased life expectancy and available European foodstuffs.

In spite of the initial optimism of the traders, it also became apparent that the region was not an unlimited source of furs. As the decline in large game animals was occuring, a result of the interplay among the new technology introduced by the traders (e.g., guns), increased population drawn to the mission, school and trading posts and possibly natural game cycles, the fur trade companies were spurring trappers on to produce more furs.

An intense rivalry between companies emerged, and incentives were offered to produce more furs. The 1921 and 1922 *Annual Reports* from the James Bay District suggest the intensity of this rivalry. In 1921 it was noted that

> Revillon Freres are adopting what they intend to be an aggressive policy...Revillon Freres have secured a hold on the trade of Attawapiskat from which it will be difficult to shake them...They have always paid great attention to this Post, considering it their most profitable Post, they have given it of their best in men and supplies... (HBC A.74/50)

In 1922 it was observed that

> Only at Attawapiskat Post...have Revillon Freres been at all aggressive...they very early in the Season adopted a policy of 'unlimited debt'...Attawapiskat is considered as the stronghold of the Opposition... (HBC A.74/51)

The other side of this observation, of course, is that the source of the wealth being enjoyed by Revillon Freres and the HBC was the Cree. Liquor, large trapping outfits offered on credit and even houses for exceptional trappers were all part of the incentive packages offered (Honigmann, 1961:15). It is apparent that by the second decade of the 20th century, the process of encapsulation, in terms of economics and religion, was in full force.

DEPLETION OF RESOURCES AND CONFLICTING CULTURES

With the emphasis placed on hunting for trade products as opposed to hunting for subsistence products, it was inevitable that there would be a reduction of fur-bearers in the region, which was never particularly rich with fur-bearers anyway. At the same time, both the mission and the fur traders were providing the people with Euro-Canadian foodstuffs, thereby hoping to reduce the possibility of starvation while at the same time intensifying the shift in a hunting-for-subsistence to hunting-for-trade attitude. Thus, a number of factors came into play that influenced the resource base and ultimately, it is argued, traditional approaches to land tenure: an increasing population in the region (many from Sutton Lake, Sutton River and Winisk River), accessibility to guns and steel traps, high prices for furs as a result of competition and intense pressure on the part of the companies to produce. What must also be considered, however, is the possibility of an underlying shift in ideological perceptions of the place of humans in the environment and their relationship to it. The goals and objectives of the missionaries and fur traders in James Bay were at odds with the fundamental cultural values and beliefs of the Cree. The missionaries sought to recreate the Cree in their image. This, by necessity, meant changing their social, economic, political and religious beliefs, all of which were inextricably part of their relationship to the land. The fur traders, for their part, did their best to keep the Cree on the land, rewarding them with European trade goods and, at times, liquor. Traditional beliefs and attitudes were seen as inconsequential in terms of the need to produce furs.

The mission sought to "civilize" and Christianize the Cree by introducing sedentary Euro-Canadian economic pursuits and activities, such as the sawmill and garden. With this, of course, came a shift in the belief and value systems. With the help of the denominational boarding schools, the missionaries succeeded in implementing a new religious belief system while attempting to eradicate the old one.

At mid century, the Aboriginal past was reinterpreted as a time of sorcery and evil, when the devil allied himself with **shamans** (Honigmann, 1958:60, 1966:205). Thus, in some respects, the Attawapiskat Cree have embraced Christianity's notion of what pre-contact life was like. But, while it seems that traditionally there was always uncertainty associated with travel and the quest for food, there also existed a relatively elaborate set of agents or powers that worked for the benefit of humankind and that functioned to restore order in an unpredictable world. The Mushkegowuk or West Main Cree, it seems, abandoned these, in contrast with the East Main Cree, who continued to respect much of their traditional beliefs and rituals. The degree to which this shift in religious/ideological practice affected resource harvest is hard to measure but must be borne in mind in any historical examination of land use. The fur companies' insistence on fur production, and the availability of foodstuffs from the mission and fur companies' stores, must have affected traditional notions of conservation and reverence for the land, although these factors were present on the east coast as well.

The Church promised a better life for the Natives. This is a *de facto* assumption. The fact that in 1990 all members of Attawapiskat were Christian (all but five being Roman Catholic, four of which were Anglican, and one Pentecostal) suggests that conversion, at least ostensibly, was successful. While replacing traditional beliefs with something else, Catholicism did not provide for *all* of the spiritual and physical needs of the Cree. Although it provided ritual and ceremony and the promise of an afterlife for those who believed, the Church did not alleviate all hardships. As noted above, starvation persisted and mission support was inadequate.

The basic shortcoming of the Church was that it promised much but did not alleviate suffering. Nor did it provide the Natives with a replacement set of beliefs that allowed them to cope with the difficulties of a hunting/trapping life. The religious ideology that Christianity had replaced was a complete one; one that acknowledged hardship but provided the spiritual means with which to cope. The religious encapsulation, in one sense, was only partial. The missionaries had convinced the Cree that pre-Christian life was spiritually evil and dangerous. The frequent periods of starvation and disease (both introduced in part by White traders and priests) helped to drive the point home. The bush was materially as well as spiritually dangerous. Nonetheless, the fur traders insisted upon fur production.

The issue, then, is that while the fur companies and the mission promised (either by implication or directly) a better life economically, materially and spiritually, neither could change the physical suffering of the Cree. And, indeed, the two major Euro-Canadian forces at times appeared to be in contradiction with each other. Therefore, the *expectations* of the Cree *vis-à-vis* the Church and the traders during times of hardship were not met. The source of material wealth and the new religion could not always be counted on to alleviate the suffering.

Preston (n.d:65) notes in reference to Attawapiskat that, in 1947, it was observed that "people don't like to go very far in the bush, for fear of starvation, and boast if they do go far." One man did not want to go upriver "because I do not know that area and might get lost." Today, there are people in Attawapiskat who either remember themselves, or who remember being told by their parents of being afraid to leave the post out of fear of "dying in the bush." The possibility of starvation and disease, and the teachings of the Church, found a basis in reality: the bush, which had sustained them for uncounted generations and which could be dealt with on its own terms through traditional skills and cosmology, was to be feared. People *did* die in the bush. The following entry was made in the Weenusk Post Journal, June 6, 1930:

> Peter Patrick and Jacob Anashoppie came in today. Report Attawapiskat Indian died of starvation during the winter (HBC B.493/a/1).

In Attawapiskat, the following entry was made on March 21, 1920:

> ...arrived today from his camp starving and also sick...his family...had nothing to eat when he left them (HBC B.243/a/1).

On March 13, 1930, the trader at Attawapiskat made the following entry:

> David Ookiitigoo's wife arrived at the post and reported that her husband was sick and that they were entirely out of "grub" (HBC B.243/a/1).

Cooper (1933) gives us a clue as to changing perceptions and land tenure patterns. He refers to the following hunters: George Edward, who "hunted near Winisk with his father before the latter died, now hunts at Attawapiskat and never leaves the Post;" "John Swanson – only at Post. Father hunted on Cape;" and John Takasam (Chookasim), who "stays at Post."

To their credit, the Church and the fur companies did attempt to aid the poor and destitute during periods of stress. The records of the HBC make numerous references to the issuing of rations: The trader made the following entry on February 1, 1930:

Issued rations to...destitute Natives (HBC B.243/a/4).

Six months later, the situation had not improved, as suggested by this entry made July 26, 1920:

Issued rations to sick and destitute Natives... (HBC B.243/a/4)

Nonetheless, we must regard the response of the fur companies to the Attawapiskat Cree's plight as ambiguous at best. While there are weekly references in the journals to the issuing of rations (and, at times, clothing) to the sick and destitute, it is also apparent that the profits of the stores were a priority. The following post journal entry was made January 24, 1920:

Frank Rickard and Dan Wesley came in this evening and reported being nearly starved, their families having had nothing to eat for two days. I gave them some grub but can't do much for Frank as he has an old balance (HBC B.243/a/1).

A decade later, company profits were still a priority as indicated by this entry from March 14, 1931:

Issued rations to...destitute Natives...brought a few skins to trade, the half value of same being retained for his debt at Albany (HBC B.243/a/5).

The Church, for its part, also offered help to the sick and starving. Honigmann (1961:17) quotes one Attawapiskat resident:

Since the government has been in the Bay the people have been hard up. I don't know how people would have been if the priests had not helped. They had a big potato garden and they did their best to feed the Indians with potatoes when the country was poor. They couldn't give enough lard when they didn't have too much for their own use but they did the best they could to give us a little.

While not denying the undoubted decency of intent through the giving of food, we must examine the underlying message of this benevolence. It is rather clear: life as the Cree knew it was evil and dangerous; the more desirable ideology was that offered by the Church: White education, White religion and subsistence based around the garden, the farm and the sawmill. As was plainly visible, the missionaries and the traders were not subject to disease and starvation. Indeed, they had surplus goods to share—if they wanted to. Life as the Cree knew it was not only dangerous; it was unrewarding and undesirable. And the "superiority" of the White man and their ways were reinforced.

Honigmann's (1961:17) same informant stated that appeals to the Post's managers and doctors for food were met with admonitions of "Go out and trap" when there were no fur-bearers left. The relationship that had been established, one that was relatively symbiotic when times were good and animals abundant, was drastically changed.

RELATIONSHIPS FROM A CREE PERSPECTIVE

We must attempt an analysis of the relationship that existed between the Cree and Whites in Attawapiskat from a Cree perspective. Cree society is based upon a number of given assumptions: **egalitarianism**, **balanced reciprocity** and political leadership that amounts to little more than *primus inter pares* (first among equals). These must be examined in turn to appreciate the unfolding of events during the lean years in the first half of the 20th century.

In egalitarian societies, a member has as much right (with some exceptions) to the resources of that society as do any other members of the society. Thus, a poor hunter is not discriminated against because he is not as proficient as his brother. Therefore, he cannot be denied food because he is a poor hunter (or having poor luck due to game shortages); nor can he be denied the right to be heard. Admittedly, this is an ideal anthropological type. As Rogers (1972:123) phrased it for the Mistassini Cree, "...it is not the land itself but rather the resources of the land that are considered the property of the group, although not in absolute terms." He concludes by noting that a hunter has the right to take game whenever he finds it if he and his family are starving.

Similarly, in Cree society the basic system of exchange is **reciprocity**, that system which is found universally among hunters and gatherers. In its simplest form, reciprocity rests upon the fundamental understanding that there is an exchange of items of, in some sense, equal value. There need not be an immediate exchange; rather, it is understood that at some point *all* exchanges will balance out and everyone will be satisfied.

Finally, it is essential to note that, among the Cree, the political structure is largely informal, based on age and sex. The leader, such as he is, has informal influence and does not have the means to enforce his decisions or his advice. Honigmann (1957:369) has stated of the Cree that "ambivalence characterizes thinking about leadership. Indians regard firm leadership as desirable and yet no pleasure comes from exercising power. Too great evidence of power is resented and feared by those whom it affects."

Honigmann (1956:58) further explains Cree leadership and reciprocity:

> [M]embers [of a band] recognized a kind of leader (or "boss"). This man advised his followers on the basis of his expert knowledge, telling them where to travel for meat or fish..."in the old days no Indian had the right to tell the people what to do. The people together decided." A leader represented a "wise man"...who helped others to make advantageous decisions. Atooket [an informant] pointed out that the band chief "gave orders because he was the oldest in the bunch...because he know all about things." A leader worked industriously so that he frequently had surplus meat to distribute to his followers who, however, were often his kin.

During my fieldwork in Attawapiskat in 1990, I spoke with some male members of the community. They stated that leadership as such does not really exist. Rather, when out on the land one man assumes a greater role in decision making because he is older, wiser and knows the land better. One man, for example, had as his partner his brother-in-law. He observed, however, that he made the decisions because it was his land and he knew it better than his brother-in-law did.

In much the same way that people (especially leaders) distributed food decades ago, it was being distributed in the village in 1990. Hunters frequently shared food among six to ten families. In one instance, after some caribou were killed, eight different families and groups (including the hospital) were given caribou meat by one hunter. Five of these were in some way related to the hunter. Three were not (one of which was the hospital). I inquired as to the relationships of those who received meat. I was told that although some people were not related it was not unusual, nor was it shameful or embarrassing, for non-kin to ask for food. A number had, in fact, come to the house asking for a share of the meat. It was expected, I was told, that one would share, especially since the hunter in this case had no wife or family to feed. If he ever needed meat, he could expect to receive some from those to whom he had given. Honigmann (1953:815) observed that borrowing of food by married persons, even from a parent, is not unknown.

Egalitarianism is reflected in part by attitudes towards leadership and how leadership is perceived. The fact that leaders had no coercive power, and that men and their families could and did change bands and territories, reflects an essentially egalitarian attitude. A society is not made up of equals if one person or group of people has coercive control over others. Hence, the Cree were (and still are) essentially egalitarian. This is reflected today in their attitudes toward the use of land and access to resources.

How, then, does this relate to Cree–White relations in Attawapiskat? The Cree saw the initial relationship as one of equals. Between the fur traders and the Cree there was a balanced reciprocity. When furs were abundant, the Cree produced them in exchange for the items they desired or needed. Similarly, the post journals contain references to gift exchanges between the traders and Cree of food and other items such as clothing, when times were good. In terms of the Church, they gave up their non-Christian ways in return for the blessings of the White man's god.

DIFFERENT SETS OF RULES

But the White institutions operated within a different set of guidelines. The fur traders were business- and profit-oriented and, in the words of Governor Simpson, "It is fair to say that our major purpose is not philanthropic." Their society did not operate under notions of reciprocity, egalitarianism and informal leadership. Therefore, the expectations of the trader and the trapper were not similar. When times were difficult for the trader, profits and productivity took priority. Thus, the order to "Go out and trap" was a reflection of the trader's primary motivation and the dictates of the trading company. In non-Native society, competition produced leaders, and the trader stepped out of a perceived role as an equal in the eyes of the Cree to assume a leadership role in maintaining and perpetuating the trade that the trading companies were there to establish. The basic assumption that the Cree held, that the trade existed between relative equals, was violated. The withholding of goods and foodstuffs in times of need violated this basic trust. Thus, on a number of counts the traders overstepped what was understood to be a relationship between equals: they withheld goods from those in need, they assumed an aggressive leadership role by giving orders and they denigrated the most competent of trappers. When times were good, the traders could be depended upon for material items. When times were bad, they could not be depended upon. A fundamental Cree tenet was breached.

The Church fared better in the eyes of the Cree. For the most part, the Roman Catholic fathers were respected. No doubt, this is partly due to their learning the Cree language. In addition, in Attawapiskat the mission's garden kept the Cree supplied with potatoes during periods of starvation.

For its part, the Church required every Cree man who used its sawmill to reciprocate by cutting and hauling one log for the mission for every log that was cut and hauled for the Cree's own use. Through it all, though, there was the belief that somehow the Church was working for a higher order, a better way of being:

> Sometimes people like to mistreat a dog...And when they do, the dog...will dodge or put their head down. That's just how it was with us in the past, when the White man first came to us. They thought of him as a God. That's what my mother told me. They thought the priest was a God. She was so wrong... (James Carpenter, cited in *Native Studies Review*, Vol. 5 #2).

When the missionaries came from the south...they did not think much of our ways...when an Indian does anything they don't think much of it...when we speak, they don't want to listen... (John Mattinas, cited in *Native Studies Review*, Vol. 5 #2).

Bailey has suggested that encapsulation is a function of the greater economic resources of the dominant society. As demonstrated in Attawapiskat, this was indeed the case, as economics in association with cultural differences led to further subjugation of the Cree people. And it was clearly the fur companies that, in times of difficulty, had economic control, as suggested by the following entry in the HBC journal from November 4, 1930:

Issued *small* outfits of necessities to several of the coast hunters who are now to commence fox trapping" (HBC B.243/a/5) (emphasis added).

Six months later, HBC company policy had not changed, as indicated by this entry from March 1, 1931:

[A number of hunters] report having very poor hunts, as they say, that most of their time is occupied hunting food, now that they only receive *very small* amounts of advance before leaving for their hunting grounds (HBC B.243/a/5) (emphasis added).

What occurred, then, was that the terms of trade had been altered. Items for trade had become economic weapons, items to be used or withheld.

But the trader must be understood in terms of *his* society. He was a minute but vital part of a much larger society, that of the HBC itself and the world, insofar as the individual posts were subject to the vagaries of the world market in furs. This concern with the larger society, of which the trader was the representative to the Cree people, was reflected in the post journals from May 10, 1920 and May 18, 1920 respectively:

The price of rats [i.e., muskrats] at Holt and Renfrew are up to $5 today (B.243/a/1).

Rats are up to $6 today (B.243/a/1).

The fluctuations in the fur market and in natural game cycles adversely affected the Attawapiskat Cree. On June 3, 1921, the trader at Attawapiskat made the following observation:

Business is very quiet this spring due to the Indians making poor hunts and to the low fur values as compared to last spring (HBC B.243/a/1).

The White trader, while being part of the encapsulating machinery of the Euro-Canadian society, was also part of the *encapsulated*. The policies of the HBC and the markets of the world, far beyond his control, largely determined his movements and decisions. While this is not meant to confuse matters, we must be aware of the fact that Whites in the north functioned under constraints not of their making.

All of this is not to suggest a Native-as-victim scenario. The HBC journals suggest a manipulation of the traders as a coping strategy. An entry in the post journal from May 30, 1931 suggests how the Cree coped:

A number of the inland hunters...who did not pay were permitted to trade their entire winter catch at Weenusk, despite the fact that the Company's manager at that post had a list showing the amount of debt each Attawapiskat native had on leaving for his hunting grounds last fall (HBC B.243/a/4).

The above discussion serves to illustrate that the initial relationship between the HBC and the Church and the Cree had been altered. Able to wield economic control, the HBC was able to change the rules of the game. The Cree/White relationship in Attawapiskat would be largely played in White terms.

THE ARRIVAL OF THE GOVERNMENT

Treaty 9

It is time now to turn in more detail to the government—the one major remaining encapsulating factor. With the Church and the traders in the Bay, it was inevitable that the government would arrive shortly. As Honigmann (1961:16) has written, "with two trading companies in the area, the time had come for the Canadian government to conclude a treaty with the Indians."

As noted by Long (1978), economic factors prompted the signing of Treaty 9, namely economic development in the south and economic depression in the north. The Albany River marked the dividing line between the north and south. Logging, hydro-electric development, minerals and farming had all been undertaken in the so-called New Ontario. These, in turn, meant the building of roads and railroads in these areas. Ontario, unlike Quebec, intended to meet its obligation to extinguish Native territorial rights (Long, 1978).

The depletion of game and fur-bearers, in conjunction with an increase in population, served to create endemic poverty and hunger. Long (1978) notes the relief paid out to Natives in Attawapiskat following the treaty signing in 1905: $32.41 in 1906–7, $716.19 in 1909–10, $2,959.00 in 1923–24 and $9,155.51 in 1929–30. What these figures suggest is an increasing entrapment within the economic pattern created by hunting for trade as opposed to hunting for subsistence.

The suggestion that there was economic depression north of the Albany River does not preclude non-Native interest in that area. Robert Bell of the Geological Survey of Canada (GSC) travelled the Attawapiskat River in 1886. In 1901, Dowling, also from the GSC, explored the Ekwan, while his colleague McInnes went down the Winisk. Thus, while there was the ostensible intent to alleviate the suffering of Natives in the North, there existed as well an economic and political interest north of the Albany River.

The Attawapiskat band was included with the Albany Cree in the signing of Treaty 9 on August 3, 1905. According to Long (1978), "the Treaty 9 commissioners were given no latitude in negotiating the terms of the treaty; these terms were decided before the Commissioners left Ottawa." Essentially, then, the treaty was a take-it-or-leave-it offer. Fumoleau (cited in Long, 1978) states that the Natives "were simply submitting to the inevitable."

Furthermore, Morrison (1986) notes that Treaty 9 is significant in that it was the first time that a province took an active role in the negotiations. But, he asks (as does Long), what was there to negotiate? The only negotiations were between the provincial and federal governments.

> [L]et us suppose that some of the Indian people had refused. What then? Ontario...would have continued with the settlement and development of the lands anyway. That fact, coupled with the province's claim to veto power over the treaty terms, had effectively removed any negotiating power the Indian people might have had. The treaty commissioners...were perfectly aware of this (Morrison, 1986:32).

Treaty 9 was a *fait accompli* before the commissioners even approached the Native bands. The governments never intended negotiations. Later, Duncan Campbell Scott would write that "there was no basis for argument. The simple facts had to be stated...the King is the great father of the Indians, watchful over their interests, and ever compassionate" (Morrison, 1986:23). Paternalistic to a great degree and totally subsuming in its intent, Treaty 9 would pave the way for subsequent non-Native incursions. In the words of one Attawapiskat elder, "in 1905 it was said that things would not change. But things changed so fast. The culture and language, etc." (Janet Nakogee, cited in *Native Studies Review*, Vol. 5 #2). It would appear that for the most part the Cree had great expectations in terms of what the treaty would provide. Treaty 9 contains a statement from the Cree, presented to the commissioners at Fort Albany, August 5, 1905:

> From our hearts we thank thee, O Great Chief, as thou hast pitied us and given us temporal help. We are very poor and weak. He (the Great Chief) has taken us over, here in our own country, through you (his servants)...Thou hast helped us in our poverty. Every day we pray, trusting that we may be saved through a righteous life; and for thee we shall ever pray that thou mayest be strong in God's strength and by his assistance...we and our children will in the church of God now and ever thank Jesus....

The prayerful attitude expressed here indicates the religious hopes of the Cree for the new regime. For the most part, the reception was similar wherever the commissioners went. Morrison (1986:43) cites the warm reception the commissioners received at Moose Factory, Matchewan and New Post. What is important to note here is how much the Cree had internalized the White religion, the White paternalism displayed toward the Natives, and the demonstration of reciprocal obligations. Implicit in this statement is the expectation of help in return for their commitment to the White god and faith.

The issue of Native understanding and expectations of the treaties has been debated since the treaties were signed. Based on the commissioners' notes from their travels, Morrison (1986) emphatically states that Natives were invariably told that hunting and fishing rights "would not be taken from them." He argues that this amounts to a serious misleading of the First Nations people as to the exact nature of the agreement they were signing. Based on this, he contends that most of the Albany River bands (hence, Attawapiskat) would not have signed had a clear explanation of the treaty terms been presented to them.

Morrison (1986:51) cites an example of the guarded answers that the government submitted to Native queries. Chief Newatchkigigswabe of Long Lake Post thanked the government for its generosity (including annuity payments) and hoped that provision would be made for his sick and destitute because they found it difficult to make a living. The commissioners tried to guard against "such unrealistic expectations," telling the people that the government was always willing to help those actually requiring help, but that the Cree must rely as much as possible on their own exertions.

James Wesley is a Cree historian at Kashechewan. He quotes Commissioner Scott on August 3, 1905:

> There will not be any legislation governing trapping, hunting animals and hunting birds and fishing, if you are in favour of the treaty. If something happens to you as to sickness or need of help the Government will help you, all the people from Albany, Attawapiskat, Winisk, Fort Severn, will have this help. This will be all for now, I will give you one hour to think it over. If you do not accept this treaty, the government will do whatever it wants with you. Where we have come from, all the Indians have agreed to sign treaty; if you don't you will find it hard for yourselves.... (Morrison, 1986:53).

There are considerable grounds to argue that the people signing the treaty did not have a very good idea as to what they were signing. Janet Nakogee, an Attawapiskat elder, has said that "The ones who signed didn't know or understand very much when the land was signed for, because it was the first time they heard about this agreement...They did not know how things would change. That is why they signed..." (*Native Studies Review*, Vol. 5 #2). And, as noted above, the people were given one hour to decide, under duress.

We have argued throughout that the process of encapsulation is very much a function of the various state agents working in harmony, whether intentional or not. This has been demonstrated on a number of occasions: the Church following the traders into Albany, the latter following the former into Attawapiskat and the federal and provincial governments working together to "negotiate" Treaty 9. The HBC and federal government also negotiated to determine the fates of those Natives in what was then the Northwest Territories (NWT). In 1904, Indian Affairs told the HBC that no people living beyond the Albany River in the NWT would be included in the treaty signing process. However, on July 6, 1905, while the commissioners were in the field, the government, under pressure from the HBC, issued an order-in-council empowering the commissioners to set aside reserves in that area between the Albany River, the District of Keewatin and Hudson Bay and to admit to treaty any Native living in that area (Morrison, 1986:58). This, in part, was due to a mistaken belief that these large, disparate groups of Natives represented a "community of interest" for trade purposes. That is, for purposes of trade and for purposes of government administration, all the Native people in the region were recognized as being one unified group, regardless of any traditional social or political social groupings that the Cree themselves might recognize. Under these conditions, Attawapiskat was included as part of the Albany Band. During the next several years the more remote groups began to pressure the government for separate band and reserve status. Thus, in 1930, under the conditions of the adhesion, the Attawapiskat Band was recognized and given a separate reserve on the Ekwan River. They were separate and apart from the Fort Albany Band to which they had originally belonged.

The petitions that were submitted by various bands to the government suggest the degree of poverty in the north. Long (1978:21) cites one of these petitions from Severn, written by Chief James Stone in 1915, prior to the adhesion:

> My band of Indians include Weenusk Post, 110 miles east of this place, situated on Hudson's Bay. We would like to join in a Treaty as the other Indians at York Factory on the west of us, or Albany, Fort Hope, Osnaburgh, Attawapiskat on the south of us...We are practically surrounded by the Indians who get help from the Government, and our hunting grounds in this cold northern climate are very poor, and we would be very pleased to be able to join in any of these treaties, now...that white men are coming into this northern country we will be driven from our land.

If the HBC was able to initiate its encapsulation through the use and manipulation of its greater economic resources, the government was able to implement Treaty 9 through its greater political machinery, that is, by means of acts of parliament, duly elected representatives, government ministries and the (theoretical) backing of the (White) Canadian public. The implementation was the product of negotiations among the provincial and federal governments and the HBC. The Cree were becoming increasingly bureaucratized. Against this conglomerate, symbolized by flags, Mounties and flotillas of canoes, the Natives, demoralized, famished, weakened and impoverished as they were by White encroachment, could offer little resistance. Further, in light of the promises made, what advantage was there in resistance?

In much the same way as the fur traders represented a much larger society outside, the commissioners represented a political and social system that, by virtue of its size, complexity and self-legitimation, could subsume the Native communities it encountered. And the process by which the treaty signing process unfolded virtually guaranteed its acceptance by those upon whom it was imposed: consciously misleading people with vague and ambiguous statements, utilizing considerable pomp and ceremony and guaranteeing of annuities in times of privation. By the time of the second summer of "negotiations," the discussion period that the commissioners "allowed" the Cree was increasingly unnecessary (Morrison, 1986:43).

It is essential to examine the signing of Treaty 9 from a government perspective. Undoubtedly, the government believed that its legal and political right to enter into treaty was unassailable. Having mandated itself the role of guardian of the Natives under Section 91 (24) of the British North America Act of 1867 (which created Canada as a country), and having developed the Indian Act in order to fulfill this role, there was, in the eyes of the government, no issue. Lending additional credibility to their action was that the government was following precedent established by the British Crown and codified in the Royal Proclamation of 1763 (i.e., entering into treaty and paying for lands taken by the government). Furthermore, any treaty that was signed was done so in the interests of the majority of Canadians. One of the fundamental reasons for the extinguishment of Aboriginal rights in northern Ontario was to enable non-Natives to gain access to the resources of that region. Therefore, they enjoyed not only a legal and political right, but also a moral obligation to non-Native Canada. Economics, Bailey (1969) reminds us, will determine the nature of encapsulation.

There is still considerable anger in Attawapiskat regarding the alleged promises made by the government. Honigmann (1949:25) states that "psychologically, the Attawapiskat Cree has defined the government as a responsible protector and 'giver' from whom sustenance may properly be expected." The Cree expected that they would "never be hard up" for anything and that the government would supply what was needed. Further, it was understood that no Native would ever starve. Given that starvation was common during the winters of 1902–03 and 1903–04 in Attawapiskat, we can appreciate their concerns and expectations in this matter.

Following the signing of the treaty, starvation occurred in 1909, 1928, 1930–31, 1934–36 and 1946–48. Assistance from the government was little or non-existent. In 1934–36 the government responded to starvation by providing lard and flour. It is on the basis of incidents like these that the Attawapiskat people contend that the government has failed to meet its obligations to them. And, despite all best intentions, attempts at talks with Indian Affairs representatives often met with failure. The HBC post journals from July 24, 1930 make the following observation:

A number of the inland hunters returned today to meet the Indian Department commissioners who are due at the post tomorrow (HBC B.243/a/5).

A week later, on July 30, the following entry is recorded:

Natives who returned from inland to await arrival of Indian Department commissioners preparing to leave for their hunting grounds (HBC B.243/a/5).

They left the following day, July 31, without having met with the government representatives:

All inland hunters now preparing to leave for their hunting grounds, being unable to await the arrival of Indian Department commissioners any longer (HBC B.243/a/5).

Perhaps predictably, the commissioners arrived the following day, August 1:

Indian commissioners arrived about 2 pm (2 hours and 40 minutes from Weenusk) (HBC B.243/a/5).

What was undoubtedly frustrating was the fact that while there existed the expectation of help from the Church and the HBC on moral grounds, the expectations of help from the government were based on legal obligations. And this help was seldom forthcoming.

The signing of Treaty 9 was the final major Euro-Canadian incursion in the lives of the Attawapiskat Cree. The coming of the Church affected them religiously and culturally, and the fur companies brought them into a new economic sphere, but the treaty signing would tie them forever to the government. All subsequent changes would be legitimized by government dicta.

Finally, in terms of the breakdown of the traditional family territory system, we must examine closely the role of the government and its representatives. John M. Cooper, in a letter to Frank Speck dated October 14, 1933, suggests the degree to which the State had an impact on this breakdown.

In those sections of the Indian territory in which the Indians are under treaty (in Ontario particularly) I have been told over and over again by the Indians that immediately after the treaty the Indian agents began systematically drilling it into the Indian mind that henceforth there was no such thing as family hunting grounds and that each Indian had the right under treaty to hunt wherever he pleased. All along the Albany River and *all along the west coast of James Bay this systematically carried out policy has been an enormous, perhaps the chief, influence that has broken down the whole land tenure system* (emphasis added) (John M. Cooper Papers, B. 7–9, "Indian Affairs Department, Canada", Catholic University Archives).

If this is indeed true, the government enacted the registered trapline system that was to follow to correct its *own* policy implemented with the signing of Treaty 9. If the government did encourage the Cree to give up their family territories, it would not be surprising if they followed the suggestion, given the depletion of resources and the fact that they had been admonished to give up their ways and follow the example and advice of the White people. It is interesting to note as well that Dr. Orford's observations of trespass by Natives from Attawapiskat and Albany were first articulated in 1941, twelve years after the signing of the treaty. Perhaps the Cree did heed the government, for it was in the 1930s that Cooper also observed the "breakdown" of the system. The government, in implementing the registered trapline system, quite likely was acting to correct its own blunder.

The Registered Trapline System

Of the various non-Native incursions into James Bay that directly affected land tenure and use, it is the **registered trapline system** that has perhaps received the most criticism from the Attawapiskat people. The reasons for this are not surprising. It is this system that was most obvious in its intent, most measurable in its consequences and most blatant in its impact.

Brody (1981:88,89) has contended that the registered trapline system in British Columbia was an attempt to bring what were considered the Natives' unusual economic practices in line with ideas of ownership and exclusivity in the interests of rational production for a market economy. He argues that Native interests were not a priority, but nonetheless First Nations everywhere were urged to register lines and accept the rules of the colonial (i.e., Canadian) powers. This, he contends, was the first direct attack upon and restriction of Native life.

The registered trapline system was the culmination of a number of Euro-Canadian efforts designed to cope with general fur and game scarcity and the breakdown of the traditional harvesting strategies and practices of Native people. While apologists suggest that the system was introduced at the request of Aboriginal people, it is fair to suggest that its implementation was as much a response to the needs of the fur companies and to the movement of non-Natives into the region.

In 1928, Duncan Campbell Scott, the head of Indian Affairs, informed Walter Cain, the Deputy Minister of Lands and Forests (Ontario) that "the Indians residing in the District of Patricia [hence, Attawapiskat] are much exercised over the rapid disappearance of the furbearing animals" which they attributed "to the inroads of white trappers." Scott suggested to Cain that he hoped that the latter would suggest to his government "the justice of setting apart various tracts in which the Indians shall have the sole right to take game, or that the game laws may be so modified as will preserve to the Indians a continuance of living" (Morrison, 1986:68).

The invasion of White trappers was attributable to rising fur prices during the 1920s, which brought non-Natives into areas previously only exploited by Natives. It has been suggested that as increasingly large numbers of Whites encroached on traditional lands and trapped beaver indiscriminately, Natives were obliged to do likewise, irrespective of traditional laws of conservation. The result was a free-for-all exploitation, reaching a climax between 1922 and 1929.

The registered trapline system is ultimately the result of a number of endeavours, beginning with the HBC. In Quebec, the HBC, in conjunction with the provincial government, established their first modern beaver sanctuary at Rupert's House in 1931. Covering an area of 7000 square miles (11,265 square kilometres), it employed those Natives whose territory it usurped as "game guardians." Some fifteen families were thus employed and paid by the company (as per contractual obligations with the provincial government). Every summer eight to ten survey parties of Cree were sent out to make an annual inventory of beaver lodges in the sanctuary.

Following the Rupert's House endeavour, the Charlton Island beaver sanctuary was re-established in 1934, having initially been developed 80 years earlier. In its second incarnation, the sanctuary was under the control of the federal government (in its capacity as administrator of the Northwest Territories, which owns the islands in Hudson and James Bay). Twenty breeding beaver were imported from southern Ontario and placed on the island, in the hope of restocking the island's only viable resource.

The third modern sanctuary was established on Agamiski (Akimiski) Island in 1935, again in agreement with the federal government, when eight beaver were placed on the island. An additional 14 were relocated there the following year. In 1936, the only adult pair of the initial eight placed on the island produced a litter. The strategy was to revive the numbers of beaver through the sanctuary so that they could restock the depleted numbers on the rivers of the west coast of the bay. So rare were beaver in the 1930s that Anderson observed that several of that generation of Attawapiskat Cree had never seen one (1937:11). Although the preserve was established in 1935, when Honigmann visited Attawapiskat in 1947/48, the Cree had had only two trapping seasons on the Akimiski sanctuary.

Following the creation of the Akimiski sanctuary, another was established at Albany, and another near Attawapiskat in 1944 that would last until 1951. The Attawapiskat preserve extended from the Kapiskau River on the south to 54 degrees 30 latitude north (16 kilometres above Lake River) and west to longitude 85 (12 kilometres west of Sutton Lake). With the development of the beaver preserves, there was a mapping of the various family territories and the registration of senior males as "talleymen," setting of individual "quotas" and mapping of hunting group "territories" (Preston, unpublished ms.). Preston notes that these concepts are rough approximations of Cree notions. Thus, there was an ostensible effort to have the sanctuaries resemble Cree territorial patterns. The setting of territories was to ensure the accuracy of the head count of beavers and their lodges. The trader at Attawapiskat acted as an intermediary between those who disputed boundaries, reconciling their differences and usually establishing precise boundaries along creeks.

In the late 1940s, in an effort to keep the territory system strong, the manager assigned areas, ostensibly along "traditional rights." The underlying assumption is that this would guarantee rights and ensure an economical use of resources. To this end, the manager apportioned tracts to two or three related or unrelated families. However, despite urging from the manager to conform to the pattern established, people did not adhere to the plan. As Preston observes (unpublished ms.), kinship organization is stronger than territory organization.

For a while, there was a process of consultation between the federal government and the HBC. Increasingly, however, Ottawa and the provincial government assumed more authority, and consultation diminished. In 1952 (officially, 1948), Ontario government personnel assumed control of the federal government/HBC beaver preserves, making them into licensed and registered traplines.

Two Views of the Registered Trapline System

We must examine both Native and government expectations of the registered trapline system to appreciate the reactions of the Attawapiskat Cree to the system. The Cree had come to see the government as a provider, and expected help from the government in times of need. The Cree expected protection by the authorities from White trappers encroaching in the north; hence, a recognition of their rights to the land, and protection from starvation.

And what of the government? The transition to the registered trapline system in the Attawapiskat region was one more step toward regulation of trapping throughout the province, a process that had begun years earlier in more southerly regions. The province had, since the late 19th century, been establishing legislation to control hunting and trapping activities in Ontario. Honigmann (1961:119) suggests that the policy was to prohibit White trappers from operating north of Cochrane. As well, licensing Natives to trap particular grounds would afford them protection against encroachment by members of their own community. Honigmann suggested that there was encroachment by Cree from Winisk as well as by some Ojibwa. What this latter contention suggests, however, is yet another paternalistic overture on the part of the government, protecting Natives against unscrupulous Whites as well as against themselves. It must be stated, however, that in some areas there was legislation allowing Natives to trap, to the exclusion of White trappers. During the 1920s, for example, when beaver and otter populations were declining, only resident Native trappers north of the Canadian National Railway line were allowed to trap these species.

The problem, however, is that the imposition of the registered trapline system was yet another piece of legislation that hindered and restricted First Nations people. Furthermore, it extended the net of encapsulation. In theory, Aboriginal people are the "responsibility" of the federal government; the registered trapline system brought them under further bureaucratic control, this time under the auspices of the *provincial* government. The registered trapline system was entrenched in legalese and, using strict Euro-Canadian definitions, spelled out the terms and conditions of use.

> [R]egulations stipulated, among other things, that a person granted a "Trap-Line License" would "have the exclusive right to trap fur-bearing animals on that portion of Crown Lands described in the License." The area described in the "Trap-Line License" was referred to as a "trap-line area" and was assigned a number by the Ontario Department of Lands and Forests (now MNR) (Hansen, 1989:30).

The legislation outlined other conditions: no person could hold more than one trap-line license at any time; the holder could trap in open season one beaver in each beaver house in the area covered by the license but only where at least five houses were reported in the application. Further, the 1947 regulations under the Game and Fisheries Act, 1946 also stipulated that the holder of a "Beaver License" could trap a limit of 10 beaver in open season in an area that was not a registered trapline area, but was land owned by the applicant. In short, the system reflected the White, legalistic, bureaucratic machinery that created it. It did not acknowledge the conservation traditions of the Cree. And, in Cree terms, it was far too rigid, restrictive and impractical. Elders in the community with whom I spoke during my fieldwork in 1990 commented on the system:

> The government [allotted] territories, and this led to aggression among the people. Hate, anger and conflict started when MNR started [the Registered Trapline].

The truth of these words are shown in some informants' comments:

> A lot of people were protective about their land, not letting others use it, but I was not.

> It was my father's land, but now I own it because I have the permit (#2332). I allow my sons and sons-in-law to trap because they have no land of their own.

> People trap all over but I don't understand why unless they are invited.

Other informants voiced concerns of a more pragmatic nature:

> The MNR interfered by asking people to [obtain] licenses.

> The MNR system was too inflexible, too impractical.

> The area was too small; therefore, it restricted people into a land of insufficient resources.

Especially important is the fact that the trapline system was couched in White culture. The notion of "exclusive" right, for example, is essentially foreign to Native culture. But it is apparent that in some instances, traditional ideas and ideology were altered. Thus, some Cree that I spoke with seemed to have internalized at least some of the dominant Euro-Canadian values.

> There is a lot of conflict if people don't share the same view and beliefs regarding the land. The government system made some people change their views, so we didn't all think the same way.

It is important to realize that in many cases the registered trapline system was allotted along the lines of traditional family territories, although the extent to which this is true is difficult to determine. When this did occur, though, problems developed when the need to procure game arose. A number of elders in Attawapiskat indicate that their moose and caribou hunting areas were the same as their trapping areas, whereas previously a different set of "rules" governed the hunting of game.

> Anybody can hunt and trap on my land. A long time ago anybody could trap on my father's land but then the government set up the grid [the registered trapline system] and things changed.

Peoples' attitudes and expectations of behaviour changed as a proprietorial attitude that had never existed before took hold. Particularly among older men (between the ages of 50 and 80) there was a tendency to restrict moose and caribou hunting to their own territories, although they were receptive to the idea of other people using their land. When moose or caribou were scarce there may have been a reluctance to hunt them outside of their territory.

> I hunt moose and caribou irregularly now. Last moose hunt was two years ago. Last caribou hunt was 10 years ago. Moose and caribou are not common in my area now.

What the government failed to recognize was that there was a logic to what appeared to be a breakdown in the traditional system. Cultures are dynamic. Cultures adapt and change when situations warrant it. Thus, while there was trespass and encroachment, these were not new. Traditional culture had ways to cope with breaches in protocol. And while people were seen to be "hunting all over," this was not a chaotic, random rambling. Rather, hunting all over reflected the environmental reality of the times. Further, it reflected conventional *social* understandings. The depletion of large game in the Attawapiskat region following the arrival of the fur companies and the Church (and the accompanying large immigration to the coast) necessitated new adaptive strategies. And, of course, the new economic realities introduced by the fur trade also meant shifts in traditional subsistence patterns. The system that emerged was one that acknowledged a depletion of both fur-bearers and large game and the increased utilization of a new material culture. It was also one that might have reflected the demands of the Indian Agent following the signing of Treaty 9. However, at the same time there still existed a recognition of traditionally held territories. What changed, then, was the nature of relationships between people in terms of land use.

What I am arguing here is that what Cooper (1933) defined as a "breakdown" in the traditional system was, in reality, a system in the process of change and adaptation. Cooper had argued that "the Indians [were] drifting rapidly from private ownership of real property to a system of communism..." However, what he failed to recognize was that the system was adapting to other, external considerations.

Cultures are not static. The demands of a new economic system being introduced, coupled with an increasing population and a dwindling resource base, made a change in the traditional system a necessity. Hunting all over was essential to survival. Today, when people refer to the days when "people hunted all over," it is a harkening back to a time when Cree norms prevailed regarding land use. Territoriality, land tenure, land use—they are all, fundamentally, sets of relations between persons or among groups of people and the land. To look at the shifts in traditional land use in the 1920s and 1930s and label it a breakdown is to miss the point: what was occurring was, rather, a change in the nature of the relationships among the people.

So what went wrong with the system? A number of ill-conceived ideas plagued the registered trapline system in Attawapiskat. An examination of the trapping areas reveals a disproportionate number of people exploiting the area immediately around the community; hence, the informant's comment above regarding the insufficient resource base for the numbers of people. While ostensibly allotting territories along traditionally held family territories, the fact that such a large number exists near the coast suggests that a significant number of territories did not follow this pattern. The Attawapiskat people were not coastal people. The abrupt allocation of a significant number of people to a relatively small area, bound by imposed Euro-Canadian standards of behaviour, would inevitably lead to conflict.

The allotment of tracts to unrelated (as well as related) families undoubtedly contributed to the system's malfunctioning. As evidenced in numerous studies, both today and historically, kin links are fundamental in hunter–gatherer societies. To some extent, this tenet appears to have been overlooked in the apportioning of territories among families.

Similarly, the apportioning of territories did not recognize the population fluctuations of game species. The Attawapiskat Cree had, at the time of the implementation of the system, experienced numerous periods of starvation. The restriction of hunters to bounded territories had a considerable effect on their ability to pursue game. Bearing in mind that the implementation of the system also altered notions of propriety, it would seem that conflicts would be inevitable.

Another fundamental reason for the resentment and ultimate rejection of the MNR system is the fact that it virtually ignored Cree notions of territoriality. The implementation process did not incorporate Cree protocol of land and resource use. Instead, there were fixed boundaries and rules regarding exclusivity of use. The system reflected the traditional government attitudes of paternalism that existed at the time. The consultation process, such as it was, established boundaries, designated "talleymen" and established quotas. These are only rough approximations of Cree concepts. Furthermore, they constitute only a minute part of the complex whole that makes up the Cree relationship to the land. The MNR registered trapline system was, in essence, a foreign system imposed on Cree people.

There is also a sense of formality with the MNR registered trapline system that is a function of the codification and registration of the various territories. This formality is in direct opposition to the informal (yet equally valid) flexibility that existed in the so-called traditional system. It might be argued that this codification and formality, in association with the deliberate efforts to convince Native people of the superiority and rightness of Euro-Canadian systems, led to the internalization and acceptance of the system which one still finds today in Attawapiskat, albeit in small numbers. Thus, a stage was set for a dispute between those who adopted the new system and those who did not.

The formalization and codification of trapping areas also meant that these areas were no longer solely the purview of the Cree. The relationship between Cree and land was no longer mediated only by environmental, spiritual and kinship concerns, but was now enjoined by the State. An outside body had, in part, usurped the rules based on age and sex that had governed tenure. The people were aware that the larger society, as manifested by the MNR, had entered into traditional land use activities.

Finally, we must examine the expectations that the system brought with it. Given the experiences of the people (starvation, disease, White trapper encroachment), and through misrepresentation and misunderstanding, the Cree expected that the registered traplines would recognize and protect their treaty rights. Cooper, in 1933, advised the federal government that the Cree in James Bay sought "some form of recognition or guarantee of the individual and family hunting grounds." Unfortunately, the form this guarantee took did no such thing. Government officials operated under the assumption that registration provided no substantive protection against competing land uses (Hutchins, 1986:19). Brody (1981:99) has observed that "in Canadian law, registered traplines grant no hunting rights and no protection against other activities that would destroy the wildlife on them."

Hutchins goes a step further in criticism of the system.

> ...the very existence of traplines has been used to deny the survival of aboriginal rights and titles. Not only is it argued that government regulations respecting the establishment and management of trapline systems may indicate an intention to exercise complete dominion over a territory inconsistent with the survival of aboriginal title, but the very fact that the trapline system is a more individualized form of land use has led to conclusions that it does not fit the test of lands held in common for the use of benefit of an "organized society". To complicate matters, impacts on one or a limited number of traplines might well be judged not to affect sufficiently the rights and interests of a collectivity so as to justify enjoining development activity (1986:17).

In the end, the MNR registered trapline system only served to exacerbate the very problem it sought to correct. The Attawapiskat Cree argue that problems of conflict and aggression were initiated with the imposition of the system. Perhaps this is an idealized notion of what the pre-MNR period was like. Regardless, in 1990 the community contended that adherence to the system was abandoned 15 or 16 years after its introduction. They argue that the problems it caused in terms of fighting and restrictions on hunting and trapping rendered it unfeasible. This is not to say that it does not exist on paper; it is still there. Rather, the people do not subscribe to it in any way. Instead, they work out their own resource harvesting practices among themselves. It is a system, as was the "hunting all over" strategy, in the process of change and adaptation.

CONCLUSIONS AND DISCUSSION

Between 1901 and 1952 the Attawapiskat Cree saw an unprecedented number of changes imposed upon their culture by traders, missionaries and the Canadian government. Cultures, we are told, are integrated, and a change to one part of the culture will affect other parts. It was inevitable that the changes imposed by these foreign institutions would have a ripple effect upon the Cree.

Drawn to the coast by the mission and the fur trading posts, there were shifts in the demographics of Cree society. An increase in the population of Attawapiskat had an impact on the area's resources, resulting in a number of periods of starvation. Possibly, as well, it exacerbated trespass, as people spread further out on the land looking for game. The Cree, expecting help from the missionary, trader and government, often found themselves without the assistance they thought should be forthcoming. Accustomed to operating in reciprocal and egalitarian relationships, they quickly discovered that Euro-Canadians operated with a different set of rules.

The government, when it arrived, codified and formalized its relationship with the Cree. Usurping their land through Treaty 9 and then imposing upon them the registered trapline system, the government sought to regulate Cree subsistence practices with Euro-Canadian concepts that failed to recognize the Cree understandings of territoriality and land tenure. After a decade and a half of trying to accommodate this foreign imposition, the Attawapiskat Cree jettisoned the system in favour of their own, demonstrating again that encapsulation, more often than not, is met with resistance.

CONTENT QUESTIONS

1. Upon what three notions of relationship is traditional Cree society based?
2. Describe the nature of leadership in traditional Cree society.
3. What is meant by "balanced reciprocity"?
4. What were the expectations of the Cree in terms of Treaty 9?
5. What were the concerns of the Cree with respect to the registered trapline system?
6. What alternative interpretation is made of the notion that there had been a "breakdown" in the traditional Cree hunting/trapping system?

Contemporary Attawapiskat Cree Land Tenures

LEARNING OBJECTIVES

After reading this chapter, students should be able to:

1. Distinguish between the two conflicting positions held by the Attawapiskat Cree concerning traditional ownership.

2. Describe the land tenure practices of the Attawapiskat Cree concerning the goose hunt, and explain why they have taken the form they have.

3. Compare the prevailing social expectations regarding the hunting of moose and caribou.

4. Describe the different means through which rights to land are obtained.

5. Explain what is meant by the statement "rights to resources are species specific."

Any attempt at analysis of contemporary Attawapiskat Cree land tenure is inevitably faced with a barrage of apparent contradictions of both theory and practice. These contradictions are the products of the following three factors: the academic literature that has been written about the West Main (Mushkegowuk) Cree; the historical events of the last century that impinge on the people and their land use; and what appear to be discrepancies among both ideologies and practices and between these ideologies and practices among the people themselves. Thus, land tenure is not, and has never (in the last 100 years) been, straightforward or easily defined and explained.

In the community in 1990 there was a divergence of positions regarding "ownership" of land and protocol regarding its use. While we cannot quantify the strength of a commonly held ideology, we can state that in the Attawapiskat case two positions held sway. One is the commonly held view that "people can hunt anywhere." This position dates back several decades and was noted by Cooper in 1933. This stance has assumed a political dogmatism and is used to refute the registered provincial trapline system. The other, conflicting, position is not so much an ideology as it is a recognition of traditionally held family hunting territories.

To have validity, an ideology must have an underpinning of logic, a rationalization for its being. Informants' statements suggest the logic and rationale underlying the "hunting anywhere" ideology. These statements are rooted in the most irrefutable of bases—the religious. "The Creator made the land to be used." "Only God can own the land." "It is a free country." "Nobody can own the land." We could, as well, argue that the ideology is rooted in traditional notions of (non)ownership, as perceived through Cree eyes.

The discrepancy between the "hunting anywhere" ideology and the second position is to be found in people's statements. "I own the land because I inherited it from my father and grandfather." "I own the land because MNR [Ministry of Natural Resources] (or the government) gave it to me." "I own the land because I hold the license (or permit)." "My family has always used this land." "If the "hunting anywhere" ideology is based upon religious grounds, the "ownership" stance finds its rationale in both Cree tradition, that is, that of the family "ownership" of territories, and the perceived legitimacy of White legal/political bureaucracy.

We could easily reconcile these two positions through a variety of means, for example, by saying that these are social statements and are not meant to be finite legal/political decrees. However, actions on the ground indicate that in many instances behaviour follows ideology. We find, for example, that a couple of older trappers strongly adhere to the allotment of territories by the MNR. They do not hunt or trap outside their land and strongly voice their objections to those who "hunt and trap all over." For them, there should be no issue: territories were assigned and people should abide by the government's dictum. There are also others who do not trap around Attawapiskat because their traditional family lands are not in close proximity to the community. In other words, they strongly respect traditional family territories and would not trap on land that is not theirs. Yet other people trap "anywhere" because: a) that is where the beaver, marten or mink happen to be most plentiful; or b) it is conveniently close to town. However, it should also be noted that some people (mostly men aged fifty or older) who do move from their own territories into someone else's ask permission.

When we examine the protocol that governs notions of land tenure in Attawapiskat, we begin to realize that it is not so much rights to land that prevail; rather, it is the rights to the resources. In particular, there is evidence to suggest that rights to resources are species specific, and that certain social expectations and obligations with regard to these different species apply. Another dichotomy that must be borne in mind is that of hunting for subsistence versus hunting for trade. Whether an animal is to be consumed for food or sold for profit determines where it is hunted.

There are other social understandings that also must be explored. In Attawapiskat, it is understood that trespass and poaching do not occur until the animal is caught. "Anybody can trap on my land as long as they don't steal." "Anybody can trap on my land from outside the family. Relationships are not based on blood, but upon a sharedness of the trapper's lifestyle." "I'm not aware of territories in a general sense, but I'm aware of my father's land." "Nobody can own the land, but an animal is 'owned' once it is trapped." "Animals belong to people only once they are trapped or shot." These statements will become meaningful as we examine the protocol that prevails in Attawapiskat regarding trapping, hunting and fishing.

GOOSE HUNTING

Of all the various Cree natural resource harvesting activities, none is pursued with more enthusiasm and anticipation than the spring and fall goose hunts. The majority of hunters report using the same hunting areas that their fathers (or fathers-in-law) did, demonstrating continuity. This continuity, however, must not be confused with the continuity of traditional family lands. Rather, in most cases they are sites that were used only for the seasonal goose hunts. Thus, continuity is such for semi-annual, relatively brief periods. Nonetheless, there is a long-term pattern to most goose hunting sites, demonstrating strong kin links to the land.

The expectations are not rigid, however. Some hunters have more than one preferred location, alternating between or within seasons. Similarly, a number of hunters may establish temporary blinds (i.e., shelters made by hunters from branches to conceal themselves from the geese) near the community during the early part of the season, during which time they will make day trips to their blinds. Later, during the peak of the season, they will move to their more permanent sites for the remainder of the fly-over.

Two factors that affect notions of tenure as they pertain to waterfowl hunting are the number of hunters (well over 90 per cent of men aged 15 to 65) and the number and availability of geese. The fact that most men return to the same sites reflects three main concerns: 1) it is a proven area for goose hunting; 2) in some instances it is on traditional family lands; and 3) frequenting of sites over the years creates knowledge of predictable patterns; hence, a social equilibrium and set of expectations regarding dispersal of hunters over the land is created and maintained. Encroachment upon and usurpation of goose hunting sites are neither expected nor do they occur. There are unspoken understandings. Two factors are key to this respect for people's use of particular goose hunting sites. One is the predictability of the geese. Their numbers have been constant or increasing for decades. Thus, there is no competition for them (neither would there be if they were scarce, we may speculate). The second factor has to do with conventional understanding of the coastal strip where most fowling occurs. Honigmann (1961:119) observed years ago that the coastal strip was open to everyone. When the HBC apportioned tracts of land, the coastal area was deemed to be "open."

It would be unrealistic, though, to expect that the dictum of the HBC would alleviate any notions of trespass or territorial violations. We have seen how the externally imposed registered trapline system was tried and rejected in favour of a local system. It is clear that the Cree themselves have worked out a viable system of land tenure and use regarding the goose hunt. It is this, as well as the nature of the hunt itself, that allows for a smoothly working system. The spring goose hunt, in particular, is as much a celebration of life as it is a primary source of subsistence. Beginning in early March, the community virtually hums in anticipation of the hunt that begins six weeks hence. Honigmann (1961:79) posits that the "wavy" hunt is one of the few emotional releases for the Cree.

Given that the goose hunt is a celebration as well as a minor competition (to see who gets the first bird of the season), the emotional framework surrounding the twice yearly hunt works against notions of trespass and transgression. The hunt is a holiday, a period of feasting and thanksgiving and a celebration. Food is abundant and easily accessible, in contrast to the energy, exertion, expense and time invested in the uncertainty of trapping or moose and caribou hunting.

MOOSE AND CARIBOU

The nature of game will determine the protocol that prevails regarding its use. Caribou and moose are not sedentary as are, for example, beaver. Neither are they directly trans-formable into cash. However, moose and caribou do provide thousands of kilograms of meat that are distributed throughout the community. In addition, the pursuit of both of these species quite often entails the crossing of numerous territories.

Moose hunts typically occur in the fall, although occasionally they occur in the winter. Caribou hunts invariably are in the winter. The former almost always involve the traversing of the major rivers (the Lawachie, Kapiskau, Albany, Attawapiskat and Ekwan) that cut through family lands. Caribou hunts are usually conducted January through April when the snow is crusty, and involve long distance searches for, and pursuit of, the caribou. Again, numerous family lands may be criss-crossed in the quest for caribou.

A set of social rules (more correctly, social *expectations*) prevails regarding the hunting of moose and caribou. During the fall hunts along the rivers, moose are "anybody's game," regardless of where they are found. During the winter, however, moose will not be shot on another person's land, should they be found there. This probably has to do with the vulner-ability of moose at this time, when the deep snow hampers their mobility. Under such con-ditions, moose could easily be cleaned out of a given area fairly rapidly. It may also be that, at this time, a hunter could be taking food away from those people who are staying on the land for the winter. Further, it might be because moose are moving less and staying in a yard. Caribou, however, are pursued across vast distances and are not subject to such restrictions. They are "anybody's game." A number of men suggested that the protocol regarding caribou hunting was still "being worked out."

TRAPPING

The social relations that exist among trappers are complex, exacerbated by the large num-ber of traplines assigned in close proximity to the community. Further complicating these relations are the volatile nature of the fur business and the cyclical nature of fur popula-tions. Finally, there is also a species specific protocol that figures into the formula. This is based on the value of the fur, the degree of sedentarism exhibited by the species (i.e., how much it stays in one place) and the difficulty associated with its capture.

Relations to ancestral lands are complex. Rights to land are based upon time spent and experience gained on a piece of land. One man, for example, stated that he "spent [his] entire life in the bush until five years ago" [he was then 76 years old]. He "trapped on land that [his] father trapped and hunted on." However, he concluded that because "nobody is using the land now, anybody can use it, nobody owns it."

Rights may be conferred upon an individual who has never spent time on the land. These rights are conveyed through the parent who used the land. For example, one man, who was born on Akimiski Island, trapped there between the ages of 15 and 25, and then trapped elsewhere with his father-in-law. Following that, he worked for the HBC at an inland outpost store. While there, he sought and received permission to exploit the surrounding area from the land's "owner." Although it was the mid 1950s when he last trapped on Akimiski, both he and his sons (who have never trapped or hunted there) have rights to the land. Similarly, another man trapped on his uncle's land and his cousin's land. He did not trap on his father's land because his sons were going to school and he wanted to be close to his sons. He asked and received permission to use his relatives' land. Nonetheless, his sons have a right to their father's and grandfather's land even though they have never used it. Several people who have had similar experiences took this position. Another man stated, "as long as my brothers are trapping, even if I am not, I belong to the land." Rights to land are gained through *experience* on the land and through *kin* links to the land.

It is also clear that while, ideally, land is passed down directly from father to son, at times it may pass through a man's widow. One man, well over 80 years old (and whose mother is frequently referred to in the HBC journals as an active widow), stated that his father died when he was young but his mother continued trapping. Therefore, it was his mother's land. His son was his trapping partner and the son was now using the land.

Another man inherited his land through attrition and then had it legitimized by the MNR. He was raised on his father's land, and when his father died another man introduced him to the land he now claims as his own. Initially, there were several people using that particular tract but, as they "thinned out," only he remained, and when the Ministry allotted traplines, this piece was allotted to him. He asserts that a number of hunters were proprietorial about their government allotted land, but he never was. This individual was also a tallyman for the ministry.

Further confusion is created when trappers (typically younger men) claim to trap on land that is "open" or for which there is no acknowledged "owner." This is due, in part, to the considerable number of trappers licensed for the immediate vicinity of Attawapiskat. An examination of the licensed trapping grounds illustrates the considerable congestion around the community. The further one travels away from the village, the larger the trapping territories and the fewer the number of license holders.

But "open land" also has a specific meaning. In practice, it means that one may set up traps on land that is not being used by its present owner. For example, a trapper had heard of an abundance of a particularly valuable species in the proximity of the community. He set out on his snowmobile and travelled until there was no evidence of traps. Here he set up his own temporary trap line. He was completely aware of who "owned" the land, but because that section was not being used it was acceptable to trap there on a temporary basis.

Also figuring into this particular equation is the population cycle of the species. Beaver, otter and marten are important species for a number of reasons. They are particularly valuable as fur-bearers, they are comparatively difficult to catch, they are sedentary (hence, subject to unscrupulous depletion) and they are relatively scarce. Additionally, beaver is highly valued as a food item. For these reasons, trappers respect the rights of territory "owners" to these animals and will not trap them on land other than their own. Under certain conditions this rule might be relaxed, for example, during periods of high popula-tion. Also, a hunter might ask permission to trap on another's land.

Rules generally do not apply to such species as muskrat and fox. They are not especially rare, or valuable, and they are comparatively easy to trap. Wolves also fall into this category, albeit for different reasons. They are quite scarce, and to catch one is considered more luck than anything else. Also, trappers will not spend the time and energy for dubious results.

BERRIES, SMALL GAME AND FISH

Berry-picking sites and small game harvesting areas are open in Attawapiskat. That is, people will pick berries anywhere, although some families have preferred areas that are used by tradition. Rabbits and ptarmigan are generally snared or shot within a maximum 16 kilometre radius of the community or camp, with 5 kilometres the norm. Territories do not apply to these resources.

Likewise, fishing sites are open. As discussed elsewhere, there is not a high value placed on fish as food, and this may account for the fact that people can, and do, fish "any-where." While some people state that their sites are on traditional family lands, an equal number also claim to fish anywhere. A significant number of people claim to have discov-ered the sites themselves or to have been introduced to them by "friends." One man stated that "his father and a bunch of other people" used the site years ago. There were also some observations that Winisk people also share sites with Attawapiskat Cree.

The "I can hunt anywhere" statement, then, is ultimately and truly a *social* statement. Fish, small game and berries may be harvested literally "anywhere." In terms of hunting and trapping, a hunter, having been introduced to land by a relative (usually a father-in-law, brother-in-law or cousin) *can* hunt or trap anywhere. The operative word is *kinship*, for a hunter is always related to the person who "owns" the land.

CONCLUSIONS AND DISCUSSION

In 1990, there were two views regarding land tenure and land use. One held that "people can hunt anywhere." The other recognized an "ownership" of traditionally held hunting ter-ritories. While these views may seem conflicting, in reality they are based upon a socially recognized set of rules pertaining to harvestable resources. These, in turn, are based upon the nature of what is being harvested as well as kinship.

Kinship, the relative abundance of a resource, the value attached to different species, the mobility of game animals, seasonality and whether or not a species is being harvested for subsistence or trade all come into play when considering land use. There is a set of mutually understood social conventions that people recognize and by which they abide. It is recognized, for example, that fish, ptarmigan and berries may be harvested anywhere, but beaver will be trapped only on a person's own land. Similarly, a moose may be shot "anywhere" during the autumn but, for a variety of reasons, hunters will not shoot a moose in winter on somebody else's land.

Kinship is the essence of contemporary Attawapiskat Cree land tenure, for it is through kinship links that a person gains access to land and the land's resources. Through kinship, people gain rights to the land. Once a person has been introduced to the land through kin-folk, that person may harvest the resources that are found there.

CONTENT QUESTIONS

1. What are the two positions held by the Attawapiskat Cree regarding "ownership" of land and protocol regarding its use?
2. What is meant by the statement "the rights to resources are species specific"?
3. What are the limitations put on the statement "people can hunt anywhere"?

chapter six

Attawapiskat Cree
Land Use: 1901-1952

LEARNING OBJECTIVES

After reading this chapter, students should be able to:

1. Describe the differences between the subsistence patterns of the Inlanders and Coasters.

2. Explain how competition between fur trading companies contributed to starvation among the Cree.

3. Describe how depletion of resources led to a diminution in size of the winter hunting group.

4. Explain the changing role of women in Cree society in the first half of the 20th century as a result of the fur trade and depletion of resources.

5. Define "environment" in terms of Bailey's concept of encapsulation.

Non-Native incursions into the Attawapiskat region put into motion the process of encapsulation and its accompanying resistance. As we examine this process over time, a discernible pattern emerges. First, there was an apparently innocuous incursion by the church and the fur companies. Then came a codification of relationships between the

Cree and the State as embodied in the registered trapline system and Treaty 9. Third, there was an assumption of non-accountability on the part of the State in terms of its relationship with the Cree. The initial encroachments appeared to be subtle and seemingly harmless, and the Cree, for the most part, were accommodating. Their resistance, when it was manifested, was equally subtle. Both the fur traders and the church, to a greater or lesser degree, allowed the Cree some autonomy. In brief, they did not exert any legal or political control. Subsequent incursions, however, were rooted in law and government bureaucracy. Any resistance mobilized by the Cree would contravene the dictates of the government.

This period, then, demarcates the time frame of the following major non-Native incursions into the Attawapiskat region: the fur companies, the church, Treaty 9 and the registered trapline system. It was also characterized by starvation, disease, shifts in the pattern of traditional land tenure and great demographic changes.

An examination of land use indicates a systematic, consistent and logical exploitation of resources. This pattern, however, was not inflexible or rigid. Rather, it was modified and adapted to exigencies as they arose. As noted elsewhere, the Attawapiskat region is "chronically poor" in such large game species as moose, caribou and beaver. Thus, there is a considerable reliance upon fish, waterfowl and small game and birds. Bear in mind this "chronic shortage" as we examine land use, for periods of great starvation occurred in the period under discussion. The Cree adopted a number of strategies to cope with these stresses.

HUNTING FOR SUBSISTENCE PRODUCTS

Unlike the case with hunting for trade products, it is difficult to quantify and delineate patterns of hunting for subsistence products. Prior to Honigmann's 1948 analysis, *Foodways in a Muskeg Community*, there had not been any systematic examination of exploitation of resources for consumption purposes. Further compounding the problem is the fact that it is (and was) impossible to keep track of the resources harvested by those people who reside in the bush year round. Therefore, extrapolation from the extant data is difficult at best. The material to follow is therefore derived from a limited database, mainly the work of Honigmann, the HBC and a government study.

Inlanders and Coasters

Honigmann (1961) wrote the definitive work about subsistence and consumption patterns at the middle of the 20th century in Attawapiskat. Based on fieldwork from July 1947 to June 1948, he produced copious amounts of data concerning diet, trapping and hunting patterns and overall economics within the community. His period of study coincided with one of the numerous starvation periods that have occurred in the region.

To best appreciate the cycle of subsistence hunting, we must examine it in terms of the seasonal round. This was the pattern throughout the first half of the 20th century and beyond.

The HBC journals suggest that two yearly patterns were in effect, essentially defined by the proximity of one's land to the post. Throughout the James Bay literature, these have been associated with the "**Inlanders**" and the "**Coasters**." It is fair to suggest that the cultural and social distinction between the two groups was perhaps much more sharply defined on the Quebec side of the bay than it was in the Mushkegowuk region. This is particularly true of Attawapiskat, where the people originally were inland people.

Hunters typically arrived from their lands in May and June, after (generally) occasional trips to the post in midwinter or early spring for supplies. Historically, the arrival date in the post was a function of the distance of the territory from the post, the weather conditions and the productivity of the hunting/trapping season.

All the Attawapiskat Indians are now in (HBC B.243/a/1; June 2, 1920).

Most of the Opinaga Indians are in too (HBC B.243/a/1; June 12, 1920).

The first contingent of northern Indians arrived this afternoon (HBC B.243/a/1; June 16, 1923).

First lot of inland Indians came in this morning (HBC B.243/a/2; June 2, 1925).

Northern Indians still along the coast (HBC B.243/a/2; June 24, 1925).

[Indians] arrived late in the evening...having left their camps owing to the early thaw in March. Serious business, this year especially (HBC B.243/a/2; May 20, 1927).

For the Coasters, those whose lands were in greater proximity to the coast, the preceding month or so (roughly April 10 to the beginning or middle of May) provided the opportunity to procure the bountiful harvest of geese that sustained them over the long summer months. For the Inlanders, the relative lack of geese inland was offset by the usually greater abundance of larger game (including beaver) in the hinterlands beyond the post. During the 1920s (and perhaps until as late as 1947/48 when Honigmann did his research) there was a discernible pattern whereby the Inlanders and others would depart for their lands after only a brief stay of a few weeks. This is in contrast to what was noted by Nonas (1963) at the beginning of the 1960s. He found that people viewed Attawapiskat as home for "three or four months a year."

Busy with Indians who are leaving for winter (HBC B.243/a/2; August 15, 1927).

Outfitted Jacob and David Chakasim for winter this afternoon (HBC B.243/a/4; July 19, 1930).

All inland hunters now preparing to leave for their hunting grounds (HBC B.243/a/5; July 31, 1930).

Indians now leaving for winter (HBC B.243/a/2; July 10, 1928).

Almost all of the Inlanders having taken up the advances prior to their departure for the winter (HBC B.243/a/2; July 14, 1928).

Fixed up last of the departures (HBC B.243/a/2; July 18, 1928).

It is quite apparent, then, that in the first three decades of the 20th century, Attawapiskat did not serve as a "summer home" for a substantial number of people. A large number of people had virtually a total reliance on bush food on a near year-round basis. This contention is in opposition to later findings by Honigmann (1961), Hoffman (1957:50) and Nonas (1963:1). They found people residing in the village for anywhere from two to four months over the summer. This is not to suggest that there was not a three to four month village residency on the part of some Attawapiskat people (undoubtedly Coasters whose lands were nearby). Rather, the point is that summer sedentarism was not the norm for all of the Attawapiskat Cree. Further, while waterfowl were and are of inestimable importance to the people, it is apparent that some Cree bypassed the greater abundance to be found on the coastal flyways in favour of the resources inland.

Spring and Summer

The staple bush foods during the spring and early summer were fish and waterfowl, with geese being the favoured and most commonly killed birds. Honigmann (1961:99) states that geese constituted half the food supply in Attawapiskat during the mid 1940s. Coincidental with the spring arrival of the geese is the emergence of muskrat, which, by virtue of their numbers, were sought for both their food value and fur. Men typically alternated between hunting geese and trapping muskrat during the spring goose migration.

Waterfowl hunting is a food getting activity in which the greatest interest and positive emotion are invested and from which the people derive their choicest foods. This is as true today as it was 75 years ago. It is important as much for its social and cultural components as it is for the food it brings to the table.

The continued hunting of the birds year after year shows the importance of waterfowl in the diet. In 1947–48 the population of Attawapiskat was 470. Honigmann (1961:152) was able to determine that, in 1947–48, the Attawapiskat Cree consumed an estimated 6280 wavies (blue and snow geese), 1720 Canada geese and 2800 ducks. Most of the wavies (5840) were killed in the autumn, while only 440 were killed in the spring. On the other hand, 1400 Canada geese were killed in the spring and only 320 in the autumn. Of the ducks, 1960 were harvested in the autumn and 840 in the spring. It is important to note that due to weather conditions, this particular period was considered by the Cree not to have been a particularly good one for geese. To appreciate these figures, bear in mind the population in 1947 and compare the kills with those in 1951, 1952, 1974–77, 1981–83 and 1989 in the pages to follow. The data provide clear evidence of sustained, measured resource use.

We may use a formula employed in 1990 in Attawapiskat to extrapolate from Honigmann's data. Informants suggested a consumption rate of 1.75 pounds (0.79 kilograms) per adult per meal twice a day during the seasons when goose is available (i.e., late spring, summer and fall). Approximately 25 per cent of the population is unable to eat meat because they are too young (under two years of age), too old or too sick.

Based on Honigmann's figures, the total weight of wavies would be 21,195 pounds (9614 kilograms), and of Canada geese it would be 13,975 pounds (6339 kilograms), for a total of 35,170 pounds (15,953 kilograms) of meat. At a consumption rate of 1.75 pounds (0.79 kilograms) per meal, this represents 20,097 meals. At two meals a day, this means 10,048 days of goose eating. Attawapiskat's meat-eating population in 1947 was 351 people; therefore, the total geese killed would supply the population of meat eaters with 3.5 pounds (1.59 kilograms) of goose a day for 29 days. If we substitute the figures used in Attawapiskat in 1990 (4 pounds (1.81 kilograms) per wavy, 7 pounds (3.18 kilograms) per Canada goose) the meat supplied by the goose harvest would last for 32 days.

The breakdown of consumption cited above must not be interpreted strictly. The not inconsiderable harvesting of ducks, fish and species such as muskrat, game birds and rabbits should be kept in mind. In addition, the 3.5 pounds (1.59 kilograms) of meat per day per person might be high; women and younger people might consume less. Finally, according to Honigmann, the 1947 harvest figures are low. Evidence from subsequent studies (including this one) support that position. Regardless, the point is clear: geese and other waterfowl were and are fundamentally important in the diet.

The discrepancy in the fall and spring kills in terms of species reflects the availability and number of the birds during the seasons. The Canada geese, for example, are the first to arrive in the spring; hence, the greater number of that species in the earlier part of the year. Also, hunters in 1990 suggested that wavies tend not to spend much time in James Bay in the spring on their way to more northerly breeding grounds. It is interesting to compare the figures above with the observation of Barnston (1862, cited in Prevett *et al.*, 1983:191), who cited a kill figure of 30,000 geese (all species) in Attawapiskat and Fort Albany (and Kashechewan) in 1862. In Prevett et al. (1983), the mean for these communities in the 1980s was 39,632. A sustained, measured yield indeed.

It is also interesting to note the apparent greater reliance upon ducks earlier in the 20th century than in 1990. While ducks were shot in 1990, they did not appear to be actively hunted the way they were previously. This could be a reflection of a number of factors: a preference for geese; a greater availability of geese; a greater availability of other game (for example, moose and caribou); or a cost/benefit factor, that is, a greater amount of meat gained from shooting geese over ducks.

There are reasons (largely anecdotal) to believe that people simply prefer goose on the basis of taste. Since geese have been abundant in recent years, we have a simple case of taste and availability coinciding. In the 1920s and 1930s, however, there was a concerted effort to hunt ducks.

Aleck Wesley [shot] four wavies and ten ducks (HBC B.243/a/2; May 19, 1927).

Indians returning from marsh with a few ducks (HBC B.243/a/3; July 16, 1929).

Outfitted [Ekwan hunters] and their families for *loon hunting* (HBC B.243/a/2; May 30, 1927) (italics in original).

Quiet day in the store as most of the Indians are off hunting ducks (HBC B.243/a/2; July 15, 1927).

What these entries suggest is not only a considerable reliance on ducks, but also a seasonal pursuit of them. As the dates suggest, duck hunting tended to occur after the spring goose hunt, although not exclusively so. Therefore, duck was a welcome and available option during the lean summer months. Also, ducks were a viable trade item.

It is not surprising, then, to find a large reliance upon waterfowl and fish as subsistence foods, particularly during the summer. These were the only species that could be relied upon in large numbers, when store food could hardly be afforded. Fish were caught year-round, especially during periods when other, more favoured foods, were unavailable. It is suggested that this ready availability rendered fish somewhat less desirable as a food item than, for example, moose or caribou. Also, many people believe that fish is less tasty than other meat, and that fish does not result in "feeling full" as does red meat such as moose.

Whitefish, the most commonly eaten species, migrate from the rivers to the bay in late spring/early summer and then back inland in September and October until freeze-up. That is when the people, especially the women, set their nets. The only times when whitefish were infrequently eaten were in late winter and midsummer, when few or no whitefish can be expected. Conversely, people in Attawapiskat in 1990 reported fishing "all year 'round."

It seems that whitefish was perhaps more important in the Attawapiskat diet in the early decades of the 20th century than it was in the 1980s. This is not to suggest that whitefish is unimportant. Rather, in recent times, more numbers of fish of different species are taken. Honigmann's (1948) *Foodways in a Muskeg Community* stresses the primacy of whitefish, whereas later in the century it had become just one of many species commonly caught, including suckers and "trout", the latter a generic name for speckled, lake and other trout. There are at least three possible explanations for this change. First, it could be that there were fewer whitefish in the 1980s than previously. Second, the possibility exists that with the greater abundance of large game and (it would seem) geese being killed and with more store-bought food being consumed, fish did not generally figure as prominently in the Attawapiskat diet in the 1980s as they had previously. Third, people might have come to want greater diversity in the fish they ate.

What is essential to note is the undeniable importance of whitefish prior to 1950, not only as a subsistence item but also as an item for trade and as dog food.

> A number of White Fish are now being caught in the river opposite the post (HBC B.243/a/4; October 24, 1929).

> Natives around the post now getting a few white fish in the nets (HBC B.243/a/5; November 8, 1930).

> White fish are now fairly numerous; the Natives in the vicinity of the post are getting fair quantities in the nets daily (HBC B.243/a/5; May 22, 1931).

While fish were and continue to be free goods, there was a protocol that prevailed regarding their capture. Essentially, then, as now, families were free to use their nets or hooks anywhere. No resentment was expressed, nor trespass inferred, if one group established its nets upstream from another group. Social conventions hold, however, that a feeder stream must enter into the main river between nets so that the lower nets may be supplied with fish. The number of nets that were set was a function of the work (or number of people) needed to check them and the productivity of the nets themselves. Honigmann (1961:146) observes that nets must be checked frequently so that they do not become tangled under their own weight and become no longer able to trap fish. Also operating on net productivity is the season. During the heavy migration periods it might be necessary sometimes to check nets two or three times daily. The norm would be once a day. In the winter, once every three or four days was the norm during the 1940s (Honigmann, 1961:146).

As reliable as fish generally are, they, too, are subject to availability cycles, possibly influenced by the weather. This pattern of availability reveals itself not only in seasonal runs but also within smaller time frames and geographical areas.

> The seine was tried just below the rapid this morning but there were few fish. Some hauls were made in the evening at the point of the island, where a good catch was made, and up near last year's scene (or seine) of activities, but here were not so successful (HBC B.243/a/2; October 22, 1928) [pun in original].

For comparative purposes, in 1990 informants suggested that approximately 40 fish (different species, including whitefish) were taken weekly in one net over the course of the winter. Winter supposedly is the poorest time of the year for catching whitefish.

Fishing was typically women's work. Archival evidence suggests that fishing lent itself to women's work groups that set and maintained the nets. "Mary Kamalatsit and Christina Toomagatsik arrived at the post from a fishing place up the river" (HBC B.243/a/4; March 14, 1930). This is not to say that fishing was exclusively the domain of women. The flexibility of Cree culture would preclude such rigidity. Indeed, as the fall run of fish preceded or coincided with the return migration of waterfowl, the need to procure large numbers of fish and geese for the coming winter was addressed by all family members. "Jacob Tookate, Sr. and John and George Edward left with their families for the coast where they will remain for several weeks hunting fish" (HBC B.243/a/5; August 19, 1930).

There were few other fish species pursued with the vigour that was expended on white-fish. In the 12 years of the HBC post journals, only trout is mentioned by name as being pursued by the Cree (February 1, 1930). Honigmann (1961) lists jackfish or northern pike, speckled and lake trout, sucker (carp), walleye (yellow pickerel), ling (loche) and sturgeon as other fish species that were consumed.

During the summer months few other resources were pursued with any effort, as people lived on fish and the large numbers of geese that were usually harvested during the spring hunt. Evidence from 1990 suggests that an average hunter often shoots enough geese in the spring hunt to sustain him and his family until the fall hunt. Honigmann's data above indicate that this would have been unlikely in the 1940s. Typically, the food supplied by the spring kill would have been exhausted by June. Therefore, the diet would be supplemented with ducks and rabbits (if available) during the summer months until the arrival of geese in the fall and the return migration of whitefish.

Autumn

The arrival of fall, of course, meant the return of a large harvest for those Attawapiskat hunters who stayed near the coast. Historically, the fall goose hunt has produced more wavies than Canada geese, while in the spring the opposite is true. Little has changed in the hunting of geese since Honigmann's fieldwork. Men still go out to blinds, typically with kinsmen such as sons, brothers, sons-in-law or uncles. Decoys are used to lure the birds within range. Charred wooden decoys are used for Canadas in the spring, white wavy wings in the fall. Blinds normally are set half a mile (0.8 kilometres) apart so as not to interfere with those of other hunters. Considering the importance of geese as food, and the emotionally charged nature of the hunt, there is little dispute or disagreement. It is understood that there is no shooting after dark because it affects the geese, frightening them away. There is no clamouring within groups of men for the first shot, for that is a sign of greed and aggression.

One element of the goose hunt that has persisted over the generations is the prestige of being the first in the community to kill a goose in a particular season. Hunters who have been fortunate enough to accomplish this can relate in minute detail the facts and circumstances surrounding their kill. Eight decades ago this was still a *coup*.

> First goose killed on Saturday (HBC B.243/a/2; April 28, 1924) [This is quite late in April for the first kill, which "tradition" in Attawapiskat says is *always* on the 10th. It was on the 11th in 1990].
>
> The first goose was seen (HBC B.243/a/3; April 17, 1929).
>
> Allan shot the first goose right in front of his house (HBC B.243/a/3; April 28, 1929).

In terms of food availability, autumn much resembled spring when, to a large extent, whitefish and goose migrations overlapped. While not a universal practice, both fish and geese (wavies) were dried in preparation for winter consumption. Also, in fall, berries were picked in great quantities, an activity in which children played a considerable role. Honigmann (1961:147) cites an average of 9.5 quarts (10.5 litres) per family, with 760 quarts (837 litres) (estimated total) consumed per year by the village. In comparison with the somewhat meagre faunal resources, the Mushkegowuk region has a considerable variety of berries. In 1990, people identified up to 15 species that were picked and eaten. As innocuous as berry picking may seem, it was not without its hazards.

Aleck Wesley's daughter who was out picking berries at 8 o'clock tonight failed to return. All hands went off to look for her but at midnight had not found her (HBC B.243/a/4; August 28, 1923).

There is no indication if the child was found.

Thus, we have an ecological distinction between the Inlanders and the Coasters in the fall. Geese and other waterfowl remain relatively available along the coast until quite late in the autumn.

Wavies going south in big flocks (HBC B.243/a/2; October 25, 1927).

Wm. Allan returned from hunting having killed nearly 100 ducks (HBC B.243/a/1; October 21, 1921).

As a result, there existed the possibility of a greater and longer dependency on geese, especially if efforts were made to preserve them by drying. Inland, there existed a greater reliance upon fresh fish, especially just prior to freeze-up when whitefish are particularly plentiful. As well, the coming of autumn marked the greater availability of rabbits and ptarmigan, particularly for the Inlanders, whose supply of geese (had they accumulated one) was usually exhausted.

Following the fall goose hunt, the people gradually started moving back to their lands for the winter trapping season. There was a conundrum that faced the inland hunters. Inland families were obliged to leave the coast before being able to amass large stocks of geese. To delay departure might mean having to wait until the ice was firmly frozen or it might delay arrival at the trapline until late in the season. As a result, the average inland family used one-third fewer geese for food than did the average coastal family. Elsewhere, we have discussed the movement of people to the coast where the goose migration guaranteed a source of food. For the Inlanders, fish remained a staple, supplemented by rabbits, grouse and partridge.

Winter

Winter, of course, is the peak trapping season. During the first half of the century it was interrupted by trips to the post at Christmas and at Easter. For the Inlanders, trapping provided an opportunity to combine both subsistence and trade hunting, for beaver supplied both meat and fur. By the 1930s, beaver were only available inland.

During winter, the Coasters tended to leave their families at the post, while the Inlanders did not. The Inlanders went deep into the bush where game was more available. With the opening of the Akimiski preserve to trapping in the mid 1940s, more beaver meat arrived at the post. It is fair to suggest, however, that the Inlanders probably had a more varied diet than the Coasters did. The Coasters tended to subsist on dried wavy, rabbits and the occasional beaver during the winter. The Coasters hoped for moose meat to be brought down the river. None was in 1947/48. The Inlanders, in contrast, had greater access to moose, caribou and beaver, as well as ptarmigan and rabbits. Among both the Coasters and the Inlanders, women played an important role in procuring both these species. Among the former group, women would go out in small groups some distance from the post to snare rabbits, spruce hens and ptarmigan. Women inland would set up snare lines around the camp, contributing to the family's subsistence and trapping income.

The lack of moose and caribou obliged people to rely heavily on smaller game. Data from Honigmann (1961) and the federal government (1951, 1952) suggest how volatile the population cycles of Attawapiskat primary game species were in the late 1940s and early 1950s.

It is useful to look first at James Bay as a whole. In 1951, there were 1862 Natives on reserve in James Bay. In that year, they harvested 191 moose, seven "deer" (species undetermined), 41 caribou, 14,700 geese and 1000 each of ducks and grouse. A year later, in 1952, the population of the region had dropped to 1840. The Natives of the region killed 480 moose, 40 "deer", 125 caribou, 35,490 geese, 30,000 ducks, 5000 grouse and 35 hair seals (Agency Report on Game Taken by Indians on Reserves for Food, 1951 and 1952).

The population of Attawapiskat was 468 in 1947, 669 in 1951 and 600 in 1952. Honigmann (1961) states that in 1946/47, the Attawapiskat Cree killed 50 moose and 14 caribou. In 1947/48, the numbers were 15 and 11, respectively. In 1951, according to the Agency Report, there were 63 moose and 22 caribou killed by band members. The following year, 1952, 20 moose and an undetermined number of caribou were harvested. The Attawapiskat Cree killed 5000 geese in 1951, while 10,700 were shot in 1952.

It should be noted that the data from the Agency Reports are "rough." H.R. Conn, who submitted the data, stated that they were not "an entirely accurate picture of the Indian game take." Nonetheless, it is the only study, outside of Honigmann's, undertaken prior to the 1970s. Its figures are suggestive, if not 100 per cent accurate.

Based on archival records and the academic literature, there are reasons to believe that perhaps there is a greater abundance of large game (i.e., moose and caribou) today than there was during the period from 1901 to 1952. An alternative hypothesis is that perhaps modern technology, in the forms of better firearms, outboard motors and snowmobiles, allows for a greater number of kills than previously. Whatever the reason, there are considerably more moose and caribou being killed today than at any point in the first half of the 20th century.

The HBC post journals cover the period from 1919 to 1931. These journals offer considerable insight into the daily life of the posts, including hunting and trapping by both the Natives and post personnel. While there are references to the ubiquitous fur-bearers for trade, as well as to geese, ptarmigan, ducks, loons, bears and seals, there are very few references to moose, and none to caribou. We would expect that when rabbit and fish are bought as meat for the post personnel, as the numerous journal entries attest, moose and caribou would be bought in the same manner. It does not, however, appear to be a frequent occurrence. It is hard to believe that, in over a decade of journal entries, the absence of references to caribou is simply an oversight when such trivial matters as the purchase of rabbit and fish are religiously noted.

The appearance of big game in the Attawapiskat region was, as suggested by the post journals, a matter of significant rarity to generate considerable excitement.

We hear talk of moose being close to the fort but very few are being killed (HBC B.243/a/1; January 29, 1920).

We are receiving plenty of moose meat now. John [illegible] and Jacob [illegible] off for a load and John Nakogee brought us a load (HBC B.243/a/1; February 3, 1920).

When moose was available to the Cree it was both a prized subsistence food and a valued item for sale as "**country food**."

Jeremiah came in with a red fox and a little moose meat (HBC B.243/a/1; April 4, 1923).

Bought some moose meat from [illegible] Toomagatik today (HBC B.242/a/2; October, 6, 1927).

The scarcity of moose is suggested by the following entry:

> Big William brought in our first snack of moose meat since the end of the summer today (HBC B.243/a/1; December 11, 1922).

What is most interesting to observe about the hunting of moose in the period under discussion is that virtually every reference to moose hunting occurs in late March or April, in contrast to the overwhelming tendency today to hunt moose in the fall.

> Jacob Tookate killed a moose yesterday (HBC B.243/a/2; March 29, 1924).

> 3 moose were killed yesterday half a day from here (HBC B.243/a/2; April 12, 1924).

Undoubtedly, this is due to the ease of killing during the early spring. A number of reasons have been suggested for this. Some suggest that the spring snow will support a man on snowshoes, while it will not support a moose. Others claim that moose are weak after the lengthy winter, and hence less able to escape a hunter. Others assert that moose are disoriented in spring and are thereby susceptible to approach by a skilful hunter. The Attawapiskat Cree do not only kill moose with guns. Snares have been used, and continue to be used in Attawapiskat today, by at least one man.

With the arrival of spring, people would start to move toward the coast in anticipation of the spring goose hunt. As noted above, not all people arrived there in time for the hunt, nor did all stay at the post for the fall hunt. But a number did, and the returning geese, and emerging muskrats, promised meat for a number of weeks. Some people in Attawapiskat today continue to eat muskrat.

HUNTING FOR TRADE PRODUCTS

The Trade Begins

Historically, Attawapiskat has proved to be an erratic post in terms of its fur production. This is undoubtedly due to the scarcity of fur-bearers in general, as well as the population cycles to which they are subject. Nonetheless, the area proved to be one in which the fur industry concentrated its efforts, particularly the Revillon Freres company.

It is difficult to avoid giving a Euro-Canadian slant to any fur trade history, given that history is generally written based on archival and other evidence written by non-Natives. At the same time, it is essential to place Native trade within a larger framework, for the context within which the fur trade played itself out involved the larger Canadian and international societies.

The Attawapiskat fur trade essentially began when C.C. Chipman, in his *Annual Report on the Fur Trade for Outfit 1900-01*, remarked in the section dealing with the Albany River District that

> The country to the North of the Albany will be better hunted by the establishment of an Outpost at Athawapiscat [sic], which, with the reduction in expenses which is to be looked for, ought to bring about better results (HBC A.74/10).

Previously, Alexander Milne, who had inspected the Company's stores in the Albany district during June 1901, had recommended such an outpost for winter use only, noting that there was already a Roman Catholic Church at "Athawapiscat [sic] River." Milne included with his report a copy of a letter from George McKenzie, the officer in charge of the James Bay District, in Albany, dated June 21, 1901, to Junior Chief Trader David Armit, the officer in charge of Albany:

> I have decided to establish Atawapiscat [sic] to be connected to Albany as an Outpost. The master of the sloop...could be placed in charge with instruction to trade only in even barter, and under no consideration to give any debt except ammunition, and that only in small quantities – to be paid for out of the first hunt they bring in.

> It will be necessary for you to take a run up there, as soon as convenient, and report to me the nature of the trade to be done (HBC Arch.B.3/e/29).

There were sound economic reasons to establish a post at Attawapiskat.

> [The Natives] frequently waste much valuable time during the hunting season in travel to Albany...[The post] will be a distinct encouragement to Indians to hunt more zealously while the only expense...will be the wintering of a Servant (HBC Arch.B.3/e/29).

On July 18, 1901, Armit, in the company of P. Faries, J. Carpenter, J. Hunter and W. Loutit, left Albany for Attawapiskat. He was back on the 22 of July "having made the quickest trip known of." He reported on his trip in a letter dated July 27.

> I left here on the 18th...found the places [at Attawapiskat] spoken to you...all too low and exposed to ice also liable to get flooded the only apparent safe place being near where the R.C. Church is which I decided on...Sufficient timber can be got for the building from a mile & a half to two miles, this they will ralf [sic] down what sawing required will be done in the bush...Wood is scarce being mostly small poplars until the Rapid is reached; above that it is reported to be more plentiful...I do not see that the place will be anything else but a fur Post...there may be a possibility of killing porpoises...The distance from the mouth of the South branch to the place decided upon (which is on the North bank of the River) is about 8 miles as near as I can judge. I think that by the last week of September the places will be completed (HBC Arch. B.3/b/100, fos. 357–8).

The four men who accompanied Armit had remained behind and returned on August 20 after having constructed "two houses 20 X 16...sufficient for the present." On September 7, 1901, Armit reported that he was sending the boat to Kapisko and "Attawapiskit", "taking Barrels Salt and Ammunition for the Goose hunt and as much Flour as the boat could carry for the trade at Attawapiskit" (HBC Arch.B.3/b/100, fo. 367). Old Louttit [Peter Louttit "A"] was to look after the goose hunt and the camp until George Linklater arrived. Linklater departed Albany on foot on October 22, 1901, under instructions to "trade nothing but Furs and Feathers, and a little food for Dogs what you think will be sufficient." He was also advised to "give no advances as it is thoroughly understood that it was only for trade purposes, this place was put up..." (HBC Arch. B.3/b/100, fo.378). Peter Louttit "A" was back at Albany on November 2.

The initial reports from Attawapiskat suggest the promise of a bountiful fur harvest, but also indicate the volatile nature of a primary industry. Armit wrote on January 16, 1902 that

> ...furs are numerous... Foxes are reported fairly plentiful, but hard to trap, very few of the good hunters had come in to Attawapuskit, what furs taken there are chiefly poor people that stay around that place fishing. Most all the Indians have gone inland as they can make nothing of the Foxes, no one has arrived from Agrunisko [sic] Island, it is expected that they have done well as it is good for Foxes (HBC Arch. B.3/b/100, fo. 394).

In the *Annual Report of 1902*, Armit was able to state that "the Winter Post at Attawapiskit [sic] has answered the purpose well and has been of good use." No advances were given to the Cree at this time; it was simply straight trade and collecting of Albany accounts. C.C. Chipman, the Commissioner, wrote to London in his *Annual Report on the Fur Trade for 1901-02* that the Attawapiskat trade was "now efficiently catered for and the expense in Staff and equipment which [had] been incurred [had] been fully justified." Furthermore, the "Outpost...kept at Attawapiscat during the winter [brought] excellent results" (HBC Arch. dated February 3, 1903). The fur trade for the Albany district in 1901/02 was profitable, due to the "great abundance" of fur-bearers. It was not to last.

Cree Starvation and Trader Competition

The winter of 1902/03 marked the first of several periods of starvation and depletion of fur-bearers and country food in the Attawapiskat region. Nonetheless, the HBC encouraged trade in fur-bearers, prompted by the arrival of opposition. The fact that many of the Natives were severely ill and undernourished seemed to matter little. In his instructions to George Linklater on February 23, 1903, Armit encouraged him to "[get] all the furs you can as it is reported...that we are to have opposition" (HBC Arch. B.3/b/102, fo. 52).

The summer of 1903 saw plans for an outpost on the Ekwan River to accommodate the trade in the northern regions. The purpose of this post was to "have the principal Rivers guarded between this and the Cape." Armit also instructed Linklater "to keep the Indians coming in here as much as possible so as to keep them from meeting [the] opposition" (HBC Arch. B.3/b/102, fo. 67).

Starvation and sickness plagued the Attawapiskat people throughout 1903/04. In June 1903, Armit reported that most of the Cree, including the best trappers, had done poorly in comparison with the previous season because of sickness and hunger. Six months later, the news was equally grim. Sickness was still rampant. Many of the best hunters were so indisposed that they could not even travel to their hunting grounds. The concern was that this would adversely affect the winter trade.

The trade for the following winter was indeed slow, but activities would pick up over the next decade. A letter from Armit to McKenzie dated March 17, 1904 stated that "Very little trade has been done at Attawapiskit this winter the Indians have not come in as formerly, the prospects for Otter is good, Marten uncertain, none of the Inland Indians from the Marten country coming..."(HBC Arch. B.3/b/102. fo. 133). In 1906, Revillon Freres opened a post in Attawapiskat "under the charge of Mr. Daillaire, a French-Canadian, and a Roman Catholic." It would provide stiff competition for the HBC over the next couple of decades, frequently securing the bulk of the trade. The *Report on the Trade of Albany District, Outfit 1908-09* claimed "the competition to be very keen and active, the Revillons agent being an ex H.B. man and very enterprising" (HBC Arch.B.3/b/103, fos. 777). This "enterprising" nature took the form of large advance credits and other incentives.

Starvation again struck the region in 1909 and saw a significant number of Natives, including some from Winisk, staying at the post. A lack of caribou was one of the main reasons for hunger. But, as seems characteristic of Attawapiskat and *environs*, the pendulum swung the other way, and by 1914/15 the post was again being seen as a potentially lucrative one, if only for the opposition. The *Annual Reports from District Officers, 1914* suggested that Attawapiskat be run as an independent post (rather than as a sub-post from

Albany) because it was "an important Post, especially in good Fox years, 124 Indians making it their trading headquarters." 1914 was not a particularly good year for the HBC in terms of the fur trade in Attawapiskat. This was largely due to the inexperienced manager and his unfamiliarity with the book work involved. It was also due to the aggressive trade of Revillon Freres. It was observed that Revillon Freres had made its presence felt by "taking more than their share of the Fur, and consider it one of the best Posts they have in the Bay..." In contrast, Attawapiskat "show[ed] up worse than any other Post in the District [for the reasons cited above]. Valued at the tariff of 1913, returns showed a decrease of over $20,000" (HBC A.74/23).

In 1915 there was an upswing, returns totalling $6241 more than in 1914, with an increase in fisher, silver, cross and red fox, lynx, mink and otter (HBC Arch. A74/45). By 1916/17, Attawapiskat was holding its own in the fur trade. In the *Annual Reports from District Officers, 1916* (HBC A.74/46), it was observed that "Attawapiskat is almost equal to that of Albany. The returns...show an increase of $4868 over the previous Outfit." Attawapiskat was hailed as "a very important Post." The fur harvest showed an increase in all but fisher, otter and wolf, which were slightly less than in 1915. A comparison of the 1916 and 1917 fur harvests for the HBC is shown in Table 6.1 below.

TABLE 6.1	Principal Furs Comparison (Attawapiskat) 1916-1917[a]	
Species	1916	1917
Black bear	5	8
Beaver	58	31
Ermine	43	285
Fisher	22	26
Cross fox	137	149
Red fox	347	442
Silver fox	27	24
Lynx	164	89
Marten	141	86
Mink	221	204
Musquash	2424	2069
Other	246	113

[a] Source: *Annual Reports from District Officers–Outfit 1917* HBC Arch. A74/47

These figures hint at the tremendously erratic nature of the fur trade in general in James Bay and, in particular, in Attawapiskat. Subsequent figures (to be given below) illustrate dramatically the game fluctuations and, as well, the ability of the Cree to predict game population cycles. It is also important to bear in mind that these figures represent half or less of the Attawapiskat fur harvest, in that Revillon Freres was taking a considerable number of furs.

Revillon Freres had built up considerable business in the decade that it had been in Attawapiskat. By 1918, Attawapiskat was "almost the biggest Fur Post of James' [sic] Bay", and it was acknowledged that at the helm of the opposition was "the smartest and most successful of Revillon's Masters" (HBC A.74/48). In his *Inspection Report on the James Bay District, June, 1917 to June, 1918*, Inspector L. Romanet concluded that Revillon's business—"sorry to state"—was much better than the HBC's. It was at this time that Attawapiskat established outposts at Opinaga and on Akimiski Island.

The intense rivalry between the companies would escalate until the takeover of Revillon Freres in 1936. There is little doubt that it was in large part due to the increasing demands of the companies that the depletion of fur-bearers occurred toward the end of the 1920s. The preoccupation of the HBC with their main opposition (there had also been a free-trading company, Dory and Spence, during 1930/31 (Preston, mss: 1990:32)) is noticeable in the *Annual Reports From District Officers, 1920*:

> Messers. Revillon Freres Bros. have stations at the following points: Moose Factory, Attawapiskat with outposts at Opinega [sic] and Weenusk. At Attawapiskat, which has been their stronghold in the District, I consider that they are losing ground.(HBC A.74/49).

The historical records say little about Dory and Spence other than that it folded in 1931 "after being in business in Attawapiskat for several years" (HBC RG3/2/7).

In 1921, G. R. Ray, the District Manager of the HBC, wrote that "Revillon Freres have secured a hold on the trade of Attawapiskat from which it will be difficult to shake them...they have given it of their best in men and supplies" (HBC A.74/49). Ultimately, the aggressive policy of Revillon Freres would be the downfall of the company in Attawapiskat, as their policy of "unlimited debt" brought in more furs but less profit. In 1921/22 they had 55.5 per cent of the furs at Attawapiskat and 40 per cent of the furs at Opinaga (where the HBC also had an outpost), but the HBC was increasing its profit. In 1936, the HBC absorbed its competition.

It is important to note that Revillon Freres was a major operation. Ray (1990:153) observes that, in the James Bay area, only this company provided vigorous competition for the HBC. Revillon Freres had roots in the fur business going back to 1723 in Paris. It was in 1902 that the company took first steps to establish itself in eastern Canada, and by 1903 Revillon Freres had 23 establishments coast to coast to coast. By the beginning of World War I, the "French Company" was providing stiff competition for the HBC in James Bay and Athabasca River/Peace River country (Ray, 1990:93).

The hard times for Revillon Freres began in the 1920s. Between 1921 and 1926, despite years of experience and considerable resources, the company lost $335,000 overall. This was largely due to the fact that post operating expenses exceeded the profit margins earned on merchandise sales. The company began to retreat from the north. In 1925, Revillon sold its operations in Labrador to the HBC. In the spring of 1926, negotiations began for the sale of controlling interest in the remaining fur trade business. According to the terms of the agreement, the HBC secured 51 per cent of the stock of Revillon Freres. Direction of Revillon Freres was left in the hands of the current managers.

Ray (1990:161) notes that the takeover had several significant implications for the HBC and the fur business. The directors did not seek to eliminate competition that they saw as "sane and reasonable." They feared adverse reaction from both Natives and government at the loss of competition. Therefore, the HBC sought to run Revillon Freres as a separate entity without the merger becoming public knowledge. They sought by this means to regulate debt, curtail trade in less-than-prime fur, reduce labour costs and implement other cost-saving measures.

Such a peaceful takeover was not to be, however, as rumours of the merger circulated within the industry and among Natives. Revillon Freres and HBC managers often refused to co-operate, contrary to the instructions they had been given. Finally, in 1934, Revillon Freres had to liquidate its assets to pay debts. The HBC made a buyout offer that was initially refused, but the following year Revillon Freres sold three James Bay posts and eight Athabasca/MacKenzie posts to the HBC. In 1936, Revillon Freres sold its remaining shares to the HBC.

Cree Responses to Competition and Resource Depletion

And what of the Cree during these three decades of intense fur trade rivalry? Honigmann (1961:15) contends that the period must have been an "exhilarating" one for the Cree, as "both organizations spurred them on to intensive trapping by offering more and more alluring prizes for furs at several outposts." If it was exhilarating, it was not to be without a price. Liquor, large outfits on credit (unlimited credit by Revillon Freres), transportation to trap-lines and even houses were offered to those trappers who could secure a good number of silver fox pelts. Honigmann (1961:15) contends that many of these incentives appear to have been initiated by Revillon Freres managers. The ultimate result, not unexpectedly, was the depletion of fur-bearers.

It was also during this period that we begin to see a shift in demographic patterns, with a population "boom" in Attawapiskat as people moved to the coast. There may also have been a change in traditional patterns of tenure as hunters spread out to secure the highly prized furs, as the following HBC Post Journals attest:

All the coast Indians are said to be away up inland now (HBC B.243/a/1; March 12, 1923).

James Mud left for Fox River this afternoon where he will spend the spring hunting musquash (HBC B.243/a/5; April 16, 1930).

James Mud (according to Cooper, 1933) was originally hunting 100 miles (161 kilometres) inland along the Lawachie River, but turned to hunting in the Fox River area.

Thos. Weesk and Family [sic] left for their "spring" hunting grounds this morning (HBC B.243/a5; April 24, 1930, quotation marks in original).

This last entry might be referring to the spring goose hunting area; however, according to Cooper, the father of Thomas Weesk hunted in the vicinity of the Attawapiskat post, while Thomas hunted on Akimiski Island. An entry on September 14, 1929 states that "Thomas Weesk and John Pakany [?] and families left for Agamiski Island...where they will remain for the first part of the hunting season."

Again, what is suggested by these entries is the possibility of movement from territory to territory over the course of the season. Perhaps the most telling example of changes in land tenure and use is provided by the following entries:

Wm. Etherington arrived from Lake River (HBC B.243/a/3; July 17, 1929).

Wm. Etherington arrived from I'berry [?] Island for some supplies, he intends spending the remainder of the hunting season on Agamiska [sic] Island (HBC B.243/a/5; February 25, 1931).

Willie Etherington was originally from Albany; his two sons hunted at Lake River. When he first went to Opinaga, some Cree (at least Tookates) objected to his hunting and trapping in the vicinity of the post (Cooper, 1933). Etherington, then, is a good example of the change in land tenure behaviour: an Albany man and his sons utilizing a number of territories from Albany north to Opinaga and Lake River and including Akimiski Island. The objections to his encroachment in Opinaga might have been based on the fact that he was an "Albany" man, as opposed to an Attawapiskat Cree. Regardless, it is apparent that during the late 1920s strict adherence to family territories was beginning to lessen. Dwindling fur and food resources, a burgeoning population (especially from Sutton Lake, Sutton River and Winisk) and, it is argued by the Cree, the arrival of White trappers in quest of the beaver during the peak years from 1922 to 1929 are all reasons for the change. The movement of Cree people to the coast, of course, was a result of the availability of trade goods, and of geese, which were now easier to procure with guns. Additionally, one must consider the fact that there were White trappers inland. Finally, the intense competition between, and the incentives offered by, the HBC and Revillon Freres made the fur market very attractive.

The degree to which the changes in land tenure occurred is visible in Honigmann's data of 1944 to 1948. At that time he observed that fully 43 per cent of the listed Attawapiskat trappers operated within 60 miles (97 kilometres) of the post (Honigmann, 1961:121). While this may not appear remarkable, it is essential to remember that Attawapiskat people were originally an inland people. While at that time (and even today), there were people exploiting the inland resources, their number was considerably lower in proportion to the total number of hunter/trappers than in the past. The irony of this is that people had been told of the more plentiful game and furs to be had inland, but were reluctant to venture far up the streams, out of fear of starvation and disease. By this time, of course, sickness and hunger had already been far too frequent occurrences, and people's fears were legitimate.

It is both interesting and useful to look at the fur harvest of the mid 1920s, when the peak years were being experienced. While we do not have harvest records for Attawapiskat specifically for 1924, we do have figures and a "prospectus" for the James Bay region generally. It is interesting to observe Native predictions for the following year. "Indians report good prospects of a coloured fox year" (HBC A.74/53). Indeed, the harvest of coloured foxes did increase.

In 1923, Natives in James Bay sold to the HBC 6239 beaver, 4793 fox (all species and colours), 3888 marten, 2202 mink and 23,698 muskrat. In 1924, the numbers were 6762 beaver, 2216 fox, 2400 marten, 3878 mink and 26,385 muskrat. In 1925, the numbers were 5602, 4851, 2783, 3387 and 21,764, respectively.

The late 1920s were the end of the peak trading period in the first half of the century. The overall harvest figures for 1927 show some decrease over the previous year and also show trade in rabbits, the first time that this species shows up in the fur records. In Attawapiskat, the HBC bought 65 beaver, 1041 fox, 113 marten, 358 mink and 6899 muskrat from the Cree, in addition to 962 rabbits. The HBC also purchased $483.74 worth of country food. This is indicative of the period of fur decrease and starvation that would follow in 1928. That year, potatoes from the mission's garden sustained the Cree. The glory days of the fur trade were close to being over.

Beginning in the late 1920s, we increasingly find a higher production of small game furs (weasel or ermine, mink, muskrat, squirrels) as the important fur-bearers become more rare. It seems that over time, only the muskrat has been a constant. It is also important to note that the Attawapiskat people have continued to attempt a viable living from a land of decreasing opportunities. Honigmann (1961:121) observed that in the period from 1944 to 1948 about one-third of the listed hunters did not use their grounds because of ill health, age or the fact that they were not residing in the area. In other words, all able-bodied men (and those women who needed to) who were in Attawapiskat worked their lands. In spite of well-grounded fears of death in the bush, and the potential availability of assistance from the White presence in the community, conscious decisions were made to pursue a hunting/trapping economy.

Between 1932 and 1940, the HBC fur purchases dropped dramatically in Attawapiskat. In 1936, 1937, 1938 and 1940, for example, the Cree did not sell a single beaver to the HBC. During that same period, the total annual fox harvest ranged from a low of 40 in 1940 to a high of 824 in 1934. In most years during the 1930s, the number of foxes sold to the HBC were between 240 to 280, a far cry from the thousands a year being sold before the 1930s. Marten, which likewise had been trapped in the thousands, never reached the double digits during the 1930s. Marten sales ranged from a single pelt in 1940 to six in 1934. At the same time, there developed a considerable reliance on small fur-bearers, especially musquash (muskrat). Also at this time, other species, notably skunk and squirrel, begin to be harvested. These were largely ignored during the boom years of the 1920s.

The growing reliance upon smaller and less profitable, but more easily accessible, fur-bearers (muskrat and squirrels, for example) must be seen as an adaptive strategy in the face of adversity. And, as noted below, the transition to less lucrative but more procurable species helped initiate a more broadly defined role for women.

From 1940 to 1950 the lack of fur-bearers continued, with a corresponding decrease in harvesting. Nonetheless, Attawapiskat trappers continued to ply their trade irrespective of the hardships it entailed. At the outset of the fur trade in Attawapiskat, it was hoped that it would be a productive post for foxes. The 1940s showed dramatically how even a "good" region for a particular species such as the fox is subject to natural population fluctuations. In 1948, only 31 foxes were traded at the HBC post in Attawapiskat. Just two years earlier, in 1946, the total number of foxes traded was 1491. As is quite apparent, 1940 and 1948 were the low point of this species cycle, producing unusually low harvests, and illustrating the need to exploit other species. This needs to be borne in mind as we examine trappers' incomes below.

Beaver, too, showed a significant decrease. In 1941, 1943 and 1945, no beavers were traded in Attawapiskat. Between 1941 and 1945, a total of 33 beavers were traded, 25 in 1944 and 8 in 1942. In the latter half of the decade, beaver bounced back somewhat, with the number being traded ranging from 58 in 1946 to 336 in 1949.

There was a moratorium on beaver harvests within the beaver sanctuaries, established in 1935 on Akimiski and in 1944 near Attawapiskat. It was not until 1946/47 that the first beaver were harvested on the Akimiski sanctuary. Beaver also had been rendered "extinct" in the coastal areas several years earlier. Therefore, those people whose lands were affected by the coastal depletion of beaver, or by the beaver sanctuaries, would have their incomes greatly curtailed in comparison to those who trapped inland where this species was more readily available. Another factor is the inclusion of a high number of traplines within close proximity of the village. The 43 per cent of the trappers operating within 60 miles (97 kilometres) of the post from 1944 to 1946 accounted for 36 per cent of the average income. The 57 per cent of the trappers operating beyond 60 miles (97 kilometres) earned 64 per cent of the average individual income (Honigmann, 1961:121).[1] A substantial reason for this discrepancy is the greater number of resources inland, especially "free" beaver. What must also be considered is the fairly large population of trappers, that is, those trapping near the post, exploiting a modest area of meager resources. There is little reason to believe that there was a discrepancy in skills between those who trapped inland and those who did not. Thus, the difference in income must be seen as a function of difference in resources, the amount of time spent in pursuing those resources, and the size of the trapping family unit. In this instance, wives and sons, should they be part of the trapping unit, may provide considerable assistance; hence, contributing to a greater income. Tables 6.2 and 6.3 detail trapping incomes in Attawapiskat from 1944 to 1947.

These figures are meaningless without context. The more than doubling of family income between 1946/47 and 1947/48 is due to the opening of the Akimiski Island beaver preserve in 1946/47. Secondary and tertiary reasons are the fluctuating fur markets and the animal population cycles discussed above. Overall, Honigmann (1961:128) states that the "chronically low incomes" for the Attawapiskat Cree are due to reduction of fur-bearers as a result of too intensive trapping, the ill suitability of the area to maintain species diversity and a relatively great concentration of human population along the coast.

TABLE 6.2	Distribution Of Trapping Incomes Among Families In Attawapiskat 1944 to 1947[a]					
Income Range	1944/45		1945/46		1946/47	
	Number	Per cent	Number	Per cent	Number	Per cent
$ 0-100	10	10.5	6	6.0	36	34.7
101-200	13	13.5	7	7.0	18	17.3
201-300	22	23.1	13	13.0	17	16.3
301-400	15	15.7	18	18.0	6	5.8
401-500	8	8.4	6	6.0	5	4.8
501-600	8	8.4	8	8.0	7	6.7
601-700	1	1.0	7	7.0	1	0.9
701-800	0	0.0	8	8.0	2	1.9
801-900	3	3.1	2	2.0	1	0.9
901-1000	2	2.1	9	9.0	1	0.9
1001-2000	3	3.1	5	5.0	1	0.9
2001-3000	0	0.0	1	1.0	0	0.0
Not Available	10	10.5	10	10.0	9	8.6
Totals	95	99.4	100	100.0	104	99.7

[a] Source: Honigmann, 1961:127

---

1. Honigmann states that these figures pertain to average income; what he apparently meant was 36% and 64% of total income.

TABLE 6.3	Total And Average Incomes Derived From Trapping Attawapiskat 1944 to 1948[a]	
Years	Total Income	Average Family Income
1944/45	$30,800	$362.00
1945/46	$40,800	$542.00
1946/47	$ 22,700	$238.00
1947/48	$ 41,097	$ 513.71

[a] Source: Honigmann, 1961:128

Trade in Country Food

Finally, we must examine the hunting of country food for trade. There has been a tendency to overlook this aspect of Native/non-Native relations in the north, although, in the Attawapiskat case at least, it played a significant role. This was particularly true during lean times. In addition, the production of country food considerably enhanced the roles of women in both the domestic and public domains.

It is most useful to examine the trade in country food in terms of the location of the people (in terms of geographical proximity to the post) conducting the trade, the items traded and the temporal patterning of trade. We typically associate the production of country food for post use with the "Home Guard" Cree; historically a select (not elite) group who, by virtue of their proximity to the post, were able to supply it with country produce (Ray, 1978:41). In the Attawapiskat case, it is evident that such trade was not restricted to those whose lands bounded the post. While the archival evidence suggests that the so-called "post families" conducted the significant majority of such trade, it is also quite apparent that Inlanders and others conducted trade in country food.

A number of people are repeatedly referred to in the journals as provisioners to the Attawapiskat post between 1919 and 1931. These include the Wesleys (Abel, Alec, Thomas and William), all of whom hunted the Lawachie River. Cooper (1933) does not consider them a post family; in fact, they are sometimes associated with Albany. "Big William" Nakogee is cited as often providing country food. While the "Nagodgis" are considered by Cooper to be a post family, he also states that William hunted "Swan River" near the Attawapiskat River. There were apparently two Swan Rivers. On current maps only one is designated, and it is between the Attawapiskat and Opinaga Rivers and does not meet the former. The Weeks (particularly Aleck, for whom Cooper has no reference) were frequent provisioners. They apparently were a post family who hunted on Akimiski as well.

John Tookate was the son of Jacob Tookate. According to Cooper, the father originally hunted along the Opinaga River, but between 1919 and 1931 hunted "at Attawapiskat." In addition to John, he had two other sons, Xavier and David. They were frequent conveyors of country produce. Jacob's father hunted Cape Henrietta Maria. Following 1931, Jacob hunted the Lawachie.

In actuality, we might argue that there was an equal distribution of country produce if we look at the diversity of source locations of that food, not solely the volume or amount. For example, there is evidence of hunters from the Kapiskau River (John Nakogee), Cape

Henrietta Maria (Joseph Carpenter) (who is referred to in the journals as simply being "inland"), the Lawachie River (James Mud), Swan River (James Spence) and Little Ekwan River (John Longpeter) all providing country produce. Others (e.g., Joseph Okitigoo) are simply reported as arriving "from inland." Akimiski Island is often referred to as being a source of hunters who provisioned the post.

The point of this discussion is to illustrate that, contrary to a generalized perception of the fur trade, post provisioners were not solely those whom we label as "Home Guard." The circumstances surrounding Attawapiskat post, (e.g., a chronic shortage of game and, at times, fur-bearers, a large traditional territory, and a fur trade exacerbated by intense rivalry between companies) might have affected the typical role allocation. In our case, it is apparent that there was not a limited number of "Home Guard" Cree provisioners. Rather, hunters from virtually all corners of Attawapiskat territory participated in the use of country food as currency.

The trade in country food is important for four basic reasons. First, it expanded the traditional exploitable universe by a significant degree. It meant that the Cree were not restricted to conventional fur-bearers in terms of marketable resources. Standard trade was no longer restricted to beaver, marten, fox and other fur-bearers. Second, this trade did not oblige the Cree to step out of their traditional roles as hunters and gatherers. Instead, through the pursuit of country food for trade they were able to merely extend their efforts in their own food search to accommodate that which could be traded. Third, in times of scarcity of fur-bearers, the market in country food could be expected, within limited reason, to offset the economic hardship. Fourth, it expanded the role of women within the economic realm. This is discussed below.

The inventory of traded country foods reads like a list of the subarctic flora and fauna. The Cree provided a large range of food items to the post, from berries to moose meat. The only significant species missing in the historical records as country food is caribou, and its absence does not necessarily indicate that it was not, in fact, traded.

While wavies (blue and snow geese) and "geese", that is, Canada geese, predominate as country food, a number of other species were bartered.

> Jos. Carpenter arrived from inland with a quantity of fish to trade (HBC B.243/a/5; October 29, 1930).

> Abel and Alex Wesley arrived from Lawachie today with rabbits and wavies (HBC B.243/a/1; November 29, 1923).

> Indian women bringing quite a few berries (HBC B.243/a/1; September 6, 1923).

> Jeremiah came in with a red fox and a little moosemeat (HBC B.243/a/1; April 4, 1923).

The volume of this trade was substantial, with one entry recording a trade of 100 ducks and 3 wavies, while on the same day a trade of "over 300 ducks" was made (HBC B.243/a/1; September 16, 1922). Elsewhere, 400 rabbits were purchased (HBC B.243/a/1; March 14, 1923). The Attawapiskat people also fulfilled a vital function in the feeding of the post's dogs. While fish and rabbit were staples of human consumption, they also were prized dog "feed."

> The team from Agamiski brought 300 rabbits for dog feed (HBC B.243/a/1; February 12, 1923).

> ...a load of rabbits for dog feed (HBC B.243/a/1; March 13, 1923).

> ...purchased a supply of fish from several of the Natives for dog feed (HBC B.243/a/5; September 6, 1930).

It is apparent that feeding the post's dogs could be almost a full-time occupation, as four days later the following entry appears "...purchasing a supply of fish from the Natives for dog feed" (HBC B.243/a/5; September 6, 1930), while less than two weeks later (HBC B.243/a/5; September 22, 1930) the post was again "trading fish for dog feed."

It was not solely smaller animals like geese, ducks, rabbits and fish in which the Natives traded. The data suggest that it was in the harvesting of larger species that Natives excelled, thus filling a vital role in the larger post community. "Alec Wesley and John Chakasim returned with...2 seals — which will come in handy for dog's feed" (HBC B.243/a/2; January 5, 1924). On September 18, 1923, 10 seals were reported as having been killed, four going for dog food while the remainder were put aside for "winter use." Nine days later, three more seals had been purchased and "put away for dog feed." Elsewhere in the journals, there are references to the use of bears for dog food. On September 12, 1927, an entry records buying three "white" bears from Joachim Spence and Philip Tookate for "dog grub." The latter hunted at Lake River and up Opinaga River, while it is believed that the former hunted along the Swan River between the Attawapiskat and Opinaga Rivers or possibly at Lake River as well. Honigmann (1961:161) suggests that seal is not eaten except in cases of extreme need. Rather, as suggested here, it is fit for dogs. The stomach, liver, kidneys and brain of bears (both polar and black, it is assumed) are avoided for food, and the paws eaten only in times of extreme need. In 1990 I was told that "only the Inuit eat seal."

It is also useful to examine the context within which much of the trade in country food took place. While there always existed a country food trade, it is apparent from the records that it was enhanced during periods of fur scarcity. Thus, we find increasing references to Cree bringing in country food to trade but few or no furs. For example, "Charles Kayshooke, Jr. arrived from inland bringing a few fish to trade and reports having killed only 1 otter since he visited the post last month" (HBC B.243/a/4; December 26, 1929). This situation was particularly true beginning in late 1929 and through to 1931 (the end of the HBC journals). This period, of course, was one of scarcity in furs, following the "fur boom" of the 1920s.

There are about five times as many references to trade in country food during the lean years of the fur trade as during the boom years. Increasing reference to trade in country food must be seen as reflecting an attempt to retain a hunting economy in the face of adversity. What is equally compelling is the fact that as little time as possible was spent at the post, essentially enough to negotiate trade and depart.

Jos. Carpenter arrived at the post at noon and left for hunting grounds two hours later (HBC B.243/a/5; March 25, 1931).

John [Chakasim] and son who arrived last night left again for their hunting grounds this morning (HBC B.243/a/5; March 31, 1931).

David Mud, Jr. and step son arrived from inland in forenoon...Left again, afternoon (HBC B.243/a/5; April 24, 1931).

The reason for these abrupt visits is simple: when country food is scarce, it is especially so in proximity to the post. It is therefore important to get back to one's lands as quickly as possible to resume the hunt for meat. To spend time at the post is to waste valuable time that is better spent hunting.

One might question why, if country food and fur-bearers were both scarce, people would trade in country food instead of hoarding it for their own use. The reason is not so perplexing. The items that were (or had become) essential for hunting and trapping were obtained from the HBC. These include such items as steel traps, bullets, guns, matches and snare wire. In addition, food staples like flour, lard, sugar and tea were also available only from the stores. The options were limited, but the people could deal in what they could produce through their labours, that is, country food, to barter for those items that allowed them to produce more. This is not to suggest that there was hoarding of country food to the point of hunger in order to trade. Rather, after meeting their own needs first people then traded in country food in order to obtain those items needed to survive on the land. Experience had shown that neither the HBC nor the government could be relied upon to help the Cree during periods of hardship. But they could try to retain their independence and dignity through their labours. Thus, there was an increasing trade in country food during the lean years.

Women in the Economic Sphere

Kupferer (1988:46), speaking of the "Swampy" Cree generally, has noted that traditionally the work of women was valued, that men did not lose status if they engaged in what was typically women's work and that older women—widowed or childless—often had reputations as good hunters. Similarly, Honigmann (1961:59) denies the existence of any rigid sexual division of labour, with men, women and children often participating in diverse tasks.

Traditionally, certain tasks were the responsibility of women. Fishing was one of these, as was rabbit and sometimes ptarmigan snaring in the winter. These were not (and are not) the exclusive domain of women, however, as both men and youngsters continued to fish and snare in 1990. Rather, women typically assumed these activities, and frequently made all-women group excursions out of these endeavours (Honigmann, 1961:91), creating a "picnic" like atmosphere. More important is the fact that women, by virtue of being the more active of the sexes in procuring fish, rabbits and small birds, might have at times been the major providers of food items. During periods of starvation this might be particularly true, as small game replaced moose and beaver in the diet. This suggestion makes for an interesting comparison with the !Kung San, a society in which women also provide the bulk of the diet (Lee, 1979:309). As shotguns, snowmobiles and outboard motors made hunting easier and more effective in the late 20th century, the productivity of men, in terms of country food production, undoubtedly increased while the productivity of women did not experience as great an increase. At the same time, the Northern Store, the hospital and the band office employed more women than men. Therefore, their contribution should be measured in terms of cash income, a task that is beyond the scope of this study.

Women (and to a lesser extent children) played a significant or dominant role in the harvesting of fish and small game such as birds and rabbits. The difference lies in the fact that qualitatively more importance is attached to the produce provided by men.

> ...fish are not really highly valued – in comparison to meat, for example...The capture of fish is not usually accompanied by excitement or great pleasure. In brief, they are a routine food only slightly more attractive than...flour and rolled oats. To these facts is related the allocation of most fishing to women (Honigmann, 1961:149).

While we could make an eloquent Marxist feminist criticism of these observations, suffice it to say that the reason for the low value placed on fish and the high value placed on meat lies in their relative availability and, hence, desirability. The reality of the situation, that is, that Attawapiskat is not a particularly biotically rich region, results in a premium on those items that are not readily accessible. That, of course, includes moose, caribou and other large game. The argument might also be made that fish is a "monotonous" diet, and that in Attawapiskat, it is perceived as a food that is not particularly filling or providing of energy.

Honigmann (1981:224) has suggested that the depletion of resources—both for food and for trade—contributed in part to the diminution in size of the winter hunting group. It is difficult to measure how this decrease in size affected the roles of women and younger people in terms of division of labour, but it is not unreasonable to suggest that there *was* a change in domestic roles.

What is interesting to note, however, is that in the early decades of the 20th century, probably due to the depleted environment, rapacious disease and restructuring of social groups, women and younger people began to play a more diverse role in economic activities.

The West Main Cree, in the 17th century, typically chose several "chiefs" (in reality, headmen) to take charge of the trading for their people. A "chief" spoke for his people, requesting the trader's consideration. How long this custom persisted is unknown, but by 1920 it is clear that, in Attawapiskat, women and "boys" had assumed some of the "chiefly" duties.

Alex Weesk's boy arrived from coast for some supplies (HBC B.243/a/; October 17, 1929).

...James Mud's wife arrived from Lawachie with a few ermine to trade (HBC B.243/a/4; December 9, 1929).

Wm. Nakoge Sr.'s wife arrived with several musquash in evening (HBC B.243/a/4; May 25, 1930).

This is not to argue that women and boys had assumed control; rather, that their roles in conducting trade had expanded.

It is suggested that if there was a decrease in the size of the winter hunting group (and an increasing scarcity of resources would suggest that, by necessity, there was), then women and younger people would assume more varied and active roles. The HBC records suggest an unusually large number of single-family winter groups, particularly during the periods of peak starvation. Rogers (1969:28), in reference to the Eastern Subarctic generally, has stated that the winter hunting group was typically ten to fifteen people in number, comprising two to four families. This, of course, represents (in the ideal form) one or two groups of trapping partners. Tanner (1979:45) observes that, in Mistassini, informants spoke of a preferred form of large hunting groups of four or five commensal units, but which could only rarely be used because of resources. In this preferred form, as well, there were trapping partnerships of two or more people. Honigmann (1981:224) indicates that the hunting group was eventually down to one to three family units in the West Main region.

With hunting groups essentially one-family units (in some cases), it is not surprising to find boys and women taking over the role of "partner."

Aleck Weesk's boy came in with several ermine to trade (HBC B.243/a/5; November 9, 1930).

Jacob Issapie's Boy [sic] came in from Equan River in afternoon (HBC B.243/a/5; December 1, 1930).

Joseph Mud's wife arrived from Fox River with a few rabbits to trade (HBC B.243/a/4; April 28, 1930).

It was the inherently flexible nature of Cree society (e.g., informal leadership, mobility between hunting groups, unrigid sexual division of labour and permeable territorial boundaries) that allowed for the development of expanded roles for women and children during the early decades of the 20th century.

It is clear that women did not function solely as adjuncts to their husbands. There are numerous instances of women working as independent hunters and trappers.

A few old widows coming in now and again with rats [muskrats] (HBC B.243/a/1; November 10, 1923).

Mary Kamalatsit arrived in the afternoon (HBC B.243/a/2; May 28, 1927).

Widow Janet [was] in today with [a] small hunt (HBC B.243/a/3; March 18, 1929).

Widow Janet and widow [illegible] arrived today pm (HBC B.243/a/3; June 11, 1929).

A number of the inland hunters came in with their final hunts – Chas. Fireman, Matthew Okimaw, John Longpeter, Jr., Joseph and David Okitigoo, Janet Martinas (HBC B.243/a/ 5; May 30, 1931).

The HBC records support the contention that women played a fundamental role in economic activities. It is apparent that women not only provided the needed foodstuffs for their own use but also turned harvested goods into trade items. A wide range of harvested goods was used in bartering.

Some women brought in a few ducks (HBC B.243/a/1; September 15, 1922).

Indian women bringing quite a few berries (HBC B.243/a/1; September 6, 1923).

Some women came in during the day with a few fish (HBC B.243/a/1; May 15, 1923).

James Mud's wife arrived from Lawachie with a few ermine to trade (HBC B.243/a/4; December 9, 1929).

In addition to being viable trapping and economic partners, women were indispensable in the bush in times of disease and starvation. Given the new structure of the winter hunting groups, that is, often reduced in size, men oftentimes had to rely on their wives for their very lives. This sometimes took heroic proportions.

David Okitigoo's wife arrived...and reported that her husband was sick and that they were entirely out of "grub" (HBC B.243/a/4; March 13, 1930).

David Ookitgoo's [sic] wife was brought to the post today by John Chakasim's and Alex Wesley's wives in a semi-conscious condition. Indians who had passed her camp had noticed that she had no fire, so the two women mentioned above left the post this morning to search for her and found her in the condition stated. This woman left the post on the 14th for her husband's camp but was only able to proceed a few miles as she had frozen her feet (HBC B.243/a/4; March 19, 1930).

When Honigmann undertook the research for *Foodways in a Muskeg Community*, it was a period of scarce resources. This fact helps to illustrate the significant contribution of women to the household diet. Honigmann (1961:91) cites the case of a number of women who spent 10 days in early March at Amiskosiipii, 10 to 12 miles (16 to 19 kilometres) north of Attawapiskat. After leaving their children in the care of older sisters and a grandmother, they set out their snare lines for rabbits. One woman caught 25 rabbits, 1 spruce hen and 10 squirrels (some women also had rifles). Another woman killed 37 rabbits and 4 spruce hens. Portions of these kills were distributed among other families. Given that it was a bad year generally, and especially for rabbits, which were at the bottom of their population cycle, this was a major contribution to the community larder.

In sum, it is argued here that the role of women, both in terms of their provisioning of food and in their overall status within the fur trade economy, merits re-examination within the Mushkegowuk region. Such an exercise would contribute greatly to existing "feminist" literature of the fur trade (e.g., Brown, 1980; Van Kirk, 1980).

NON-TRADITIONAL ACTIVITIES: LOGGING, GUIDING AND GARDENING

In addition to subsistence hunting and hunting for trade, there were other aspects of land use that merit mention. Some of these were of a direct nature, others were indirect but called upon Native familiarity with their land. A number of Cree were involved in log cutting for the HBC, working for wages. Those who did "log work" were active trappers who cut logs in the off-season. This, of course, was in addition to the wood cut for their own use.

> Some Indians brought down a raft of wood about 6 miles (HBC B.243/a/ 1; September 22, 1919).

> Log men started this morning for their camp with a week's supplie [sic] as they intend staying out for the week (HBC B.243/a/1; April 5, 1920).

> Quite a number of Indians are now on the post for Christmas. Four or five of them are off chopping in the bush for the Company (HBC B.243/a/1; December 21, 1922).

After the logs had been cut there was the opportunity for other work. "Indians hauling wood for $7 a pile, 6 × 8 × 4" (HBC B.243/a/3; January 25, 1929). Presumably, this hauling of wood was by dog team, and not human labour.

The HBC also employed traditional Cree skills in other areas.

> Two Indians are sawing canoe lathings at $35 per (HBC B.243/a/1; May 4, 1921).

> R.V. Cook left for the north accompanied by three native guides George [illegible], Alex [illegible – Wesley?], and David Koostachin (HBC B.243/a/4; August 2, 1929).

There is another area in which the Cree participated, if inactively. Cultivation and gardening are not traditional Cree endeavours, but in 1912 the Oblate Mission began to cultivate a large garden. One villager, Joseph Nakogee, also began cultivating a garden on the island below the village. When he left, the mission enlarged his plot and for the next 40 years this garden was worked (Vezina, 1978:5). Honigmann (1961:137) recorded that in 1947/48 there were two Cree gardens in operation. One belonged to an elderly widower (possibly Joseph Nakogee) and the other was a community garden. The latter produced twenty 75 pound (34 kilogram) bags of potatoes, which were distributed to at least 30 families. Thus, each receiving family was given about 50 pounds (23 kilograms) of potatoes. Despite these efforts, gardening has not persisted to a great extent in Attawapiskat. The Mission farm eventually was phased out, and in 1990 fewer than half a dozen volunteers tended the community garden.

CONCLUSIONS AND DISCUSSION

The period from 1901 (the arrival of the HBC) to 1952 (the implementation of the registered trapline system by the Ontario government) was a period of numerous economic and social changes for the Cree. Paramount among these were greater integration into the economy of the fur trade and shifts in patterns of land tenure. However, it is argued that integration into the economy was *not* at the expense of hunting for subsistence and that hunting for trade did *not* replace hunting for food. Further, changes in tenure must be seen as adaptations to environmental and demographic changes.

This period marked the greatest changes in Attawapiskat society, characterized by conscious and deliberate attempts on the part of the State to bring the Cree under non-Native control. Bailey (1969:181) has observed that the difficulty facing all encapsulated structures is how to maintain themselves by finding adjustment with a changed environment. "Environment" he defines widely: "a new law, a new ideology, a new technique of cultivation, a tender-hearted or rigid administrator, or many other things, singly or in combination..." (1969:191). It is quite apparent that there were dramatic changes to the cultural and natural environment of Attawapiskat between 1901 and 1952.

There was continued reliance upon the land by the Attawapiskat First Nation, despite State incursions and repeated periods of game and fur-bearer depletion. Times of hardship were met with social reorganization (e.g., diminution in size of the hunting group), redefinition and expansion of traditional roles, shifts in economic strategy (e.g., emphasis upon trade of country food when fur-bearers were non-existent), a restructuring of traditional ideas of land "ownership" and tenure and pursuit of more numerous and accessible, if less valuable, species when beaver was scarce.

A number of conventionally held ideas about the Cree in general, and the Attawapiskat Cree in particular, may not be as accurate as previously believed. Among these is the notion of prolonged summer residence at the post. While this may be true for some groups, for example, the Coasters or "post families," the data indicate that not all families resided for the summer months in the community.

Similarly, while there existed so-called "post families," it is evident that a sizable number of inland and other families helped provision the posts. This is particularly true during periods of minimal fur-bearers.

Finally, the role of women as family provisioners needs to be examined more closely. Attawapiskat (and possibly other Mushkegowuk bands) might be a unique case, given the "chronic shortage" of big game, but one cannot deny the considerable amount of food provided by women. We might suggest that the Attawapiskat case is typical for the Subarctic generally but is overlooked by most researchers. Women provide rabbits, fish, partridge and ptarmigan. While these are not prized food items like moose, goose and caribou, they provide a substantial portion of the annual diet.

CONTENT QUESTIONS

1. Distinguish between the practices of Inlanders and Coasters.

2. Briefly outline the main food resources of each season.

3. When did the Attawapiskat fur trade essentially begin?

4. What changes were taking place in Attawapiskat demographics and land tenure during the period of the intense fur trade rivalry between Revillon Freres and the Hudson's Bay Company?

5. What caused fluctuations in family income from trapping from 1944 to 1947?

6. Why was the trade in country food important?

7. Outline the role of women in providing country food.

An Attawapiskat man working on a canoe. Photo taken by John Honigmann in 1947/48.

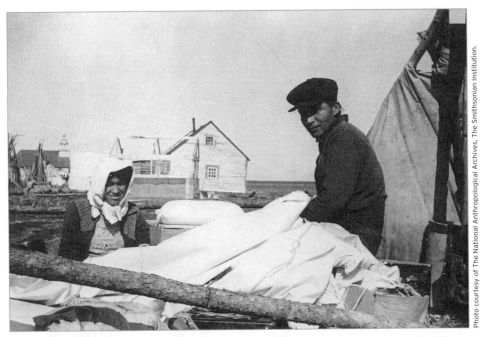

Photo courtesy of The National Anthropological Archives, The Smithsonian Institution.

An Attawapiskat man and woman preparing a tent for winter use on the trapline. Behind them is the Roman Catholic mission. Photo taken by John Honigmann in 1947/48.

Photo courtesy of The National Anthropological Archives, The Smithsonian Institution.

An Attawapiskat woman treating what appears to be a moose hide. Photo taken by John Honigmann in 1947/48.

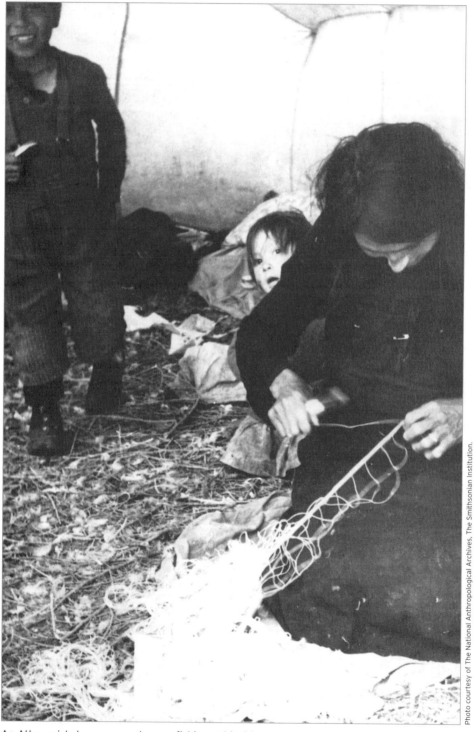

An Attawapiskat woman works on a fishing net inside a tent while her children watch her from behind. Photo taken by John Honigmann in 1947/48.

Photo courtesy of The National Anthropological Archives, The Smithsonian Institution.

A man and woman with a pail of fish, a staple food of the Attawapiskat Cree. Photo taken by John Honigmann in 1947/48.

An Attawapiskat man, wearing a rabbit skin coat, fashions a snowshoe frame. The icicles on his mustache suggest how cold it is. Photo taken by John Honigmann in 1947/48.

An Attawapiskat man, returning from a goose hunt, has two of the day's catch around his neck. Photo taken by John Honigmann in 1947/48.

Photo courtesy of The National Anthropological Archives, The Smithsonian Institution.

An Attawapiskat family travels on the frozen river during a mid-winter visit to the post in 1947/48. Note the snowshoes and child on the sled and the cradleboard the woman is carrying. The Cree didn't make extensive use of draught dogs, and this family's dog has not been put into harness. Photo taken by John Honigmann in 1947/48.

chapter seven

Attawapiskat Cree Land Use: 1953-1982

LEARNING OBJECTIVES

After reading this chapter, students should be able to:

1. Compare the perceptions of the Cree and the government regarding the registered trapline system.

2. Explain why there might be large differences in the harvesting of a single species from one year to the next.

3. Critically evaluate harvest data in terms of population and harvesting statistics.

4. Evaluate the impact—both positive and negative—of communications and transportation technology on Attawapiskat.

Between 1953 and 1982, Attawapiskat was opened up to Canada and the world through the greater provision of government services, communication and transportation access. In this 32-year period the community received telephones, television, daily flights in and out of the community, community health care and education. There was continued land use during this period as well. In addition, perhaps as a result of the greater access to the larger Canadian society, as well as the continued government pressure, the Attawapiskat Cree found themselves at times defending their rights to the land.

If the period from 1901 to 1952 was characterized by the initial Euro-Canadian encroachment and subsequent codification of relationships, the following three decades saw the State assume a position of non-accountability to the Cree. Following in the footsteps of the traders and the church, the government, through Treaty 9 and the trapline system, had furthered the encapsulation of the Attawapiskat people. Firmly buttressed by the legalities contained in and implied by the Indian Act as well as the treaty and the trapline regulations, during the period from 1952 to 1985 the government considered alternative uses for traditional Attawapiskat lands. At the same time, the government ignored Cree requests for a new, more strategically located reserve.

The significant aspect of the government's considerations is that they were conducted in a secretive manner, without consultation with the Attawapiskat people. In one case, the government intended to make the Akimiski region into an RCAF bombing range. In another, Akimiski was considered as a relocation site for an Inuit population. The Cree were, in the eyes of the government, an encapsulated people, not worthy of consultation or consideration. As Bailey (1969) contends, encapsulation is a function of the perceived economic needs and greater political complexity of the dominant nation. Nowhere is this more apparent than in these two instances. However, the Cree did not meekly accept these changes. Indeed, as the encapsulation process became more rigid and defined, the patterns of Cree resistance also became more formal.

Throughout this period there was a continued population growth with accompanying demands upon the environment. Nonetheless, the Attawapiskat First Nation continued to rely upon the land to sustain them as it had for generations. The latter half of the century brought new forms of commercialized land use—some of them introduced from outside, others developed locally. These were incorporated into the local economy, as the population sought to maintain that precarious balance between use and over-exploitation.

HUNTING FOR SUBSISTENCE PRODUCTS

We are somewhat limited in our knowledge of subsistence and trade hunting for this period. Without the extensive HBC archival data (post journals and harvest records), our information pool is diminished. What we do have, however, are two major government studies—one from the 1970s and the other from the 1980s. The former examined only waterfowl harvesting, while the latter was quite extensive, including virtually all bird and mammal species in the James Bay area.

Moose and Caribou

In the second half of the 20th century, moose and caribou were killed much more frequently than during the first half. Virtually every male over the age of 50 in Attawapiskat has killed moose and caribou, many on a regular basis. This suggests a significant increase in the availability of these species. (The age of 50 is used here because a 50-year-old man in 1990 would have been 13 years old in 1953; hence, just starting an active life as hunter).

To help put into perspective the increase in the number of moose and caribou, and the degree to which they have been hunted between 1953 and 1985, it is useful to look at some statistics. In 1990, 47 men over the age of 50 were interviewed. Of these 47, only 5 indicated that they had never hunted moose or caribou. An additional 6 stated that they had hunted moose, but not caribou. None had hunted caribou to the exclusion of moose.

That more moose and caribou were killed in the 1980s than in the 1920s and 1930s reflects, in part, the increasing mechanization of hunting in the modern era. Outboard motors and snowmobiles, as well as advances in weapon technology, greatly helped subsistence hunters. Caribou, in particular, became more accessible due to the snowmobile.

It is important to note that there are differing perceptions regarding the availability of moose and caribou. Some hunters, for example, observed that either or both species were "rare" or "scarce." This might be interpreted to mean that a) there are either fewer moose/caribou today than a number of years ago, or b) they are "scarce" in their areas. The latter is probably the case. In a study conducted by Thompson and Hutchison (n.d.), for example, only one moose was killed in Winisk between June 1982 and June 1983. A number of Attawapiskat families have their grounds near Winisk. Thus, a man stating that moose are rare in his area might indeed be making an accurate statement if he hunts in that region. The same holds true for caribou. Therefore, the discrepancy between an apparently large number of moose and caribou being killed and a man's statement that either species is rare is not a contradiction. It reflects regional availability factors, primarily the northerly location of caribou and southerly location of moose.

It might also be mentioned that increasing age does not necessarily reflect decreasing time spent hunting these two species, although poor health is a major factor in deciding not to hunt. The point is that, up to 1985, men continued to hunt as long as they were able.

Thompson and Hutchison (n.d.) conducted an exhaustive study of resource harvesting by the Natives of the Hudson Bay Lowlands. Their data are extensive and very detailed, covering birds, mammals obtained by hunting and trapping, fish and fuel wood. Their study period is 1981/82 and 1982/83. Their data, in some instances, corroborate that of this study. In other areas there are discrepancies. Thompson and Hutchison estimate that in 1981/82 Attawapiskat hunters killed an estimated 76 moose (range 55 to 95) with each hunter killing an average of 1.5 animals. In 1982/83 the estimated number of moose killed was 116 (range 107 to 126) with an average of 2.7 animals killed per hunter. "Range" refers to the smallest and largest possible number of animals killed either by a hunter or, in the case of totals, the smallest and largest possible total by all hunters.

We need to note several points regarding the Thompson and Hutchison data. They studied "male and female hunters between 14 and 75 years of age that reported moose hunting." According to one of the researchers (John Thompson, pers. comm), they recognized all male and female adults as potential hunters. However, there were no females who actually reported hunting moose, caribou or geese. Thus, one should not assume that the figures reflect women hunters of these species. This author's research found the same to be true; that is, women do not hunt moose, geese or caribou.

There are also several variations within their data. There are, for example, considerable differences in harvest figures for caribou. Conversations with one of the researchers (Bill Hutchison) confirmed that these differences reflect normal and natural fluctuations. They are not attributable to any social, cultural or demographic changes, fluctuations or aberrations within the communities. Therefore, variations in kill figures, time spent hunting and numbers of hunters are indicative of the availability of species and the environmental and meteorological conditions suitable for their pursuit. For example, he suggested that if there were a greater number of caribou killed in a particular year, it reflects that caribou were abundant and accessible. Similarly, he suggested that if the moose kill were down, it would be due to natural factors such as that river conditions were not optimal for the travelling necessary to hunt moose in the fall. It would not be due to social factors such as men being absent from the community or being occupied in building houses or other form of wage labour. He noticed no social conditions that might account for differences. The differences are naturally occurring variations, not aberrations.

In the Thompson and Hutchison data we notice a considerable discrepancy from one year to the next in terms of kills. In the moose data, the number of kills increases by 50 per cent from one year to the next. It is interesting to note that in Honigmann's work, a 300 per cent increase in moose kills was found from one year to the next. This might suggest population fluctuations within the species. What also might explain the differences is the availability of other species, for example, geese and caribou. Perhaps the greater abundance of one led to a decrease in the hunting of another.

One aspect of moose hunting in which there is variation between the Thompson and Hutchison data and the present study is in the amount of time spent moose hunting each year. Again, this discrepancy might be attributable to their sampling techniques or the particular years of study. In 1981/82 they found a mean of 3.5 days/hunter, and in 1982/83 there was a mean of 6.5 days/hunter. The latter is consistent with findings in 1990. The range for the first period was 1 to 7 days, for the second period, 2 to 12 days. The 1990 study found a range of 2 to 14 days, with a mean of 7.38 days.

In terms of caribou, Thompson and Hutchison again found a considerable discrepancy between 1981/82 and 1982/83. They estimate that in 1981/82 there were 94 caribou killed in Attawapiskat (range 64 to 135), with an average of 3.3 caribou killed per hunter. In 1982/83, the total kill was 217 (range 195 to 246), with an average of 8.7 killed per hunter. This is a difference of well over 100 per cent. As suggested above, a number of factors might account for this difference. What is undeniable, however, is that there was, and continues to be, a significant dependence upon caribou in the second half of the century that is not as apparent in the first half. Perhaps a reason for this is the greater accessibility of caribou through the use of snowmobiles. This will be addressed below.

The approximate time spent hunting caribou, as determined by Thompson and Hutchison, corresponds to that found by the 1990 study. In 1981/82 they found a mean of 5.1 days/hunter spent caribou hunting. This is based on a sample of 14 hunters, with a range of 3 to 8 days. For 1982/83, they found a mean of 6.8 days, based on a sample of 22 hunters. The range was 2 to 15 days. The average in 1990 was 4.9 days, with a range of 1 to 14.

There might be a temptation to explain the long-term increase in the number of moose and caribou kills as a simple relationship with increased Cree population. However, if we examine the relationship between population and moose and caribou kills over time, we still find that there is an increasingly large number of these species being killed. Table 7.1 relates moose and caribou kills to population.

There are several ways of examining these data. The most meaningful question is about the relationship of moose kills to population. It is apparent that the population of Attawapiskat is increasing. Is there a concomitant increase in the number of moose and caribou kills, or a decrease?

It is apparent that there is a dramatic increase in the number of moose and caribou killed and eaten in Attawapiskat over the 37-year period, and that this increase is not solely dependent upon an increasing population. It is unfortunate that the Honigmann data are

TABLE 7.1	Population and Moose and Caribou Kills 1946 to 1983		
Year	Population	Moose kills	Caribou kills
1946/47	467[a]	50[a]	14[a]
1947/48	470[b]	15[a]	11[a]
1951	669[c]	63[c]	22[c]
1952	600[d]	20[d]	no data available
1981/82	1000[e]	76[e]	94[e]
1982/83	1000[e]	116[e]	217[e]

[a] Source: Honigmann, 1961.
[b] Source: Honigmann, 1966.
[c] Source: Agency Report on Game Taken by Indians on Reserves for Food, 1951.
[d] Source: Agency Report on Game Taken by Indians on Reserves for Food, 1952.
[e] Source: Thompson and Hutchison, n.d.

taken from a particularly poor year for country food, because the 1946–48 data do not reflect typical moose and caribou years. However, if we acknowledge 1951 and 1952 as more typical years, we can definitely see that the growth in the rate of kill of caribou has exceeded the growth rate of population increase, while the kill rate of moose has remained consistent with the rate of population growth.

To put the moose and caribou harvest into an even clearer perspective, it is useful to determine the harvests as a ratio to human population. That is, how many people are there per moose/caribou killed? Let us examine the moose kill first. In 1946/47, the ratio of moose killed per human population was 1:9.34. A year later, in 1947/48, it was 1:31.33. Moving ahead to 1951, there was one moose killed for every 10.6 people, while in 1952 the ratio was 1:30. The figures 30 years later are similar to those of 1946/47 and 1951. In 1981/82, the ratio was 1:13. In 1982/83, the figure was 1:8.6.

The contrast in ratios for caribou over time is striking. In 1946/47, the ratio was 1:33.35 and in 1947/48 it was 1:42.72. In 1951, there was a caribou killed for every 30.4 people. No data are available for 1952. Leaping ahead three decades, we find that the ratio is significantly lower: 1:10.6 in 1981/82 and 1:4.6 in 1982/83.

These calculations illustrate dramatically the high degree of reliance upon moose and caribou and how this reliance has increased for caribou and remained consistent for moose over time. The notion that the increasingly technological world that has encroached upon the northern communities has eroded their relationship with the land does not hold true. Rather, technology, in the form of snowmobiles, outboard motors and other tools have allowed the Cree to make better use of the resources that they have. In a community where beefsteaks sell for $15 each, hunting is not a sport or a luxury; it is a necessity. Such use has not diminished in the last decade, nor has it resulted in a diminution of resources.

Generally speaking, Thompson and Hutchison's observations concerning moose and caribou hunting are consistent with the findings in this study. They observe that most moose are taken in the fall (which appears to contrast with the 1930s data), and most caribou are killed in the winter and spring, particularly March, April and May. This finding is similar to the 1990 data. Likewise, they concluded that Native moose hunting areas were situated along the major river corridors or coastal streams, while most caribou were taken along the coast or inland. In Attawapiskat, the latter pattern prevails. They also drew attention to the significant role played by snowmobiles in accessing caribou in the interior. Finally, they also noted the importance of the harvesting of moose and caribou to Native communities, observing that a comparatively small number of moose/caribou harvesters does not reflect a minor dependency on these species. The meat from both these animals was (and still is) distributed to numerous households throughout the community.

Waterfowl

Studies have consistently indicated the continued reliance upon goose hunting in James Bay. All of the men over 50 whom the present study addressed reported goose hunting. Some, of course, for health reasons, no longer hunt. I will again attempt to extrapolate backwards to determine the goose harvest from 1953 to 1985. We are fortunate, however, in having two major studies to draw upon, that of Prevett *et al.* from the 1970s and Thompson and Hutchison from the 1980s. While this chapter addresses land use within a particular block of time, we will compare the work of the two studies above with Honigmann's and others from previous years. One of the objectives of the present study is to determine *continuities* and *changes* over time; thus, we cannot simply look at the 32-year span in isolation.

Thirty-seven of the 47 men over the age of 50 with whom I spoke still hunt geese. This statement, however, must be modified. Some hunt only in the spring, and many do not hunt as extensively as they used to. Nonetheless, they still hunt and kill a large number of birds. A somewhat surprising result of the figures quoted showed up in the quantification of the data. Despite the fact that some hunt only one season, and others don't kill as many geese as they used to, the average per hunter is virtually the same as government studies for all hunters in Attawapiskat. In other words, men over 50 who still hunt kill as many birds as do younger hunters, although they might spend less time, for example, only in the spring, actually hunting.

In the present study, I asked hunters a number of questions relating to goose hunting. In addition to questions regarding where they hunted and why, and with whom and for how long, I asked them how many of each species they killed the previous spring and fall, whether this would be an average kill and, if not, whether it was high or low. Also, reasons for the variation from the norm (if there was one) were sought.

To reiterate, the point of addressing only men over the age of 50 in this chapter is to try to establish a quantitative profile of land use between 1953 and 1985. By drawing upon their present use patterns and/or their recollection of previous use, I can try to recreate the norm for the period under discussion.

Of the 37 men who still hunted, 8 did not hunt in both the spring and fall hunts, that is, they hunted in one season or the other but not both. Thus, their annual count of waterfowl kills was low. Seven indicated that their seasonal kills are now less than previously because they no longer provide for large families and/or their sons provide them with geese.

These potential skewing factors are offset by a couple of hunters with exceptionally large numbers of kills. One man reported killing 500 to 600 geese, another 400. A third man claimed 635 goose and 70 ducks. Two other hunters killed over 200 geese each (235 geese plus 100 ducks, 232 geese plus 50 ducks). It should be mentioned that these truly are exceptional—two to four times the average—and in Attawapiskat there is resentment and disgust expressed (by some people) at these very large kills. Those who harbour such sentiments see it as overkill and indicative of greed.

What I found was remarkably similar to the findings of Thompson and Hutchison (see below). There was an overall annual kill of 130 geese (all species). The annual "wavy" (blue and snow geese) kill was 57.18 birds, with an average of 45.56 being taken in the fall and 11.62 in the spring. Canada geese (or simply "geese") were harvested at an annual rate of 72.89 birds per hunter per year, with an average of 54.89 being killed in the spring and 18 in the fall. Ducks were killed in far fewer numbers, and a correspondingly fewer numbers of hunters killed them. There was an average of 10.56 ducks/hunter being killed in the spring, and 12.18 ducks/hunter in the fall. In sum, the average waterfowl harvest (ducks and geese) was 152.81 birds per hunter for men over the age of 50.

Prevett *et al.* (1983) conducted a major study of waterfowl kills by James Bay hunters for the period from 1974 to 1976. They found that 85 per cent of the potential hunters actively harvested geese. Of these, 98 per cent hunted in the spring and 86 per cent took part in the fall hunt. Hunters spent an average of 9 days hunting in the spring and 10 days in the autumn. These hunters killed a total of 9204 snow geese, 6370 large (or giant) Canada geese, and 905 small (or lesser) Canada geese. The duck kill comprised 105 Brant and 3187 "ducks" of unidentified species. Per hunter in Attawapiskat, this worked out to 61.6 snow geese, 39.5 large (or giant) Canada geese, 6.0 small (or lesser) Canada geese and 21.3 ducks, for a total annual average kill of 128.4 waterfowl.

It is important to note that this figure is considerably lower than that found by Thompson and Hutchison (n.d.) and the present study. It is also important to note some trends observed by Prevett *et al.* They noticed that the James Bay Native kill was approximately 13 per cent of the total hunting kill of the Tennessee Valley Population, 9 per cent of the Mississippi Valley Population and 7 per cent of Hudson Bay lesser snow geese. The Cree apparently are not contributing to goose overkill. It is useful to compare their Attawapiskat-specific data with the data of the present study as it pertains to hunters over the age of 50. Prevett *et al.* found that 70.6 per cent of the snow goose bag was killed during the fall; this study found that the number was 80 per cent. Similarly, their Canada kill was 77 per cent in the spring; the current study had 75 per cent of the Canada kill being made in the spring. Finally, Canada geese constituted 42.5 per cent of the total Attawapiskat goose kill. This study found that the figure was 56 per cent. This contrast in figures, however, is not that striking, for Prevett *et al.* make the following observation: "The kill of Snow Geese has apparently increased by a factor of 2, and that of large Canada Geese by a factor of 3, since the mid-1950s" (Prevett *et al.*, 1983:187).

Thompson and Hutchison also examined waterfowl harvests in James Bay between 1981 and 1983. Their results confirmed Prevett *et al.*'s results of a decade earlier: waterfowl are the primary source of country food for the Cree in terms of preference, abundance and enthusiasm with which they are hunted. In some respects, their results are quite similar to those of the present study, especially in terms of number of birds harvested and time spent hunting.

Thompson and Hutchison (n.d.) reported 97.5 per cent and 98.1 per cent of potential waterfowlers hunting in the fall and spring of 1981/82, respectively. For the following year it was 88 per cent and 93.8 per cent. They found an average bag of 151.5 waterfowl per hunter in the 1981/82 season. This consisted of 67.1 snow geese, 45.9 large Canada geese, 21.7 small Canada geese and 16.8 ducks. The following year, 1982/83, the average kill was

175.5 birds per hunter. The breakdown consisted of 72.7 snow geese, 62.7 large Canada geese, 16.9 small Canada geese and 23.2 ducks.

The Thompson and Hutchison study found significantly different results in terms of number of days spent waterfowl hunting, when compared to Prevett *et al.* The former study found a mean of 21 days/hunter (range 3 to 47) for the summer and fall of 1981 and of 17 days/hunter (range 1 to 93) for the spring of 1982. For the 1982/83 season, the figures were 22.3 (range 7 to 62) and 15.2 (range 1 to 93) (n.d.:68,69). The Prevett *et al.* (1983:187) study, in contrast, found means of 9 days for the spring and 10 for the fall for the years 1974 to 1977. The findings of the present study for 1989 are much more in line with those of Thompson and Hutchison.

Small Game, Fish and Birds

In terms of subsistence, moose, goose and caribou are the main species, at least in terms of preference. In sheer numbers, however, fish are at least equally important. Small game and birds must also be considered in analysis of land use.

People in Attawapiskat are often reluctant to volunteer figures for small game, bird and fish harvests, out of fear of being inaccurate. The reasons for this potential inaccuracy are easy to understand: these species are not considered as important in the diet as are the others and they do not entail as much effort to procure. Hence, they become routine, and for hunters their numbers are not easy to recall. Thus, in 1990, hunters did not readily volunteer figures even for contemporary harvesting of small game and birds. Any attempt at backward extrapolation would be feeble at best.

Thompson and Hutchison (n.d.), however, do provide us with statistics regarding these mundane food items. The most important of these are willow ptarmigan (1418 harvested in 1981/82, 1092 in 1982/83), sharp-tailed grouse (1250 in 1982/83, 1506 in 1982/83), snowshoe hare (locally referred to as "rabbits," of which there 2041 harvested in 1981/82 and only 350 in 1982/83) and various shorebirds (a mere 10 in 1981/82 but 1798 in 1982/83).

Significant is the decrease in the number of snowshoe hares taken in 1982/83 compared to the previous year. This is undoubtedly due to the downturn in the animal's population cycle. We should also note the simultaneous increase in the number of shorebirds taken during the same year of the low hare harvest. While not disputing the veracity of the data offered by Thompson and Hutchison, it might be suggested that even the snowshoe hare figures from 1981/82 are low. The snaring of hares is not limited by age or sex, and in the bush a number of full-time trappers live virtually exclusively on hares and fish. Any estimate must take into account these dozen or so families. In 1990, some people (not full-time trappers) reported taking up to 50 rabbits a week during the period from December to February. While this is exceptional, it indicates the difficulty of establishing estimated kills.

A letter from Harvey (Superintendent, Indian Affairs) to Matters (District Manager, Indian Affairs) dated August 7, 1957 suggests the degree to which the Attawapiskat Cree were dependent upon country food. The letter recounts a band meeting at Attawapiskat in which the band requested the purchase of a 150 foot seine net "to enable [the people] to put up a supply of dog food and edible fish for the winter." They also requested "wood for the Old People, shot shells and gilling twine." These last items were going to be provided "unless otherwise advised" (RG 10, Volume 6961, File 486/20-2, Harvey to Matters, August 7, 1957).

The requests for a seine net and wood illustrate how important these two items are in the everyday lives of the Attawapiskat people. It was noted earlier how suitable firewood has never been particularly abundant and, with the passage of time, firewood harvesting involves greater distances and effort. Thompson and Hutchison have attempted to quantify the number of trees consumed as fuel. They determined that in 1981/82 an estimated 30,182 trees were harvested (range of 28,944 to 31,420) while in 1982/93 the estimated number was 76,204 (range 74,414 to 77,994). Again, it is suggested that these can, at best, be rough estimates. It is nearly impossible to take into account firewood burned in the bush on brief or extended forays. In Attawapiskat today, people contend that the burning of wood in houses is dependent upon the age of the house, the weather (which is, of course, variable) and the type of wood and the species of tree. In 1990, a number of residents could not offer an estimate in the number of cords burnt. Thus, attempting to quantify the number of trees is indeed rough. Nonetheless, the estimates of Thompson and Hutchison are valuable and reflect a concern of all members of the community, namely increasingly inaccessible firewood.

It is very difficult to explain the greater than 100 per cent increase from one year to the next. In 1990, wood-burning stoves heated 95 per cent of the houses; presumably, this would be so in the period of 1981 to 83. Nonetheless, these authors claim that these estimates are probably quite close to the true values. The figures, incidentally, equate to 100 to 250 trees per family per year (Thompson and Hutchison, n.d.:32). According to the authors, next to the goose hunt, tree harvesting was the second most important resource use activity in the Mushkegowuk region. Arguably, for Attawapiskat in particular, it might be *the* most important activity, given the lack of alternative heating.

Fishing has continued unabated over the years, with whitefish being the most common species caught. Thompson and Hutchison report that most of those who fish in Attawapiskat tend to work the Attawapiskat River up to 100 kilometres from the coast. Some families, though, went as far as the junction of the Mississa and Attawapiskat Rivers and north along the coast near the Ekwan River.

They determined that five major species (brook trout, whitefish, pike, walleye and suckers) were harvested and, in 1981/82, totaled 32,250 kilograms. Of this total, whitefish accounted for 23,254 kilograms. In 1982/83, the total fish harvest was more than double the previous year: 65,162 kilograms, with whitefish accounting for 50,802 kilograms.

The data presented by Thompson and Hutchison document the continued high reliance upon fish generally, and whitefish in particular. Again, no explanation is offered for the considerable discrepancy from one year to the next; in part, it may be attributable to population cycles or weather factors. Thompson and Hutchison suggest that the fishery (for domestic use) is the fourth most important activity in the Mushkegowuk region after waterfowl hunting, fuel wood gathering and grouse shooting. For Attawapiskat, this surely isn't so, and has not been so, as an examination of fish and grouse harvests attests.

HUNTING FOR TRADE PRODUCTS

It has been argued that the period from 1901 to 1952 is one of great encapsulation. It is the time frame in which the government and other Euro-Canadian institutions saw fit to bring the Cree under legal, political, religious and economic domination and control. The following years might be seen as the period of opening up, that time when—through transportation and communication technologies—the world came to Attawapiskat. This was not entirely a bad thing, for through a judicious use of these new technologies, the people of Attawapiskat were able to increase their traditional hunting and gathering activities.

To appreciate how the introduction of various technologies affected land use activities, we must first examine a number of demographic changes in the community. First, the early and mid 1950s saw the beginning of regular air traffic in and out of Attawapiskat. The first helicopter flight arrived in September, 1953, while 1957/58 saw Austin Airways begin regular weekly flights to Attawapiskat and other James Bay communities. These were then changed to twice, then thrice, weekly flights. Previously, all of the communities had been allotted four or five trips a year for mail service. It was not until 1974 when the Ontario Ministry of Transport built an airstrip that daily flights become a reality.

The implications of this new air service are seen in population figures for the community, which had always been unstable. Simply, many of those people in the community who no longer found that the land could support them moved southward to Albany, Moosonee, Cochrane or Timmins to find jobs working for the railroad or the lumber industry. This, it might be argued, relieved some of the pressure on the land. Studies have shown that when predators are removed from an area, the prey species, such as moose and caribou, will replenish. Once a large number of Cree had moved south, such might have been the case.

Informal censuses taken by anthropologists and government officials between 1947 and 1952 indicate that the population in Attawapiskat fluctuated between 470 and 600 people. Between 1955 and 1961, similar censuses taken by anthropologists and missionaries show that the population had dropped to between 300 and 400. However, it would be simplistic to assume that that there is a single causal relationship between a decreased population in the 1950s (since the 1940s) and an increase in moose or caribou kills. Nonetheless, such a situation might be one of several factors leading to increased production in harvesting activities for both food and fur. What the data suggest is a fairly rapid depopulation following the introduction of air service to the community, a factor that likely had an impact on the taking of resources from the bush. This depopulation was followed by a population increase in the late 1960s and early 1970s.

Trapping

Surprisingly, our knowledge of hunting for trade in Attawapiskat between 1953 and 1985 is in many respects more limited than for the previous half century. This is due, in part, to the fact that there are no HBC journals after 1931 and also no HBC harvest records after 1950. Government harvesting documents are, when available, sketchy. On the other hand, we do have data on other forms of commercial harvesting. These are useful, and indicate a shift in traditional hunting for trade patterns after the mid century mark.

Despite the drastic reduction in the number of fur-bearers during the first half of the century, the people of the Attawapiskat First Nation continued to trap to the best of their abilities. At times, however, their efforts appeared to be thwarted by an unproductive environment, bureaucracy and relations with traders. A letter from W. J. Harvey, Superintendent of the James Bay Agency, to F. Matters, the Regional Supervisor, outlines some of the band's concerns as they were articulated at a council meeting. Two of these issues—the lack of productivity of the region and the licensing of trappers—still concern the band today:

The Chief pointed out that the Attawapiskat country was a very unproductive area, the Cree having to travel long distances to make a living and that only those fortunate enough to have their health and a fair hunting area were able to eke out a living similar to their blood brothers further South.

The Band Council as a whole made a request for help for those who did not receive adequate credit from the local traders and the writer promised to take this up with the proper authorities.

Councillor Iahtail requested that each trapline should be covered by one license only and that each member of the head trappers [sic] family not be required to pay an additional license (RG 10, V.6961 File 486/20-2, Harvey to Matters, August 7, 1957).

In a letter to W. J. Harvey dated September 4, 1957, J. H. Gordon of the Welfare Branch explained that the Cree request that each trapline be covered by one license only "would be a matter of grace" by the Ontario Department of Lands and Forests who were (and are) authorized not only by provincial regulations but also under the terms of the Fur Agreement to impose a license fee on all trappers without respect to racial status (RG 10, V.6961 File 486/20-2, Gordon to Harvey, September 4, 1957). The Cree would find ways over the years to cope with this problem.

As indicated earlier, the harvesting of food from the bush continued and, in fact, actually increased during the period under discussion. A dwindling population is not sufficient to explain the pattern. Other factors must be considered for the increased harvesting.

A number of factors served to coalesce the population around the trading post in the second half of the 20th century. A hospital (St. Mary's Hospital) was established in 1951. In 1953 the first students were enrolled in the Attawapiskat School, a day school that was largely religious in its instruction. Initial enrolment was 15 students. In July 1955, the government started building the first four houses in the community. Twelve months later, construction of the first streets began (Vezina, 1978:12). What this development indicates is a State-driven move to make the Cree of Attawapiskat sedentary, through the implementation of allegedly desirable goods and services.

These changes were not necessarily unwelcome. The Cree had been living near the post for years, partaking of the goose hunt and trading. However, there are some in the community today who contend that the perceived decrease in harvesting activities such as trapping was a direct result of such changes as the introduction of the school (particularly the new school that opened in October 1976), and that it cannot be considered a move for the better. However, reliance upon the bush has not decreased. Rather, it is the nature of this reliance and the forms and means by which the harvest is extracted that have changed. When the moose, caribou and goose harvests have steadily increased over time, we cannot argue that the Attawapiskat Nation does not rely on the bush.

A government report from 1963 suggests that trapping was still a viable part of the Attawapiskat economy.

...we were very pleased with the results of the trapping in [Attawapiskat] and the fact that most of the families are earning a fairly decent living from the fur this winter. A check was made on all relief recipients...and three quarters or better of these on dollar value assistance were old persons, widows, and those who were not able to earn their own living due to physical handicaps. A few others on the list were assistance cases of a very temporary nature... (RG 10, Volume 6963, File 486/20-2, *Quarterly Report*, James Bay Agency, Quarter ending January 31, 1963).

The increased localization of people around the community meant that the nature of trapping would change. A number of men found jobs with the mission and the HBC. In

1961, Nonas observed that the mission employed 10 men at a rate of $3.50 a day, while the HBC "hired fewer still, and paid less." The HBC "chore-boy" was an old man who hauled "load after load of water, wood, and garbage and was paid twenty dollars a month" (Nonas, 1963:10). Nonetheless, these jobs were readily taken when they became available.

With the school, hospital, mission and trader in the community, as well as the possibility of wage employment, it was inevitable that the structure of trapping would change. Not as many men or families would stay out for months at a time during the winter and spring. Rather, an increasing number would replace the trapline cabin with their village house as the point of departure for checking their traps. This became particularly true in the 1960s, as snowmobiles replaced the dog team and snowshoes as the primary means of winter transportation.

It is virtually impossible to overstate the importance of the snowmobile in Subarctic Native life. Dog teams were never as prominent in Attawapiskat as they were elsewhere. Prior to the arrival of snowmobiles, much winter travel was on snowshoes. Honigmann suggests that because of the difficulties of winter travel in the "pre-Ski-doo" period and the respect and prestige accrued to those who fared well under adverse conditions, people were not fond of winter travel and "are particularly proud when they successfully come through difficult weather" (1961:125). The snowmobile, with its extended range and speed far in excess of dog teams, revolutionized trapping when it was introduced to Attawapiskat. The HBC sold the first two snowmobiles there in 1962. Six years later it sold 12, and in 1976 it sold a record 62 machines in one year.

Along with snowmobiles, two-way radios or "transceivers" were also introduced into Attawapiskat. These allowed hunters to go into the bush and yet retain contact with the community. The fear of starvation and death in the bush that had characterized much of the community earlier could, to some degree, be dissipated through this means.

In brief, the considerable influx of communications and transportation technology allowed trappers a greater number of options. Further, the opportunity for full- or part-time wage employment also made part-time trapping a possibility for those who did not care to leave their children behind in town to go to school while they trapped. During the 1950s, 1960s, 1970s and early 1980s, a number of new strategies were developed.

A number of families continued to trap year-round, returning to town infrequently to trade. These trips into town would be during the summer and at Christmas. For others, trapping became a part-time activity, made easier by snowmobiles. In both of these instances, there was effort made to take children into the bush so that traditional skills could be learned. This is reflected in the large numbers of younger men who today still hunt and trap.

For a large number of families the benefits of transportation technology were reflected in two new patterns of bush access. A typical trapper would canoe into his territory in the fall, carrying his snowmobile. At Christmas he would skidoo back to town. The reverse pattern occurred in the spring. This is still the norm for some trappers today.

Other trappers would sometimes fly into their camps, arranging for Christmas pickup ahead of time. For some, whose lands were quite distant from Attawapiskat, this arrangement was made also for the goose hunts. These trappers are the ones who frequently have two-way radios, a vital link between them and outside help should it be needed. In the 1970s, the Ministry of Natural Resources initiated a programme to fly trappers into their camps and also back at the close of the trapping season. This service is maintained free of charge by the ministry.

It is tempting to look at the rapid changes brought on by White incursion into the north as inevitably detrimental to "traditional" culture and, in many cases, this may be so. However, there have been some positive aspects to the technologies brought in by outsiders—witness the increased accessibility of trapping territories and the constant communication links between isolated camps and the community allowed by outboard motors, snowmobiles and radios.

We must also bear in mind that factors such as the availability of resources and the option of working for regular wages had an effect upon the degree and nature of land use. The availability of transportation and communication technology allowed for the option of part-time or full-time trapping, as resources permitted. In other words, in those seasons when there was a bountiful harvest of fur-bearers to be had, a hunter could—if he had the material resources in the form of snowmobile, guns and traps—avail himself of this harvest. Up until this time, a person whose lands were 100 or more kilometres away was quite restricted in terms of pursuing trapping on a part-time basis. Indeed, a hunter could conceivably spend months in the bush for minimal or no returns. With a snowmobile, however, the same hunter could make a return journey of 200 kilometres in a day or so of travelling. To put this into perspective, a HBC post entry from 1930 stated that "Patromay Carpenter arrived from inland bringing the first part of his hunt – 2 mink" (December 22, 1930). In contrast, in 1990, a young part-time trapper was informed of the large marten population in the region. The trapper set out on his snowmobile, set his traps approximately 50 kilometres away and during the next week and a half caught half a dozen marten and an ermine. It necessitated just a few trips of approximately two hours each on the snowmobile. This part-time trapper was also employed as an interpreter and was self-employed selling firewood. The point is that since the introduction of snowmobiles the options open to trappers have increased. With the return to population increase during the 1970s, this option was important in terms of employment. In contrast, in the pre-snowmobile era, trappers were relegated to trapping or welfare. In the post-1950s, trapping—on a part-time or full-time basis—may be pursued. There is little evidence to indicate that trapping decreases once full-time wage employment is attained.

The most disruptive factor between 1953 and 1985 was not downswings in game population or the introduction of technology; it was the carryover of the registered trapline system. Its implementation provides a valuable lesson in the cross-cultural imposition of unilateral decisions. Suffice it to say that the registered trapline system was adhered to by the Cree for only 15 or 16 years (until the mid 1960s) and then essentially rejected in favour of their previous practices. The resentment, anger and distrust that were a product of the system largely disappeared with its abandonment. It is interesting to note that the Cree adapted readily to environmental, technological and economic change, modifying and reshaping their land use practices to meet these new challenges. Legal and ideological shifts imposed by the new trapline system, however, were too overwhelming; when this threatened to destroy the very foundation of Attawapiskat society through threats, violence and feuding, the essentially foreign trapline system was discarded in favour of what they knew worked for them.

There are few data available pertaining to trapping harvests. What we do have, however, are figures specifically for Akimiski Island for the period of 1959 to 1962. At the time the island was still a HBC beaver preserve. Between 1959 and 1962, the Akimiski fur harvest included a total of 910 beavers, 339 foxes (including eight arctic foxes) and 440 muskrats, in addition to lesser numbers of other species. Beaver and muskrat showed considerable fluctuation. One hundred and twenty-nine beavers were trapped in 1959, compared to 578 in 1960, 82 in 1961 and 121 in 1962. There were 265 muskrats caught in 1960, compared to 35 in 1959, 135 in 1961 and only 5 in 1962.

One of the trappers working on Akimiski throughout the period of 1960 to 1962 (and possibly beyond) was a woman, Caroline Wheesk. Cooper (1933) notes that Thomas Wheesk's lands were on Akimiski, while other data from 1910 suggests that they were a "post family."

It remains to compare the harvest of these furs with the harvests from previous years to determine the degree of hunting for trade. It has been argued that hunting for subsistence has increased appreciably over the years, as determined by the sheer number of moose, goose and caribou kills. When these figures are calculated on a kill/population ratio, they still support the argument for greater subsistence hunting than previously. We shall use the same method of comparison (harvest/population) to draw conclusions.

Since we do not have yearly population figures for Attawapiskat, a direct comparison is problematic. What are detailed below are harvest figures for those years for which there are available population statistics. Table 7.2 shows harvest figures and populations for 1947, 1948, 1950, 1971/72 and 1981/82.

TABLE 7.2	Comparison of Fur Harvest 1947, 1948, 1950, 1971/1972, 1980/1981				
	1947[a]	1948[a]	1950[b]	1971-72[c]	1980-81[c]
Beaver	122	273	279	1229	1183
Ermine	649	222	2360	55	31
Fox, Silver	9	–	1	–	–
Fox, Cross	52	6	15	–	–
Fox, Red	203	23	108	–	–
Fox, White[d]	7	2	–	169	81
Fox, Coloured	–	–	–	61	203
TOTAL FOX			124	230	284
Lynx	–	–	–	204	61
Marten	1	–	–	9	122
Mink	51	78	275	121	139
Muskrat	1428	2828	3627	2191	3026
Otter	192	147	174	82	231
Squirrel[e]	2665	2573	985	122+	75+
Skunk	105	24	32	–	–
Black Bear	–	–	–	–	2
Polar Bear	–	–	–	–	5
Timber Wolf	–	–	–	21	2

[a] Source: Honigmann, 1961. The population of Attawapiskat was 468 in 1947 and 470 in 1948.
[b] Source: HBC Archives. The population of Attawapiskat was 669 in 1951.
[c] Source: Ministry of Natural Resources, Wildlife Branch. The population of Attawapiskat was 1143 in 1971/72 and 1183 in 1980/81.
[d] MNR lists foxes as "Coloured", "Arctic" and "Grey."
[e] MNR lists only "Red Squirrel."

It is quite apparent from the data that hunting for trade, when measured on a per pelt basis, did not diminish between 1950 and 1985. When correlated with population, fur harvests for the most part (and in terms of major furs) showed an increase between the years 1950 and 1971/72 and 1980/81. These figures, however, do not tell us everything. We do not know, for example, how many people were trapping during these years. Are these increases the product of a smaller number of more active hunters or do they reflect an overall increase in the numbers of trappers and their production? Data are lacking on the numbers of trappers. On the other hand, we do have the observations of the 1963 Quarterly Report, wherein it is observed that, generally speaking, people made a "fair living" at trapping.

There are other points that must be noted. The data do not tell us how many part-time trappers there were in comparison to full-time trappers. Perhaps these questions need not concern us, for the incursion of White institutions and White technologies allowed for the conscious choice of part-time over full-time trapping. With what data we have, though, we can argue that hunting for trade between 1952 and 1985 remained relatively consistent and in terms of a pelts to population ratio, increased somewhat in major fur species such as beaver, fox, lynx and marten. Thompson and Hutchison (n.d.:44) state in their study of the James Bay area resource harvesting that beaver and marten are the most important furbearers in the region. It might be suggested, then, that while the harvesting of certain species may be down, in terms of the most important species, activity is increasing. Perhaps there is a cost benefit approach being taken to trapping, with effort being expended on those species that promise greater financial reward.

Commercial Fishing

Two developments in Attawapiskat between 1953 and 1985 were the creation of goose hunting camps and a commercial fishery. The latter was only of a short duration, being adversely affected by a number of factors endemic to the hinterlands. The goose camps are still in operation and offer employment to a number of people.

The commercial fishery was in operation less than a decade and in many respects is reminiscent of the economic development schemes chronicled by Driben and Trudeau (1983) for the Fort Hope band. The program began with test fishing for sturgeon in the Attawapiskat River in 1958. The tests themselves were inconclusive, the Native guides stating that the water was too high and too dirty for fishing at the time, but should be better later in the season (RG 10, V.6962, 486/20-2, Turner to Harvey, July 21, 1958). It was not until 1962 that the James Bay Indian Agency applied for sturgeon fishing licenses for the Ontario portion of the bay. The Quebec side was already conducting commercial fishing. The licenses applied for were for the French, Albany and Attawapiskat Rivers (RG 10, V.6963, 486/20-2, James Bay Indian Agency Superintendent's Quarterly Report).

A report on the James Bay fishing industry dated December 21, 1962 records the Attawapiskat sturgeon catch for 1962. On August 16, 1962, one box of sturgeon containing 64 pounds (29 kilograms) of small fish was produced. The value was $65.28. One week later, three boxes of medium sized fish, totaling 298 pounds (135 kilograms), was produced. Its value was $303.96. The last harvest, one box of 131 medium sized fish, was produced with a value of $133.62.

The very nature of the bay worked against any successful commercial fishery without considerable financial outlay. Hunter, of the Fisheries Research Board of Canada (Arctic Division), submitted a draft report on the west coast fishery in 1963. In it he stated that

> [Studies] affirmed readings of temperatures of 15 degrees Celsius. Such being the case, any fish not removed from the nets within a very limited time would result in a second-class product. Winds and rough water along the west coast of James Bay are likely to prevent regular tending of nets so that the above situation may often occur (RG 10, V.6963, File 486/20-2, Hunter to Gimmer, July 24, 1963).

He also noted an improper size and use of netting in the James Bay fisheries. The Indian Affairs Branch had provided these.

In his report, Lapp (Regional Supervisor, North Bay) observed that unless the high cost of transportation could be kept to a minimum, the fishery operation would continue to function on a marginal basis without sufficient revenue derived to pay the cost of nets and other necessities (RG 10, V.6963, 486/20-2, Lapp to Indian Affairs Branch, December 21, 1962). He noted how high transportation costs resulted in decreased revenue to fishermen (they received 44 cents a pound when sturgeon was paying $1.02/pound). Lack of communications between the fishery and the carrier resulted in a number of unnecessary trips to pick up parts. All of this resulted in high operation costs, a problem that he suggested could be partially alleviated if fish camps were provided with radios.

The commercial fishery persisted for a few more years despite the cost. In 1966/67, 219 pounds (99 kilograms) of large sturgeon were taken out of Attawapiskat. At $1.52/pound, they paid $332.88. In the overall James Bay fishery there was a gross loss of $11,764.20 that fiscal year (RG 10, V.6963, 486/20-2). There are no further data on the fishery after 1967.

In Attawapiskat in 1990 there were fewer than half a dozen people who were aware that the commercial fishery ever existed. Those people who remember it can offer some explanations for its demise. They maintain that it was pursued on a trial basis only, and that the effort put into it on the government's part reflected that fact. The equipment provided was not the proper type (see Hunter's comments, above). Furthermore, the transportation provided to fly fish out was not reliable. Between unreliable scheduling of flights and those flights that were legitimately kept grounded by bad weather, a great deal of the fish catch went bad. Thus, they maintain, the project was scrapped. Today, however, a commercial fishery might be a viable operation because of daily flights in and out by two airlines and freezer capabilities to keep the fish until it might be flown out.

Goose Hunting Camps

The Chookomoolin family tourist camp began when the family started proceedings for its establishment in 1962, and it remains a very successful operation. Goose camps are an important source of income for the James Bay Cree, four being in operation on the Quebec side and two in Albany at the time the Chookomoolins applied for their license. It is essential to examine the reasons for the success of the camp. There are a number of reasons that might be suggested. First, it was an endeavour that was proposed by the family, not one that was imposed by outsiders. Therefore, the motivation for success was personal, not bureaucratic. Second, the hunting and fishing camp is a project that is consistent with traditional economic activities. It is a form of employment that draws upon the knowledge and skills that the family and employees have gathered through their life experiences. Third, the camp does not interfere with other economic and subsistence activities. The family pursues trapping and hunting after the goose and fishing seasons. Thus, the camp is incorporated into the traditional seasonal round. Fourth, the camp was able to get off the ground and mobilized in large part due to the enthusiastic and unreserved support of the government. The various departments came together in their approval and guidance. Fifth, the fact that this was (and is) a family project is not a small consideration. Kin groups are important economic units and holders of tenure. Thus, the emergence, perpetuation and success of the Chookomoolin tourist camp may be partly attributable to the fact that it is a *kin* based endeavour. There is a collective responsibility to make the project successful. Sixth, two factors—the decline in the fur industry and the opening up of the area through transportation and communication—provided an impetus for a new economic endeavour. These factors, in conjunction with the family's ambition and industriousness, fuelled the success of the project.

Today, the camp remains successful, and family members take pride in it. They stress the many positive aspects of the camp: the outdoor living, the opportunities to educate the public about life in the bush and Cree culture, the fact that it is a business built by their own hands on their own lands, the opportunities to practice their own harvesting activities and the famous and "important" people they have met through the camp (mainly politicians and professional athletes).

During this period there was another goose camp built, this one under the initial control of the government. In 1959, the Attawapiskat band had approached the Indian Affairs Branch with the idea of establishing a camp on the Kapiskau River, which at that time was also the site of a Native game sanctuary, but this idea was initially vetoed. It was 1969 before the government established another camp in the Attawapiskat area. In August of that year, a $2500 loan was approved for the establishment and development of a goose hunting camp in the name of the Attawapiskat band. The financial administration would be under the supervision of the Department of Lands and Forests. Eventually, in 1977, the camp would be turned over to local Native control.

THREATS TO TRADITIONAL USE AND OCCUPANCY

There were a number of external threats between 1953 and 1985 that impinged on the people of Attawapiskat and their way of life. Some of these failed to materialize but nonetheless suggested the vulnerability of their position and indicated the fragility of the hunting/gathering culture *vis à vis* the larger nation-state. An examination of these reveals the machinations of the bureaucratic process, a process that is often hidden (intentionally and unintentionally) to those whom it may ultimately affect.

The RCAF Seeks a Bombing Range

Had it materialized, one of the most devastating intrusions into the Attawapiskat territory would have been the suggested Royal Canadian Air Force (RCAF) bombing and gunnery range. Proposed in 1957, it was to comprise an area approximately 25 by 50 miles (40 by 80 kilometres). This proposal is remarkable for a number of reasons. One of these is the initial confusion it created regarding the exact location of the suggested range. This confusion might be humourous except for the casual attitude shown by governmental officials concerning the fate of the local Cree and, of course, for the very real potential for suffering and the loss of human life. Nobody in 1990 seemed to be aware of the bombing range that was proposed in 1957 for James Bay. Inquiries to Indian Affairs in 1989 and 1990 brought blank responses. People in Attawapiskat were unaware that their region at one time was being considered as a military training ground. And therein lies a matter of grave concern. The communications exchanged were all, not surprisingly, confidential. The lack of famil-iarity demonstrated with regard to the proposed site is disconcerting. So, too, is the some-what casual attitude displayed toward the Cree who inhabit(ed) the area. Without consultation with the people and without environmental impact and social impact assess-ments, government bureaucrats and administrators were sufficiently happy to warn Natives that they would have to vacate the area should the RCAF need to make use of it. We can only speculate on what would have transpired had the proposal gone through. With the community's apparent lack of awareness of the issue decades later, we do not know what killed the idea. Its relevance lies in what the proposal said about State intentions and Native concerns. The later Innu crisis concerning low-flying jets and bombing runs in caribou country in Quebec and Labrador is not without partial precedent (see Wadden, 1996).

An Attempted Relocation of Inuit to Akimiski Island

The Attawapiskat people recognize Akimiski Island as being part of their traditional lands, by virtue of having lived and hunted on it for centuries. The rights to this land have come under question from a variety of sources. A brief, aborted attempt to usurp these rights was initiated in the early 1960s. The attempt never reached beyond the conversational and memo stages but it, too, illustrates dramatically how Native people are often left out of the negotiating process and, hence, are vulnerable to encapsulation. The proposal (made through a branch of the Department of Indian Affairs and Northern Development (DIAND) then called "Northern Affairs") was to have Inuit relocated to Akimiski Island. From the 1930s to the early 1960s, the federal government was actively engaged in relo-cating a number of Inuit communities (see Tester and Kulchyski, 1994). Subsequent com-munications between the various administrators within the Departments of Citizenship and Immigration (housing, at the time, Indian Affairs) and other departments reconfirmed the legal right to maintain Akimiski Island as a fur sanctuary. The proposal was dropped.

Also potentially threatening to Attawapiskat rights to Akimiski Island was a proposal to transfer control of the islands in the area from the federal government to the province of Ontario. This proposal, too, was not acted upon.

Neither of the two proposals for Akimiski came about. The Inuit were not relocated to the island, and it was not given to Ontario. But, as in the case of the proposed bombing range, the Inuit relocation proposal indicates how political machinations behind the proverbial scenes may affect those who lack political power. The encapsulation process is, in part, a function of greater political resources.

Treaty Rights Versus the Migratory Birds Convention Act

The Mushkegowuk Cree have been subjected to frequent RCMP and MNR authority arrests for violating provincial and federal game laws. This is particularly true with regard to the spring and fall goose hunts (see, for example, *The Globe and Mail*, November 11,

1987). These crackdowns on the part of the Mounties and others are a result of the discrepancies between Treaty 9 hunting and fishing rights and the Migratory Birds Convention Act restrictions. The Migratory Birds Convention Act has been given legal priority, despite what was agreed to in the treaty. Guns and birds have been confiscated, and the people have been very frustrated by the apparent duplicity of the treaty negotiators.

Subsistence Hunting Versus Hunting for Sport

In the early 1960s, propagandizing in some American newspapers and magazines also posed a potential threat to traditional semi-annual goose hunting. These articles evoked a defensive reaction on the part of the Canadian government.

The *Minneapolis Morning Tribune* (July 7, 1964) story said, in part,

> The fuse is sputtering on what could be a major explosion of sportsmen's protests over the wholesale slaughter of wild geese by Indians – who are being subsidized by the Canadian government to do the hunting....There are no restrictions on when and how many birds or animals they can kill. And the Canadian government is subsidizing the kill by furnishing the Indians with shells....At the village of Fort Severn, it is estimated that the Indians killed 35,000 geese last year with government shells [said Vern Jones, a Fort Frances bush pilot]. At Fort Albany, the estimate was 80,000 geese last season.

The article goes on to estimate the total Canadian kill to be "in the hundreds of thousands." "Indians," the reader is told, kill many of the geese while the birds are resting or in the flightless moulting stage. Another strategy allegedly used by Natives is to kill "several" birds with one shot while the geese are bunched together on the water.

An ostensible American authority who allegedly "knows more about the Canadian waterfowl situation than any other American" stated that "I know this situation exists, and I have told the Canadian authorities about the resentment building up here. It just has to stop."

The danger of such an article lies not only in its gross misinformation (subsequently established by the Canadian authorities) but also by the vast readership to which it is exposed. The article was later carried in a Canadian daily paper. One can only wonder if the same readers later read the correct figures and information.

A Decades Long Struggle for a Reserve

Finally, another struggle the Attawapiskat First Nation faced was not a threat to their livelihood but a very real battle for a reserve. The earliest record of the band's efforts to get a suitable reserve is found in a petition forwarded by Bishop Belleau (OMI) on behalf of Chief Alex Wesley, two of his councillors and nearly 200 band members. The date of the letter and petition is August 31, 1954. The process leading up to the establishment of the present reserve is a study in the workings of bureaucracy. A number of memoranda passed back and forth between various administrators between 1954 and 1958. In 1959, Chief Xavier Tookate again brought up the subject of a new reserve in a letter to the government. The final outcome of the petition begun in 1954 was that the Attawapiskat band received, on November 4, 1963, a reserve of 325 acres at the mouth of the Attawapiskat River. The original reserve, in contrast, was 104 square miles. This represents 66,816 acres. The discrepancy in size is obviously startling. The new reserve (91A) cost the government $200. The band's original proposal for a reserve was all the land from one mile north of the main channel of the Attawapiskat River, south to the north bank of the Lawachi River and inland for seven miles.

Today, the Attawapiskat people have their new reserve, although it is much smaller than the original one on the Ekwan River. It has a number of conveniences: the airport, hospital and school. However, it does have other concerns including unclean water and susceptibility to flooding. These problems remain unresolved.

Encapsulation and Resistance

The fact that the majority of these threats failed to materialize should not leave us unconcerned. Their significance lies in the way that they were constructed: the Cree were unaware of the proposed bombing range; they were uninformed of behind-the-scenes talks of Inuit relocation. The media presentation of the James Bay Cree killing "hundreds of thousands" of geese with government-supplied shells was beyond their control.

The scenarios presented above all have to do with power, and the lack of it. "Power," we are told, is the ability to bring about compliance or obedience to one's will. How this comes about is through greater political and economic control and through authority. Authority, in turn, is granted through a recognized "office." Through complex political machinery and greater economic resources, the government is imbued with power. This power is given legitimacy by the authority of its office and its mandates, the BNA Act and the Indian Act. These mandates then strip the Native people of power, rendering them wards of the state.

In the "goose slaughter" incident, the larger society, through its control of the media, was able to create damning misinformation that the Cree, through lack of capital and media voice, were unable to correct. The defence offered by the government was as much a defence of its own policies and reflection of its public face as it was a genuine concern for the Cree.

What these incidents also indicate is the vulnerability of the Cree in particular, and hunting societies in general. Brody (1981:xi) has stated that "the hunting societies of the world have been sentenced to death." Whatever truth this may bear is rooted in the powerlessness of hunting societies within the parameters of nation states. The encapsulation process strips small-scale societies of political and economic legitimacy, while the State creates and codifies the constraints of their bondage.

Knowledge and information are crucial tools in the exercise of power. Thus, when these are withheld or used manipulatively, powerful people, institutions and states are better able to exercise their power. The dramas that were enacted in the examples above illustrate how knowledge and information were employed in deciding the possible fate of the Attawapiskat people. The Cree were never informed of plans for a bombing range, or relocation of the Inuit or possible transferal of Akimiski to Ontario. Nor were they informed *for five years* of the government's plans for a new reserve *after the Cree initiated the move*. The fact that the plans for the bombing range and Inuit relocation did not materialize reflects changes in the government's agenda, not concern for or benevolence regarding the Cree.

However, we should not assume passive, acquiescent acceptance of a pre-determined fate on the part of the Cree. The Attawapiskat people have demonstrated resilience and willingness to adapt to change. The struggle for the reserve illustrates concrete efforts at ameliorating their situation. The strategies invoked for bringing about their reserve reflect thought and analysis: using the bishop as middleman, clearly stating their case with sound fundamental reasons (including proximity to White institutions such as the Church, school and hospital), including a petition with 200 signatures (surely every adult in the community, as the population of Attawapiskat in the summer of 1955 was 400) and patiently waiting for the bureaucracy to respond. These are not the actions of people who quietly accept encapsulation. However, when the dominant State withholds information, such resistance is hampered. Knowledge *is* potential power.

CONCLUSIONS AND DISCUSSION

There is a tendency among both the lay public and anthropologists to view industrial, capitalist intrusions into the hinterlands occupied by hunters and gatherers as inherently and unequivocally detrimental to the latter group. We cannot deny that European and Euro-Canadian penetration of the north has brought innumerable negative effects: disease, starvation, the diminution and eradication of aboriginal languages, attacks on traditional religion and loss of political autonomy.

As the second half of the 20th century began in Attawapiskat, the community was still reeling from many of these adverse effects. But the next 35 years would also see the arrival of new Euro-Canadian material culture—items that were not inflicted upon the people, but which could be selected and utilized through conscious choice. Herein lies a fundamental consideration. While the Cree were able to maintain some autonomy in the making of some decisions, throughout the 20th century much of their collective fate was largely in the hands of the State, many times in ways unknown to the Cree themselves. This fact has been demonstrated time and time again, from the signing of Treaty 9, to arbitrary decisions by the Church and HBC, to the imposition of the registered trapline system.

We could argue that with such relative powerlessness and the sense of futility it engenders, traditional land use activities would dwindle and wane. We could certainly understand if such were the case, especially in light of the lack of resources to be found at the close of the 1940s. But in the 1950s and beyond, the degree of land use activity (as measured in resources harvested/population) remained consistent, and indeed increased in some cases. In part, it is argued, this is due to the increasing ease of such activities made possible by the introduction of such items as snowmobiles, two-way radios, all-terrain vehicles and outboard motors. These were all items that had practical, utilitarian value for traditional activities, and that rendered those activities more viable in the face of the increasing localization around the post.

These items made trapping and hunting an optional part-time or full-time activity, a choice that many hunters and their families did not have earlier in the century. With pressure from the State to keep children in school, the choice was often between long-term separation from the family or not trapping. These were no longer the only options.

One choice the Cree did have—to adopt those items of Euro-Canadian culture that would help them in traditional activities—was made, with the ensuing result of greater production of country food and higher priced furs. At the same time, there was the further option of taking those wage labour jobs made available by White institutions—the Church, hospital and school—in the community. These wage labour jobs, it must be stressed, have not resulted in lower resource use.

The importance of Cree conscious decision making (as opposed to accepting decisions made by the State) is reflected in the success and failure of two commercial resource use activities: the Chookomoolin tourist camp and the commercial sturgeon fishery. Suffice it to say that the success of the former and the demise of the latter lie, in part, in the fact that the government initiated one while the other was established and maintained by the Cree themselves. Other reasons for respective success and failure have been addressed. These two case studies provide valuable lessons in both resource use policymaking and Native–government relations.

While there was increased land use activity throughout this period, the relative power-lessness of the Cree remained undeniable. The negotiations that were going on that directly affected the Attawapiskat people—proposed bombing ranges, resettling of Inuit to Akimiski—are indicative of the considerably weaker position of Native people *vis à vis* the State. This weakness is not only seen in the mere existence of these talks, but also in the fact that the Cree are perceived to be so insignificant that the government did not see fit to include them in negotiations. Such actions epitomize powerlessness. Implicit in the govern-ment's actions is an assumption or belief that Native reliance upon the land is non-existent or unimportant, or at least in comparison with White needs or wants. A corollary of this assumption is that Native culture is secondary to non-Native culture. Furthermore, the cod-ification of relationships between the State and the Attawapiskat people, through Treaty 9 and the Indian Act, gave legitimacy to any subsequent actions undertaken by the govern-ment. Hence, in the eyes of the government there was no perceived need to consult with the Attawapiskat people on such issues as the proposed bombing range in their territory.

We must, however, distinguish between lack of power and lack of will. Native people in Canada have been relatively powerless because of a deliberate, systematic and concerted effort at encapsulation by the dominant Euro-Canadian society. Nonetheless, there have been attempts, many of them successful, at resisting this encapsulation. Trading at Winisk when credit was disallowed at Attawapiskat, petitioning for a new reserve, consciously readapting to former patterns of tenure instead of adhering to the MNR trapline system and establishing Cree-owned and -operated goose camp are all forms of resistance. Resistance, by definition, cannot be acquiescence. It should also be noted that within this period the Cree themselves adopted more sophisticated (at least in White terms) forms of resistance, such as circulating a petition and using White allies to fight their battles for them. Therefore, just as the State codified its relationships with the Attawapiskat people, they too would codify their demands.

We have defined power as the ability to bring about compliance. By this definition, it is hard to say the Native people have power. At the same time, the Attawapiskat Cree have not acquiesced, but have quietly and patiently resisted, creating their own forms of disengage-ment from the State. And their relationship with the land has continued, although it has been reshaped to meet the exigencies of the time.

CONTENT QUESTIONS

1. Why did the Attawapiskat Cree reject the registered trapline system?
2. Why was the commercial fishery unsuccessful?
3. Outline the reasons for the success of the Chookomoolin goose hunting camp.
4. What were four major threats to Attawapiskat land use and occupancy? What do they tell you about the vulnerability of the Cree position with regards to outside influences such as government and media?

chapter eight

Attawapiskat Cree Land Use: 1985-1990

LEARNING OBJECTIVES

After reading this chapter, students should be able to:

1. Explain why the partnerships involved with the moose and caribou hunts differ somewhat from those of the goose hunt.

2. Explain why it is difficult to gather accurate data about small game and bird harvests in northern Native communities.

3. Assess the impact of the anti-fur lobby on northern communities such as Attawapiskat.

4. Identify the various types of sacred and historical sites found in Attawapiskat territory.

5. Describe how the land meets the needs (biological, social, psychological) of the Attawapiskat Cree.

The Attawapiskat Cree have continued to rely upon the land throughout the recent past. Indeed, they have expanded their means of resource use to include entrepreneurial endeavours that generate income, but that do not threaten the environment. These initiatives are reflective of the recognition of new realities in Attawapiskat, namely, that while subsistence hunting is always productive, the fur market is increasingly volatile. To compensate for this there is a diversification of land use activities, including the trapping of specific species that promise the greatest return for time and energy expended.

Paralleling this diversification of land use activities are a number of other endeavours through which the community seeks to break out of the encapsulation that the State tried to impose during the 20th century. These include the assumption of local control of education, the initiation of a pilot project for a local justice system and, along with other Mushkegowuk communities, organized protests against the enforcement of the Migratory Birds Convention Act.

There are other areas of land use considered here that are too often ignored. These include the significance of graves and cemeteries, historical and cultural sites and the construction of utilitarian and artistic handicrafts and tools. Finally, attention is also focussed on the Attawapiskat community garden, which contributes a considerable amount to the village's diet.

HUNTING FOR SUBSISTENCE PRODUCTS

The data from 1990 demonstrate a continued, if not increased, reliance upon the land to meet the community's food needs. This continued reliance is consistent with increased population. The data also reveal that there is considerable sharing of food within the community. Those who are unable to hunt for themselves are provided for by those who can.

The Goose Hunt

It is not surprising to find that the goose hunt remains a staple of the community, providing vast quantities of meat. Data from 1990 reveal that fully 92 per cent of households participated in the goose hunts during 1989. There is little unevenness in terms of participation by age, with men (although not women) of all ages participating in equal numbers. It would appear that only two factors will keep adult men from participation in the hunt: age/infirmity and being provided for by kin. One man, for example, who was fully capable of hunting did not because his sons provided for him out of their own hunts.

Men over 50 years of age comprise 30 per cent of the total hunting population. Those under 50 but over 18 comprise 70 per cent of the total hunting population. Data from 1990 indicate that men over the age of 50 kill an average of 152.81 waterfowl annually. This amounts to 72.89 Canada geese, 57.18 "wavies" or snow geese and 22.74 ducks. There is a seasonal breakdown to these figures. Older hunters kill, on average, 54.89 Canada geese in the spring and 18 in the autumn. Typically, 11.62 wavies are shot in the spring and 45.56 in the fall. There is less seasonal breakdown to duck harvesting: an average of 10.56 are shot in the spring and 12.18 in the autumn.

Among younger hunters (those under the age of 50), the average number of waterfowl killed is 149.15. This breaks down to 72.79 Canada geese (61.66 shot in the spring, 11.13 in the autumn), 56.96 wavies (24.47 shot in the spring, 32.49 in the autumn) and 19.4 ducks (7.56 killed in the spring, 11.84 in the fall).

In terms of sheer numbers killed, there is little significant variance between these groups. However, there are differences in the distribution of these kills among species and between seasons. These differences will be addressed below. The ultimate total bags, however, are almost identical.

Balancing these figures over the age spectrum (30 per cent of hunters over the age of fifty, 70 per cent under), the typical hunter in Attawapiskat kills 150.01 waterfowl annually. This figure comprises 72.69 Canada geese, 56.94 wavies and 20.38 ducks.

It is virtually impossible to overstate the importance of waterfowl in the Attawapiskat diet. Clearly, this importance is increasing over the years, if these data are compared with those of Honigmann and others. Using the formula of four pounds (1.8 kilograms) per wavy and seven pounds (3.18 kilograms) per Canada, it may be argued that each goose hunter is contributing 736.59 pounds (334.81 kilograms) of meat to his household. To this must be added 40.76 pounds (18.53 kilograms) of duck (at two pounds of meat per duck) for a total of 777.35 pounds (353.34 kilograms) of meat annually.

At 1.75 pounds (0.795 kilograms) of meat per meal, this represents 444.2 meals. Given that waterfowl is generally consumed twice a day when it is available, this equates to 222.1 days (close to 7.5 months) of meals per person. The average household size in Attawapiskat is five people, of whom four will eat meat, so on a per household basis the waterfowl kill will feed an average household for 55.5 days.[1] While we are examining these data in terms of averages, we must keep in mind the range of harvests. For example, one hunter who goes out during both the spring and fall hunts, killed "only" 30 Canadas and 45 wavies. Another hunter shot a total of 630 Canadas. These differences are partly a function of family size. Informants suggest that hunters increase their kills (particularly wavies and ducks) in relation to family size. Thus, it was suggested that 100 Canadas, 150 to 200 wavies and 50 to 60 ducks is not unusual for a "typical" family. In comparison, one hunter suggested that a single man might kill 100 Canadas, 30 wavies and 10 ducks.

Physically, goose hunts are relatively easier to engage in than are moose and caribou hunts. Therefore, older men who might be reluctant to undertake a hunt for moose and caribou continue to engage in the goose hunts. While moose and caribou hunts are usually a week or so in duration, a hunter can hunt geese on a day-to-day basis from his house, and in this way secure a substantial amount of meat. It is not surprising, then, to find a significant number of men who have long since given up moose and caribou hunting but who nonetheless bag large numbers of geese annually. If these men are single, widowers or are part of a couple whose children have left home, the goose hunts provide them with meat for a considerable period of time.

Fewer men participated in the fall hunt than in the spring. Three main reasons were offered for this. First, it was suggested that hunters don't like being out when "sports" hunters were out. Second, a significant number of men over 40 function as guides for the sports hunters, thereby removing them from their own hunts. This argument is questionable, as some people suggested that one of the benefits of guiding is that you can hunt and get paid for it. Third, the fall hunt coincides with the ideal moose hunting season and some people suggested that the availability of moose meat reduces the need for goose.

This is not suggesting a waning importance of the fall goose hunt. It still remains vitally important. As suggested by the harvest figures, hunters are killing more birds than previously to feed their families.

---

1. Indian Affairs suggests that the average Aboriginal household in Ontario is four people; in the north somewhat larger. In Attawapiskat it is five.

Hunters in Attawapiskat spend an average of 10.52 days hunting geese in the spring. The range is from 1 to 45 days. Men typically make a couple of one-day excursions at the outset of the season (often trying to bag the first goose of the year), before going to their camps for prolonged stays of a week or so. Transportation is by snowmobile during the spring hunt.

The fall hunt averages 9.2 days, with a range of from 1 to 60 days. As the hunt occurs before freeze-up, transportation is by canoe. Thus, hunters spend an average of 20 days to procure 222 days of meals.

In contrast to what has been described for the east coast of James Bay, the Attawapiskat hunt appears to be a much more individualized endeavour. The largest percentage of hunters (22 per cent) indicate that they hunt geese alone. The only hunting partnership approaching this number is that of father and son (18.5 per cent). This particular partnership undoubtedly includes men and their adolescent sons who have not yet started hunting independently. Young men typically start independently hunting geese in their late teens. The percentage of all other partnerships drops dramatically. Brother partnerships (11 per cent) and cousins (10 per cent) are the only significant combinations.

While the individualized nature of the goose hunt might suggest the absence of a kinship component, there is a temporal nature to the hunt, which supplies the kinship link. Seventy-four per cent of all hunters indicated that they hunt in the same areas that their fathers did. An additional 4 per cent hunt where their fathers-in-law did, while 1 per cent hunt in areas in which their uncles hunted. Only 2 per cent indicated that they hunt geese "anywhere." The remainder (19 per cent) claimed to have hunted in areas that they had "discovered" themselves or had been introduced to by friends. However, two important points must be stressed. A significant number of hunters who indicated that they hunt in areas where their fathers did not hunt are from outside the community, for example, Winisk or Albany. Thus, their fathers did not have the opportunity to establish a "traditional" hunting site. Further, a number of hunters indicated that their fathers' lands were quite distant from the community; therefore, their fathers' usual goose hunting areas were likewise too distant to access from Attawapiskat. The point that must be taken, then, is that the norm is for goose hunters to hunt in areas utilized by the previous generation. Therefore, there is temporal continuity demonstrated in the selection of hunting sites. This continuity establishes and maintains kinship links to specific hunting sites. This is particularly interesting because when the hunting territory system was "established" by the HBC, the coastal zone (which is where most goose hunting takes place) was ostensibly a "neutral zone" for the purposes of the goose hunt. I am not suggesting that there is a formality to the goose hunt that includes notions of propriety regarding hunting sites. What I am proposing here is the informal recognition of traditional goose hunting sites.

We can safely argue, then, that goose hunting continuity is firmly entrenched in the intergenerational use of hunting sites. Further, while the actual process of hunting, that is, building a blind, setting decoys and shooting, might be a largely singular activity, the reality is that hunting is in many ways more communal than it might appear. It is often the case, for example, that related hunters, especially fathers and sons, will establish blinds in close proximity to each other. Blinds are often less than a kilometre or so apart, so in reality, while men might "hunt alone," kin are literally and figuratively close.

The Caribou Hunt

In contrast to what appears to have been the norm during the first half of the 20th century, the harvesting of caribou continues at a significant rate. While the number of hunters is not exceptionally high, the average hunter kills a number of caribou, and there is considerable sharing of caribou (and moose) meat. From January 1989 to December 1989 there were 29 reported active caribou hunters in Attawapiskat. These hunters killed an estimated 132 caribou (range 127 to 137). These figures do not include the population with whom I did not speak, a total of about 20 households, including approximately 10 "bushmen" families. Even though a bushman spends all but one week in the bush annually, this does not guarantee that he is a big hunter of large game. Therefore, informants suggest that the bushmen families, in total, are likely to kill between 30 and 35 caribou a year. This figure, plus another four being killed by town families, suggests a total village kill of 168 caribou a year. Reported, documented kills, however, are 132. MNR figures for 1981/82 indicate an estimated 94 caribou killed (range 64 to 135), and an estimated 217 killed for the following year, with a range of 195 to 246 (Thompson & Hutchison, n.d.:85). Thompson and Hutchison report 14 hunters in 1981/82 and 23 in 1982/83. The present research suggests an average annual kill of 4.175 caribou per hunter (3.3 in 1981/82, 8.7 in 1982/83; Hutchison & Thompson, n.d.:85). The current data then, pointed to a continually significant reliance upon caribou over the decade.

Hunters generally hunt caribou "after freeze-up" until April, when there is sufficient snow for snowmobiles. Within this broadly defined season, however, a couple of months predominate as the preferred time for caribou hunting. Twenty-eight per cent of hunters indicated hunting in March, 22 per cent in February, 17 per cent in April and 11 per cent in December. Not surprisingly, the two peak months for caribou hunting coincide with the ideal snow conditions as well as that time when the fall goose and moose meat have likely been exhausted and the spring hunt is still several weeks away. Hunters in 1989 spent an average of 4.9 days (range 1 to 14) in pursuit of caribou, a figure not inconsistent with the findings of Thompson and Hutchison (n.d.:96,97) for 1981/82 (average 5.1, range 3 to 8) and 1982/83 (average 6.8, range 2 to 15).

Berger (1977:24) suggests that a caribou yields approximately 112 pounds (50.8 kilograms) of meat. Therefore 132 caribou represent 14,836 pounds (6729.5 kilograms) of food; 168 caribou (our projected estimate including "bushmen") represent 18,816 pounds (8534.8 kilograms). Hunters typically share their kills. Each successful hunter distributed meat to six to ten other families.

The nature of caribou, and the fact that hunters share the meat extensively, preclude the barring of access to one's lands. Thirty-six per cent of hunters indicated that they knew whose land they hunted caribou on, although the "owner" of the land was not one of their hunting group nor was he close kin. Twelve per cent of hunters hunted caribou on their father's land. Another man hunted on his grandfather's, another on his cousin's and a third on his trapping partner's land. An additional 18 per cent stated that they hunted caribou "anywhere" because caribou "move around." One hunter related how he had to pursue caribou for nearly 75 kilometres before making a kill. Only one man indicated that he did not know whose territory he had hunted caribou on.

What the foregoing suggests is not only a recognition of rights to land but also a recognition of the right to kill game for subsistence purposes. A number of men (18 per cent) stated that it was unreasonable to expect a hunter to restrict himself to a given territory when pursuing a highly mobile animal such as caribou. Caribou, it was said, vary in their location from year to year. Furthermore, given that men often hunt in groups of three to six, and each will share with six or more people, it is not unlikely that the "owner" of the land will benefit regardless of whether or not he is part of the hunting party. Finally, as one informant stated, one "does not own an animal until it is killed."

In contrast to the spring and fall goose hunts where "hunting alone" was the norm, caribou hunters invariably hunt in partnerships, often in groups of three or more. The rigours of the hunts, taking place as they do over several days and under the harshest of weather conditions, demand the safety of numbers. The potential dangers of the mechanical breakdown of snowmobiles dozens of kilometres from the village, in the dead of winter, virtually preclude solitary hunting, although two men indicated that they do hunt caribou alone. They were exceptions. Another practical reason for hunting in groups is that often there are multiple kills: one group of four hunters killed sixteen animals. A number of sleighs are required to haul such large numbers of animals back to the village.

There are social considerations of which we must be aware. The selection of a partner for caribou hunting does not appear to be random. It seems that specific kin are sought as companions in the hunt. Twenty-four per cent of caribou hunters stated that they hunt with their brothers-in-law, while another 24 per cent indicated that they hunt with their cousins. Brothers constituted 14 per cent of partnerships, while "friends" made up another 10 per cent. This last named, however, is misleading, as "friends" is often a generic term for such relationships as second cousins. Seven per cent of hunters stated that they hunt with "anybody" while stipulating that they "usually hunt with cousins."

With between approximately 50 and 55 per cent of hunters selecting brothers-in-law or cousins as their hunting partners, it may be asserted that the caribou hunt provides an opportunity to reinforce the extended family kinship links. As well, it might simply reflect a desire to hunt with members of one's peer group. In this sense, the hunting partnerships may be analogous to the more formal age-grades found in other societies. The number of supra-familial (i.e., beyond nuclear family) partnerships contrasts sharply with the number of hunters who reported hunting with such nuclear family members as their fathers (10 per cent) or their sons (5 per cent).

The Moose Hunt

When initial attempts were made to quantitatively analyze the moose hunting data from 1989, I was struck by what appeared to be an exceptionally high number of kills. However, the total annual kill, while high, is actually lower than that suggested by the MNR for 1982/83. Hunters in Attawapiskat killed 114 moose between January 1989 and December 1989. This figure represents actual reported kills. Including our additional 20 families, we might add 20 kills, for a total of 134 moose. In contrast, MNR data (Thompson & Hutchison, n.d.:84) indicate 76 killed in 1981/82 (range 55 to 95) and 116 in 1982/83 (range 107 to 126). The 1990 Attawapiskat data indicate an average kill of 1.7 animals per successful hunter, in contrast to 1.5 in 1981/82 and 2.7 in 1982/83 (Thompson & Hutchison, n.d.:84). In part, the large moose harvest is attributable to an aberration in the form of a young hunter who returned from a four-year absence from the community and became an especially active hunter and provider for a number of families. This man, in association with a nephew, a brother-in-law and a friend, killed 17 moose over 3 trips. Thus, 15 per cent of the total village moose kill is credited to one hunter.

Perhaps, though, we should not be concerned with what appear to be large kills. As documented earlier, the caribou harvest increased by 230 per cent from 1981/82 to 1982/83. The delineation of "large" and "average" number of kills, then, is to a considerable extent arbitrary. What determines whether there will be community success in bagging an adequate number of game species is the number and accessibility of that species, and the optimal environmental conditions under which to pursue it. For example, when hunting moose, there must initially be a significant moose population (itself dependent upon such factors as the severity of the previous winter and abundance of browse for food), adequate river depths to provide for the canoes from which the men hunt and suitable fall weather conditions. Presumably, these conditions were met in the fall of 1989. Additionally, the community's nutritional needs will also dictate how many moose are killed. A poor goose season, for example, might very well be expected to increase the effort expended in hunting moose.

Autumn is the favoured time for hunting moose. Sixty-two and a half per cent of hunters indicated hunting during the month of October, 22.5 per cent during September and 7.5 per cent during either of those two months. Others (only one hunter in each instance) stated that they hunted in August, November, January and February. Moose are usually hunted along the major waterways, including the Kapiskau, Lawachi, Attawapiskat and Ekwan Rivers. In 1989, 62 hunters spent an average of 7.38 days hunting moose, with a range of 2 to 14 days. Not all were successful

According to Berger (1977:24), a moose yields 438 pounds (198.7 kilograms) of meat. Therefore 114 moose represent 49,932 pounds (22,649 kilograms) of moose meat brought into the community, while 134 moose (the projected community total) represent 58,692 pounds (26,622 kilograms). As with caribou, a moose kill is inevitably distributed among 6 to 10 families. Again, using the formula of 1.75 pounds (0.795 kilograms) of meat per meal twice a day, a moose kill provides a hunter with 128.5 days of meals. An analysis of moose kills on a community basis is much more useful for establishing the significance of subsistence hunting. It has been suggested that, in 1990, there were approximately 900 people in the community who ate moose meat. Beginning with our 58,692 pounds (26,622 kilograms) of meat from 1989, and utilizing the figure of 3.5 pounds (1.59 kilograms) of meat per day/person, every meat-eating resident of Attawapiskat is provided with moose meat for 18.6 days. Using the same analysis, caribou meat provides these same people with meat for just under six days.

As with caribou hunting, the pursuit of moose is invariably a team effort, involving partners. However, the makeup of these partnerships does not appear to be as circumscribed as in caribou hunting, where brothers-in-law and cousins partnerships comprise approximately 55 per cent of the relationships. Rather, in moose hunting partnerships, 28 per cent are brothers-in-law, 19 per cent are brothers and 17 per cent are cousins. The remainder of the partnerships is made up of father and sons (8.5 per cent), "friends" (which might include relatives) (8.5 per cent), unidentified relatives and "friends" (6 per cent), alone (6 per cent) and nephew and uncle (4 per cent).

Again, we can speculate on the reasons for these types of partnerships. As noted above, two possible explanations might be the desire to extend and reinforce supra-familial kin links, and the conscious desire to hunt within a peer group, that is, with one's own age-mates. It was observed above that the only hunting that incorporates father/son partnerships in meaningful numbers is the goose hunt. Traditionally, the goose hunt was one of a boy's earliest introductions to hunting, the boy being accompanied by his father for a number of years. Informants suggest that a boy will receive his first gun (usually a .410 shotgun) at around the age of seven or eight, when he will begin accompanying his father on goose hunts. Thus, the apprenticeship stage for a young hunter is about ten to twelve years, during which time he is mastering numerous skills relating to hunting and firearms. With this foundation of knowledge, by the time a young man starts hunting moose and caribou in his late teens or early twenties, he is ready to establish partnerships outside the nuclear family, for example, with cousins and brothers-in-law. The particular rigours of moose and caribou hunting—160 kilometre trips and 12- to 14-hour days—necessitate strength and experience, which are gained after the long apprenticeship. Only after these are gained can a man seek companions other than his father. These new hunting arrangements are reflected in the number of supra-familial partnerships among moose and caribou hunters.

Fishing

Sixty-four per cent of all households reported doing some fishing during 1989, while an additional 13 per cent reported fishing occasionally or in the recent past. Fishing is adapted to the weather and water conditions, with three main types of strategies used: gill nets, baited hooks and rod and reel. The latter is particularly practised as recreation after the breakup of the ice.

The MNR study by Hutchison and Thompson did an admirable job of quantifying subsistence fishing in the Mushkegowuk region. They were able to quantify the fish harvests according to species, something I attempted to do, but regrettably found impossible. Respondents were, understandably, reluctant to break down their fish catches by species. Rather, they simply estimated their catches on a weekly or other temporal basis, identifying in a general way what they caught. For example, a person would say that s/he caught 40 to 50 fish, including whitefish, speckled and lake trout, every five days in his or her nets. It is estimated that in 1989, 53,855 fish were caught in Attawapiskat (range 45,895 to 61,814). This estimate is based on the number of people who indicated fishing, their seasons and their estimated catches, with additional numbers coming from the bushmen. This latter group is especially important in our consideration, because some informants suggested that fish figure prominently in the bushman diet. By way of comparison, Thompson and Hutchison (n.d:101,102) estimated 32,250 for 1981/82 and 65,162 for 1982/83. In their analysis, whitefish predominated (23,254 in 1981/82 and 50,802 in 1982/83). There is no way of determining the ratios for 1990. The MNR study indicates five species in their inventory of harvested fish: brook trout, whitefish, pike, walleye and sucker.

What the data do clearly indicate, however, is a continued undiminished reliance upon fish as a subsistence item. The current statistics fall midway between the catch figures of 1981/82 and 1982/83, suggesting that fish remain a crucial group of species for meeting food needs. Of the total fish caught, only 962 were caught by rod and reel—so-called "recreational" fishing—as opposed to those caught by nets or baited hooks. The fact that these were caught by rod in no way diminishes their relevance or importance as food items.

In contrast to moose, goose and caribou hunting, fishing is very much a family activity, with the vast majority of respondents indicating that they fish with their spouses and families. Only the recreational fishermen (usually men) indicate fishing with supra-familial partners. In these cases, partners are typically cousins, uncles or nephews and brothers-in-law.

There appear to be no rigid guidelines or rules pertaining to fishing sites. Fifty-four per cent of informants indicated that they fished at sites where their fathers had, while 39 per cent indicated that they had "discovered" their own fishing sites or had been introduced to them by friends. Three and a half per cent of informants fished where their fathers-in-law had, while another 3.5 per cent used their uncles' sites. There appears to be no hard and fast rule governing selection and use of fishing sites.

Similarly, there does not seem to be any fixed season for fishing. In a number of papers, Honigmann has suggested that fishing is used to supplement the diet during the summer between the goose hunts. In contemporary Attawapiskat, I was hard pressed to find such firm statements. Rather, some people fish year-round, while an equal number are likely to fish at intervals during the year when the situation warrants it. Several informants suggested that they fish "occasionally during the year." Likewise, fishing may last from "1/2 day three times a year" to "year-round fishing." The only consistent pattern is for people who fish for recreation. They constitute 54 per cent of all people who fish, and they do so after spring breakup for an average of two to three days.

Small Game and Birds

It is difficult to measure the number of small game and birds harvested in Attawapiskat. This is due in part to the fact that men often shoot ptarmigan and snare rabbits while moose and caribou hunting, and also because other family members, including women and girls, will frequently hunt on one-day forays. These efforts are generally so commonplace that they are unrecalled. Hence, when asked the question "do you or members of your family hunt or trap small game or birds?" the answer is likely to be "no." The reality, of course, is the opposite.

With this thought in mind, it is stated here that 48 per cent of households in Attawapiskat pursued small game and birds in 1989. Thompson and Hutchison (n.d.) have observed that, with the exception of the pursuit of snowshoe hares and willow ptarmigan, the harvesting of small game is likely to be incidental to other hunting. In 1981/82, only 10 shorebirds were killed, and only 35 spruce grouse, in comparison to 1418 willow ptarmigan and 2041 snowshoe hares. Based on my research, I am in agreement with that statement. The hunting of "small game and birds" is basically synonymous with the pursuit of ptarmigan and "rabbits" (i.e., snowshoe hares).

The nature of small game harvesting renders quantification problematic. A number of people, for example, indicated that they snare rabbits or shoot ptarmigan "on occasion" or "when the opportunity presents itself." One man stated that he takes up to 50 rabbits on occasion but could not firmly state when he snared them because "it varies." Another man indicated that he snares rabbits "every day" but would not volunteer an average catch. A very conservative estimate, then, indicates that, in 1989, 3061 snowshoe hares were caught in Attawapiskat. This estimate is again based on those who indicated snaring, their seasons and catch or range of catch. We may add 1000 to this figure to include the bushmen, who rely heavily on small game. An estimated total community snowshoe hare kill then, would be 4061.

While hares may be snared all year, the preferred months are those between freeze-up and April, with November and December predominating. March is also a common hare season, likely because it immediately precedes the arrival of geese, and meat is often low. The snaring of snowshoe hares is not restricted by age or sex. While adult men most often do the actual trapping, women, boys and girls also run snare lines. Similarly, while hunters will establish snare lines when in the bush, most often they are established within a five-kilometre radius of the community, allowing access by the very young or very old of both sexes who often monitor them. Snowshoe hares are the preferred species of those who pursue small game, being snared by 54 per cent of the small game and bird hunters.

Ptarmigan are harvested by 29 per cent of those who pursue small game and birds. They are most often shot but are occasionally snared as well. They are typically procured during the winter months (November to March, particularly November and December). As with the snowshoe hare harvest figures, the estimated ptarmigan harvest is higher than that cited by Thompson and Hutchison for 1981–1983. Calculations based upon the 1990 data give an estimated ptarmigan harvest of 2197 (range 2061 to 2334) for the community in 1989. To these reported figures we may add 500 for the bushmen, for a total of 2697 ptarmigan killed in 1989. In contrast, Thompson and Hutchison (n.d.:77,78) state harvests of 1418 for 1981/82 and 1092 for 1982/83.

Hunters also report hunting spruce grouse, although not nearly in the numbers of either snowshoe hares or ptarmigan. Total estimated kill for Attawapiskat is 117 in 1989, a figure not inconsistent with the Thompson and Hutchison MNR study (35 in 1981/82, 101 in 1982/83).

Berry Harvests

Berry picking is of less importance (but is by no means unimportant) than either hunting or fishing in the Attawapiskat economy, with only 39 per cent of households indicating active berry picking in 1989. An additional 18.5 per cent indicated that they pick berries "occasionally" (although not that year) or had picked berries in the past.

Informants suggest that as many as fifteen different species of edible berries grow and are picked by the community. These include (in local vernacular, in some instances) strawberries, blueberries, cranberries, raspberries, gooseberries, blackberries, mooseberries, muskegberries, headberries, bakeapple berries, currants, rabbitberries, whiskyjack berries, moss berries and sugar plum berries.

Cranberries are by far the most frequently picked and consumed, with approximately 39 per cent of all berry pickers harvesting that species. In decreasing order of importance are gooseberries (12 per cent), mooseberries (9.2 per cent), strawberries (8.5 per cent), blueberries and raspberries each being consumed by 7 per cent, and bakeapple berries being picked by 5 per cent of all berry pickers. The other species are all picked by less than 3 per cent of the community berry pickers.

Berry pickers do not restrict themselves to one species. Rather, they pick an average of 3.9 different species (range 1 to 10). Similarly, those community members who pick berries do so in large amounts. Data suggest that the average household picks an average of 4.49 gallons (19.78 litres) of berries annually, with a range of 1 to 10 gallons (4.40 to 40.04 litres). On a community level, this represents just under 301 gallons (1325.85 litres) of berries being harvested by the community annually. When shared among the community, this amounts to 1.4 gallons (6.17 litres) for every household in Attawapiskat. If we take into account only the younger and middle aged, this amount increases, as a number of seniors (those over 65 years of age) indicated that they "used to pick more when [they] were younger." The norm for seniors is 2 to 3 gallons (8.80 to 13.21 litres) of berries yearly.

There is no division of labour when it comes to berry picking, with husbands, wives, husbands *and* wives, children and families picking in equal numbers. For many households, berry picking is a family affair, amounting to a Sunday outing in the late summer and early fall. Similarly, no protocol obtains where berries may be picked, as people harvest them "everywhere." The only exceptions occur in those cases where people happen to know of exceptionally bountiful regions; for example, one family habitually picks berries on Akimiski Island, another on the Ekwan River. These are not "owned" sites. They simply happen to be productive areas where the families traditionally go.

HUNTING FOR TRADE PRODUCTS

Contemporary Attawapiskat sees an undiminished reliance upon the land for commercial purposes. In comparison with earlier years, however, hunting for trade has been reshaped and redefined in accordance with both a volatile fur market and opportunities for other economic endeavours.

Trapping

In trying to quantitatively determine the extent of land use, we are inevitably confronted with discrepancies and contradictions in the data. To illustrate, one man, "a bushman," claims to kill an average of 200 beavers a year. Given that one source (MNR) claims that the entire village produced 323 beavers in 1988/89 and 247 in 1987/88, the claim of 200 beavers for one trapper seems high. Similarly, the numbers of actual hunters varies depending upon the source. My fieldwork in 1990 determined that a minimum of 42 trappers were active during the 1989/90 season. To this must be added approximately ten "bushmen" who were out of town, plus a handful of others who were unavailable for other reasons. Ten other people had trapped within the last two years. Another five had trapped within the last three years. In contrast, another source claimed that there were 27 trappers in 1988/89 and 52 in 1987/88. The informant observed, however, that in the former season "not all trappers could have bought licenses." However, the present data correspond very closely (both sources indicating 52 trappers in 1987/88) in certain respects.

In recent years, trapping in Attawapiskat has been shaped by five fundamental external considerations: a wildly fluctuating fur market, the availability of species, the high cost of maintaining a trapping economy, the impacts of increased localization and sedentarism around the village (e.g., the need to keep children in school and the opportunities for wage labour) and a world-wide protest against the fur industry. Despite these considerations, a significant number of people in the community state that trapping is their preferred way of life. Many plan to return to it if they have been obliged to give it up.

Seventy-eight people stated that they had been trappers "in the past," that is, prior to the 1987/88 trapping season. Twenty-two (28 per cent) gave up trapping for either age or health reasons. Three stopped trapping for "personal" reasons, while six stated that they quit trapping because it did not pay enough or that it was too expensive. Thirteen (17 per cent) indicated that they had a choice of trapping or working full-time elsewhere and chose the latter. Another nine (11 per cent) did not cite a different job as their reason for quitting, but did indicate that they are now working at something else. Nineteen of the 78 did not give clear reasons why they quit trapping. None had assumed other jobs. Others had left the community, or had no snowmobile (also a financial reason) or had other reasons. There were 42 active trappers in the community in 1989/90. While the majority of these people did not have other full-time occupations, ten (or 24 per cent) of them did work full-time at other jobs. This quite obviously indicates a considerable amount of part-time trapping being conducted.

This part-time trapping reflects another shift in trapping in the contemporary period. When I examined fur harvest records for the latter half of the 1980s, it was apparent that there is a concerted effort to maximize returns for effort expended. It appears that trappers focus on those species that bring the greatest monetary return. This means concentrating efforts on those species that a) are plentiful, in close proximity to the community and easy to catch (e.g., muskrats), and b) might not be in such large numbers, but if caught are profitable. In 1989/90, such was the case with marten (more correctly, pine marten). Typically, muskrats are caught at five to seven times the rate marten are, but the latter are worth (generally) between $70 to $140, while the former bring $3 to $5. In between these two species are others such as lynx, mink, otter, beaver, fox and wolf. In recent years, these have not been caught (with the possible exception of beaver) in the same numbers as marten and "rats." The reasons for this have to do less with the value of the fur (although they have been worth less than marten in recent years) than with the fact that these animals (generally) are fewer in number and much more difficult to catch. Therefore, in good muskrat and marten years (the former are almost always available) effort, gas and time will be geared toward these species, which promise return on the investment. It might even be suggested, as one informant stated, that trappers are becoming specialists in harvesting certain species.

The environmental niches occupied by certain species, as well as the expertise and technology employed by the trappers, allow for species specialization. For example, the marten is an arboreal weasel that subsists largely on squirrels and jays. Trappers will exploit this niche in their pursuit of the marten, setting their traps in trees. Likewise, traps are set in proximity to beaver lodges and dams, or near otter "slides" for that species. With an intricate knowledge of their environment, the Cree are able to specialize in the most profitable species.

Within the Mushkegowuk askii region, the availability of a species near one community does not guarantee its presence in another. However, the indications of such a profitable species in a community's *environs* promises considerable reward for those with the skills and means to harvest them. As noted in the previous chapter, when word of mouth indicates that marten are present, trappers with the proper tools can get their share of the resources.

Economics has most affected trapping in Attawapiskat, with maintenance costs often seeming to be the most debilitating to those who want to trap. When I spoke to trappers who have given up their profession, they most often cited economic reasons for giving trapping up. They quit either because trapping had become too expensive, with the high cost of purchasing and running a snowmobile, or because the prices for furs were down. In either case, the returns from furs could not justify the expenses incurred. One man, for example, quit trapping around 1965 because "it was too expensive." This was approximately the time that snowmobiles were introduced. Thus, we can better appreciate the decisions of those who opt for regular remunerative employment instead of trapping, which is characterized by game population cycles and a volatile market. A decision to choose a desk-bound job at the band office is not easily made. The fact that roughly one-quarter of all active trappers choose to continue trapping after full-time employment attests to the desirability of the former for some.

For trappers whose lands are close to the community (and the vast majority of registered trap lines are close to the village), the profits to be gained from a good marten season will offset the financial cost of trapping. Ironically, it is those people who are wage-labour employed who often are better able to afford to trap. The income from their wage employment supports the economic costs. For example, in 1990, snowmobiles cost approximately $6000 and gasoline sold for $1.10 a litre in Attawapiskat. It is for this reason that there is still considerable part-time trapping, and concerted effort at killing those species that promise profitable returns. It also helps explain the considerable number of traplines within close proximity to the community.

Cited in Table 8.1 are harvest figures for 1987/88 and 1988/89. Two sets of data are given. One is from MNR, the other from Informant A, who wishes to remain anonymous. Also given are the prices paid for furs, as stated by Informant A, as well as the number of trappers. Table 8.2 (page 122) gives marten harvest figures for different years.

When comparing these data with those of earlier years, we find basis for the argument that effort is put forth when financial returns are most promising. For example, marten furs have been worth two to three times that of any other fur (with the exception of fisher, of which there was only one produced in recent memory), and the harvest of marten pelts has increased significantly.

A young trapper exemplifies the species specialization found in 1990 among some Attawapiskat trappers. With his partner, he trapped only marten, travelling by snowmobile in an area that was convenient for him. His trapping season was from November to February. By January 24, 1990, he had trapped 21 marten, when marten were paying well over $100 for an average pelt. He was not unique. That year, many, if not most, trappers

TABLE 8.1	Attawapiskat Fur Harvests 1987/88, 1988/89				
Species	1987/88[a]	Average Price	1988/89[a]	Average Price	1988/89[b]
Beaver	247	27.00	293	28.00	323
Mink	55	48.50	57	42.00	79
Marten	650	107.30	254	80.37	328
Otter	74	37.40	71	39.85	74
Fisher	1	149.31	–	–	–
Fox, Coloured	28	30.00	11	25.00	36
Muskrat	685	4.60	1813	2.73	1688
Arctic Fox	80	8.50	50	31.25	50
TOTAL INCOME		86,669.41		40,628.32	

NOTE: The number of trappers in 1987/88 was 52. In 1988/89, the number was 27. The "number of trappers" represents those who actually bought licenses, not the actual number trapping. The two are not necessarily the same.

[a] Source: Informant information
[b] Source: Ministry of Natural Resources

TABLE 8.2	Marten Harvest 1971/72, 1980/81, 1987/88, 1988/89				
	1971/72[a]	1980/81[b]	1987/88[b]	1988/89[b]	(MNR)[a]
Marten Killed	9	122	650	254	(328)

[a] Source: Ministry of Natural Resources
[b] Source: Informant Information

trapped only marten or a combination of marten, otter, beaver, mink and muskrat. One elderly widow (79 years old) was still trapping in the fall of 1989, taking 5 marten, 2 mink and 20 muskrats. One young man trapped only during the month of December. He and four others who trapped in the same region shared a main camp but then spread out on their separate traplines for a week at a time. He trapped only marten.

We must be aware that the discrepancies in these figures might be attributable to population cycles, but they probably also reflect the relative value of the fur. For example, the very large number harvested in 1987/88 undoubtedly reflects the fact that the average price paid was $107.30. In comparison, mink paid $48.50, the second most profitable species (with the exception of the solitary fisher). The following year the marten harvest dropped by approximately 400 pelts, but the value of the fur was also lower by over $25. In 1987/88, marten alone brought nearly $70,000 into the community.

The anti-fur lobby has had a major impact upon trapping. Building up its momentum throughout the 1970s, and reaching a peak in the mid 1980s, it struck the fur industry so hard that it has never fully recovered (*The Globe and Mail*, December 28, 1990). A number of trappers and former trappers articulated their concerns with the animal rights people. One trapper stated that he "used to trap full-time but the demand for fur is low today" so he traps alone (as opposed to with his brothers, who used to be his partners). In 1990, he made day trips with his snowmobile and trapped marten, beaver and otter. Another man, who trapped while also working at the band office, gave up the former occupation because "today people don't pay for fur and it is too expensive an occupation." Another 35-year-old man who last trapped two years earlier (beaver and marten) stopped "because of the lousy market conditions" and was planning to return when the market was better. Another former trapper who trapped full-time from 1978 to 1984 stated simply that he stopped because it "does not pay enough to trap."

To fully appreciate the impact of the anti-trapping lobby, we need only to note that fur sales plummeted from $30 to $9 million from 1987 to 1990, and that the price of beaver pelts similarly dropped significantly, in only one year dropping at least 50 per cent to only $11.80 in 1990 (see "Fur Trade Group Faces Collapse", *Toronto Star*, January 5, 1991).

The Ontario Trappers Association (OTA) was the only trapper-owned fur auction in the world. This gave it considerable advantage in paying fair prices for its furs. Trappers state that with the OTA they may sell their furs only at select times of the year, notably the end of December and end of February. At these times, however, they receive "full" price for their furs. In 1990, for example, marten would bring about $120 to $140 from the OTA. Thus, if you could afford to wait, you were guaranteed a fair price. The HBC, on the other hand, would buy the furs at any time. Knowing that trappers had no other outlet, except when the OTA was buying, they could afford to pay less than "full" price; typically, according to informants, about half. Trappers, then, are in a tough situation: most cannot financially afford to wait to unload their furs at the OTA but are loathe to sell them for a lower price to the HBC. Unfortunately for the trappers, however, the economic reality is that they must sell them locally in order to provide for themselves and their family. With the demise of the OTA, the situation is likely to get worse.

Shortly after these articles appeared in the papers, the HBC declared that it, too, was closing its auction operation.

Goose Hunting and Fishing Camps

A number of goose and fishing camps operate in the region, offering seasonal employment to the Attawapiskat First Nation in the forms of cooking, camp maintenance and, perhaps most importantly, guiding. The two goose and fishing camps that provide the most employment are Chookomoolin's tourist camp and Gabe's Goose Camp, operated by Gabriel Spence (sold by him during the summer of 1990 to another local Native person). Gabriel Fireman, another local person, owns and operates a fishing and moose hunting camp.

Gabe's camp is located five kilometres from the village on the coast. It consists of sleep camps, cook camp, a small store for general merchandise, freezers for preservation of shot birds, a generator for electricity and a sauna. The sleep camps are heated with wood.

Between 1967 and 1979 the camp was owned and operated by the Ministry of Natural Resources, but during the late 1970s the MNR decided it should be controlled and operated by Natives. Gabe assumed ownership and changed prices, the brochure and the hunting season. The camp is operated only in the fall. He hires approximately fifteen guides a season for four to five weeks, and three or fur cooks. Since 1980, the season has run from September 15 through October. Guides use their own canoes. Plans were underway to expand into a fishing camp during the summer of 1990.

A number of people have worked as guides for years. The average guide working in 1989/90 had 4.5 seasons' experience, with a range of 1 to 28 years. People who have worked as guides are virtually unanimous in their positive attitudes towards their experiences. Of the 43 people who worked at the camps during 1989, only 4 had negative feeling towards their jobs. This translates into 93 per cent job satisfaction. Complaints generally focussed on the hunters who "wanted to shoot all the geese," who "were uncooperative" and who were "crybabies." One guide said that he is "gradually disapproving" of guiding, while another said that it is hard work for inadequate money, but nonetheless he finds it "fun."

Despite this handful of concerns (articulated by fewer than 8 per cent of active guides in 1990), most people who work for the camps enjoy it and seek re-employment. Reasons tend to be as much intrinsic as economic. The opportunities to meet people and socialize, to share Cree skills and knowledge, to be out on the land and to demonstrate the quality of Cree life were all expressed as reasons for satisfaction with the job. Other people found the job enjoyable because it provided opportunity for their own hunting. Further, it is satisfactory because "it is what [the Cree] have been educated in." There are economic reasons as well: in addition to salary, approximately half the hunters tip.

Some local people have expressed concerns and doubts about guiding. Two people, neither of whom has ever worked as a guide, articulated, albeit vaguely, their concerns. One observed that "guiding needs examining closely," while the other suggested that "guiding is a form of employment for people if properly controlled." Both of these people have permanent jobs.

The camps are certainly not a panacea. They offer only short-term, seasonal work. With the possible exception of the owner/operators, nobody is going to make large amounts of money. Operators hire only those guides who have their own equipment: canoes, motors, gasoline, decoys and food for their own meals. Daily take-home pay is about $50. Their benefits, however, lie in the fact that they are locally owned and operated; therefore, they are economically autonomous. The high level of job satisfaction, the continued rehiring of people, and the very fact that they have been in existence for decades now all attest to their viability as businesses as well as economic opportunities for local people.

But there is more to the camps. They are means of providing income for local people in ways that are consistent with traditional Cree culture. It would be understandable if the Attawapiskat people resented outsiders arriving in their community to hunt what for the people are sources of subsistence. Such resentment hardly exists. Rather, guides are aware of the fact that the southerners who arrive are the proverbial strangers in a strange land. The Cree guides are working for employers who are neighbours, if not kin, and providing expertise far beyond the ken of the hunters for whom they guide (lifetime subscriptions to *Sports and Field* notwithstanding). At Gabe's Goose Camp, there are two hunters per guide. The guide is in virtual total control, preparing the blind, setting out the decoys, and often calling the geese (without the benefit of a commercial goose call). Oftentimes they pluck the geese for the hunters. The brochure for Gabe's Goose Camp subtly reminds the hunters to "keep low and still until your guide says 'okay.'" Those of us who have experienced the goose hunt can appreciate the true art and science that go into it. Guiding, then, allows the hunter to utilize a lifetime of skill, knowledge and experience, and to be compensated financially for it. Further, it does not interfere with his own pursuit of food for his family. In brief, guiding is a remunerative, self-enhancing, self-gratifying form of employment. And, given that non-Native hunters are restricted to five geese per hunt, there is an awareness that "sports" hunting is not detrimental to flock populations. Honigmann (1961:79) has suggested that the goose hunt for the Cree is comparable to the annual vacation for a factory worker: it is anticipated and revelled in. If this is so, we might suggest that goose guiding is a virtual paid vacation for the Attawapiskat Cree. What is fundamental to understanding the appeal of guiding for local people is an appreciation for the work environment. And the environment is one in which the Cree guide is totally familiar and one in which he has mastery: "his" hunters are not familiar with, and do not have control over, his environment. Furthermore, his "employer," such as he is, is most likely a cousin or uncle. Few jobs anywhere provide such conditions.

The success of the goose camps has generated an interest among some Attawapiskat people in the potential for other forms of tourist operations. In 1990, one elder was seeking backing for a "retreat" at his camp. Another, younger, man was considering an "adventure travel" type of resort wherein people conceivably could travel from Attawapiskat to Polar Bear Park, possibly by horseback.

The importance and relevance of these ideas is that they represent an interest in utilizing the land in a way that is not detrimental to it, while simultaneously putting to profitable use the knowledge and expertise of the local populace. While there may not be a yearning to leave Attawapiskat for the outside, there is an interest among the majority of the population in meeting the outside and presenting to outsiders their culture and history. Indeed, as discussed above, one of the prime attractions of guiding is the opportunity to meet strangers and socialize. Hence, the projects proposed above (and possibly others) would meet the criteria established by the goose camps: local control and autonomy, utilization of the land in a non-exploitative way, employment for local people, the creation of a mutually beneficial intercultural nexus and an opportunity for the Cree to put their lifetimes of knowledge, skills and expertise to work.

Firewood Vendors

A number of community people have profited economically by selling firewood. The vast majority of houses in the community are heated by wood. The average home burns approximately 31.5 cords of wood a winter. This figure is admittedly very rough: a number of people were reluctant to give estimates; many guessed, and some gave ranges. Some people suggested as few as 2.5 cords a year, others 300-plus. Averaging the estimates given by informants arrives at the estimate of 31.5 cords. A number of community people suggested it was fairly accurate, if not 100 per cent precise. The amount of wood burned is a function of the age and condition of the house, the latter, in turn, a function of the former. The house in which I stayed was one of the newer (but not one of the newest) and burned approximately 2.5 cords a month during the winter.

A number of people, particularly the elderly with no family and those who work at wage jobs, are obliged to buy firewood. An interesting exception is a 79-year-old widow who cuts her own (30 cords per year). She also still traps.

The procuring of firewood has always been a problem in Attawapiskat. Suitable trees are literally few and far between. One resident, originally from Winisk/Peawanuck, but living in the community for nearly three years, stated that he buys his firewood because he does not want conflicts over wood rights. This statement says more about the scarcity of firewood than it does about proprietorial attitudes towards it. One resident approached the government about establishing a reforestation project to help alleviate the problem in the future but his suggestion was essentially ignored. Today, residents travel an average of 25 kilometres to cut firewood. Forest fires in recent years have not helped the situation.

The selling of firewood poses somewhat of a moral dilemma for some people. It is essentially an issue of profiting by providing a necessity for those who cannot provide for themselves. Nonetheless, a number of people sell, or have sold, firewood. In 1990 there were 36 people who reported selling firewood within the previous year, and an additional eight who had sold firewood in the past. While there does not appear to be a fixed rate for wood, prices in 1990 seemed to range from between $60 to $90/cord, with about $75 being the average. Those who sell wood are noticeable by the large number of cords arranged behind their homes. These sellers frequently stockpile the wood the year before, allowing it to dry over the summer. When winter arrives the wood is ready to be burnt without the danger of creosote buildup.

The HBC journals are replete with references to rafts of wood being floated down the river to be used for firewood. This is still a preferred technique for transporting wood, and is becoming increasingly more so. Wood is cut and hauled in the wintertime using snowmobiles, but the ever-rising cost of gasoline is increasingly leading to the relatively cheaper "rafting" of wood after breakup. Similarly, the cost of using all-terrain vehicles is prohibitive.

Handicraft Sales

A number of people in the community make and sell handicrafts. Mitts, gloves and moccasins are made and sold by women. These typically are of moose or caribou hide and decorated with beads. As well, other forms of arts and handicrafts are made from bush materials, including tamarack geese, snowshoes and wood and stone carvings. Children and teenagers often act as liaisons between the artisans and their buyers, who often are resident teachers and transient professionals who are working at and/or dining at the hospital.

It is difficult to establish the number of artisans/craftspeople and the amount of work they produce. Caribou hide gloves and mitts typically sold for $85, while a tamarack goose could be purchased for approximately $15 to $20. The same goose sold for $79 at Toronto's Royal Ontario Museum in 1990. The eagerness with which these and similar items are sought by visitors to the community suggests that there might be a viable market for the products elsewhere. One does not have to be a cynic to doubt that the artisan is getting the bulk of the $79 from the goose sold at the ROM.

At least one entrepreneur has found a niche in the Attawapiskat economy selling snowmobile sleighs. Using mostly wood he cuts himself in the bush, he constructs sleighs on assignment, selling them for $500 to $800. In the year prior to the study he had sold 15 such sleighs. By March of 1990 he had made and sold eight more. In addition, the proprietor of a local grocery and dry goods store also sells locally made sleighs, although not in the numbers of the above-mentioned individual. These sleighs are an indispensable part of the local tool kit, being used for the hauling of such items as wood and water, hunting and trapping gear, geese during the spring hunt and groceries.

OTHER FORMS OF LAND USE

People in the community make vast arrays of artistic and utilitarian items from materials gathered from the land. These items are those that are usually made for personal or family use and not for commercial purposes such as the sleds, decoys and moccasins discussed above. Nonetheless, their value must not be underestimated, for oftentimes these items are used routinely and hence are of considerable importance.

When I was trying to determine the extent of craftsmanship that exists in the community, my initial efforts were usually met with the reply that "I [we] don't make anything." However, when I proffered a list of items such as snowshoes, bedding and paddles, people would invariably respond with "Yes, I make bedding and snowshoes." Thus, the *caveat*: there is more use made of bush materials than is indicated. The reason for the lack of acknowledgment of craftsmanship is essentially that for the harvesting of small game and birds: the performance of these activities is *so* routine it is mundane, hence, almost forgettable. This, of course, is in contrast to goose hunts, which are semi-annual, or moose hunts, which are generally annual. The basis for the contention that certain items are made more frequently than indicated is both empirical and anecdotal: I either saw many more than would be suggested by the response, or other people indicated that the item is made and/or used frequently. Wing dusters are a case in point. Numerous households have them for cleaning; few indicated that they are made. Similarly, tent poles are cut and used every time a tent is taken into the bush; few people indicated their use.

If we were to examine the number of items made and the percentage of households that made and used them, the statistics are impressive. For example, I estimated that 41 per cent made sleds, 40 per cent made gloves and mitts, 35 per cent made moccasins, 34 per cent made paddles, 29 per cent made duvets, pillows or other types of bedding, 27 per cent made decoys for waterfowl hunting and 26 per cent of households made snowshoes. It is not surprising that, when considering land use, many people forget the plethora of domestic articles made from the bush. However, were they to be cut off from this supply, the Cree would be subject to considerable financial outlay, as well as being denied the use of their traditional skills and artistic expression. Sale prices for goose down duvets in Toronto in February 1993 ranged from $159 to $229. Regular prices were from $280 to $400. The Cree (men and women) make these from the birds they shoot for subsistence. Denied the option of making their own bedding, it is completely within the realm of possibility that to pay for bedding of similar quality, a family would have to pay nearly $1000. The same argument (if not the same cost) holds true for the numerous articles of everyday use: sleighs, tent poles, gloves/mitts and decoys.

The construction of domestic articles, then, is both a cost-saving measure and an outlet for cultural and artistic expression. It is virtually impossible to measure the former and it *is* impossible to measure the latter.

Burial Sites and Cemeteries

There are other forms of land use by the Attawapiskat Cree that must be acknowledged. These are grave and historical/cultural sites, provenience of artistic materials and utilitarian tools, the community garden and Cree medicine and pharmacology.

It is relatively easy to measure the significance of subsistence hunting or the monetary economics of goose hunt guiding for southerners. However, it is considerably more difficult to assess the significance of burial sites in the bush for a culture whose kinship links are of paramount importance and for whom the land is fundamental to their culture.

Despite the fact that people have been gravitating toward Attawapiskat for a century and that there are two graveyards in the community, 69.9 per cent of all household heads of all ages are aware of burial sites in the bush. These are not solely incidental, singular graves. When asked how many burial sites they were aware of, fully 30 per cent stated that there were "lots," meaning they did not wish to count or identify them. In addition to this 30 per cent, one man said that he was aware of over 60 burial sites; another knew of over 100. We can appreciate the importance of these graves only by stepping into the shoes of the Cree. By considering for a moment the reverence with which we hold the graves of our own deceased, we can come to identify with those members of the Attawapiskat First Nation whose ancestors are buried on the land.

Burial sites are of significance in any culture, for they are the repository of the dead, and the respect of them by the living. The mere fact that cemeteries exist and are visited is testimonial to their importance to those who live. The dead, indeed, transcend time, for they live in the memories of those who survive them, and who carry on their names and who try to emulate those who have gone before.

For the Cree, the grave sites are yet another temporal and spiritual link to the land. Even if the present generation were never to hunt moose, goose or caribou, its ancestors are interred in the bush, providing a permanent conduit between them and the land. It is this connection that the Cree never want to see broken. And the fact that such a high percentage of the present generation is aware of these special places is indicative of the importance placed upon them. It is incumbent upon them to know of their existence and to respect them.

Historical Sites

In addition to the gravesites, a number of people are aware of other places that are of historical and cultural importance to the community. These include Aboriginal battle sites (at least two: one between the Cree and the Inuit, another between the Cree and the Iroquois), former summer gathering sites, a communal loon hunting site, winter gathering sites, old trading posts, old habitation sites (Lake River), places where **shamanism** was witnessed and battle sites where the British and French fought (one informant saw a bell from an old ship, *The Lord Strathcona*). These historical and cultural sites are virtual texts of Cree history and lore, and contain not a small amount of European history. In all, 23 people were able to speak with certainty of historical/cultural sites with which they were familiar and were able to locate on a map.

What is remarkable about these observations is the consistency of the reports; most were verified by other informants. For example, seven people were familiar with the "summer gathering site" at which people met after breakup and socialized, played games and hunted loons. Six people were familiar with the battle site between the Cree and the Inuit. Other sites were of a more personal nature: one man witnessed the footprints of a "Sasquatch" (his term); another was familiar with a place where his grandfather told him he had witnessed shamanism.

Whether these sites are of public or personal knowledge, they are important for the meanings they hold for those who are familiar with them. To the Cree, the Inuit battle site (in which 11 Cree and 16 Inuit died) is as meaningful as the Plains of Abraham are to English and French Canadians. The sites are not just locations in space (unidentified to the rest of the world but very familiar to the Cree), they are also temporal markers. They are places of meaning, taking on emotional, cultural, historical and even ideological significance. Events shape history, and history shapes cultures. The Attawapiskat First Nation seeks to retain its history and its culture.

The Community Garden

In 1912, the Oblate Brothers established a garden behind their mission. At the same time, Joseph Nakogee, a local man, built one on an island below the village (Vezina, 1978:5). When he left, the Oblates assumed control of his garden until 1970, when they turned the island farm and all of its equipment over to the band. According to the local priest, the garden produced "excellent crops of potatoes" for three years but in the fourth year a late spring ruined the potato field and discouraged the band from continuing its garden.

The garden on Potato Island has apparently been resurrected, for there are now five volunteer gardeners. Four of the five men are related. The potatoes are grown and sold locally and, according to the gardeners, the garden produces 325 seventy-five pound (30 kilogram) bags of crops annually, or 24,375 pounds (11,079.5 kilograms) of potatoes a year. This is obviously a significant amount, equating to over 9 kilograms of potatoes for every person in the village.

The gardener with whom I spoke is quite enthusiastic about gardening, observing that it is better in the long run than hunting because it is more predictable than hunting and "lasts longer," as meat is consumed quickly. To him, hunting and gardening are comparable. He sees both as ways of using the land in productive ways that are non-injurious. For economic reasons, he would like to see more people garden.

Pharmacology

Seventy-one households (41 per cent) indicated that they were familiar with traditional Cree medicine. This familiarity is not restricted to single remedies or the powers of single pharmacological plants. Rather, the degree of familiarity is high, with the average practitioner familiar with approximately 7 remedies (6.77) with a range of 1 to 15. The significance lies in the fact that these are not only known, but also practised. People find curative powers in a range of natural substances, including tamarack for stomach cramps, skunk scent glands for colds, otter scent glands for snow blindness, beaver castoreum for cuts, cones for painkillers, bulrushes for absorbents and similar uses.

CONCLUSIONS AND DISCUSSION

When I made initial contact with the Attawapiskat community in 1988, some members of the community, both Native and non-Native, suggested that fewer than 10 per cent of the Attawapiskat First Nation was involved in land use activities. This reaction, it is feared, is far too often typical. Superficial examinations (we cannot call them analyses) reveal little. The data and analysis clearly indicate that land use—in many ways—remains strong and continues to be an important part of the Cree economy and culture.

Simply because the majority of the community does not spend its winters in family hunting groups trapping does not mean that trapping does not exist. Rather, the economic reality of trapping demands that trapping be redefined and reshaped to meet financial exigencies. These include trapping those species that promise the most monetary return, incorporating trapping into other employment opportunities, carefully weighing the advantages of trapping to other forms of employment and rescheduling trapping so that it makes the most economic sense. The reality is that trapping has become an uncertain occupation and trappers must weigh their options. In spite of this, however, given a choice, a large number of Attawapiskat people would choose trapping over other forms of employment. For many, however, the initial financial outlay and the uncertain fur market preclude making that choice. With these observations, however, between four and five dozen Attawapiskat people continued to trap in 1989/90, a number of them on a part-time basis, indicating the continued interest in trapping as an economic pursuit and in the culture of which it is a part. While the structure of trapping might have changed, the desirability of trapping remains undiminished.

The Attawapiskat Cree have found other income-generating endeavours that help offset an unsure fur industry while maintaining their use of the land. Linkage with the outside world has created a local tourist industry, notably in the goose and fishing camps. These goose camps provide regular, if very seasonal, work. While wages are hardly exceptional, the hours do not conflict unduly with their own subsistence hunting, and the opportunity for tips (from approximately half the hunters) exists. Fulfilling the needs of local people also provides some employment. The construction and selling of sleighs and provisioning of firewood are two local industries where people have found niches.

Nowhere is the demonstrated continued land use more apparent than in subsistence hunting. In terms of the three major species—moose, goose and caribou—there has been no decrease, and indeed there is evidence of increase, of hunting for subsistence purposes over the last century. These three species alone contributed 234,843 pounds (106,523 kilograms) of meat to the diet. This equates to over 213 pounds (96.6 kilograms) of meat for every man, woman and child in the community. In addition, the community ate over 50,000 fish, and thousands of rabbits and ptarmigan. We must not ignore, as well, the fact that a significant amount of meat is brought into the community through the process of trapping for trade purposes. Beaver, for example, provides both meat and fur. In 1989, this meant 5620 pounds (2549 kilograms) of additional meat brought into the community. Thus, we might argue that the land provides nearly a pound (0.45 kilograms) of meat per person per day. On the basis of this evidence, one can argue that subsistence hunting does not merely supplement the diet, but is literally essential to the diet. The Attawapiskat Cree, it might be argued, could conceivably be undernourished or face starvation if denied access to hunting and fishing for their own needs, as has been documented for the hardship periods earlier in this century.

Table 8.3 below illustrates the major sources of country food in Attawapiskat and their contributions to diet.

TABLE 8.3	Attawapiskat Country Food Consumption 1989
Waterfowl	157,335 pounds (71,516 kilograms)
Moose	58,692 pounds (26,678 kilograms)
Caribou	18,816 pounds (8553 kilograms)
Hare	7716 pounds (3507 kilograms)
Beaver	5620 pounds (2555 kilograms)
Ptarmigan	2157 pounds (980 kilograms)
Fish	53,855 (total fish)
Berries	301 gallons (1370 litres)

Note: All weight estimates based on Berger (1977:24).

Needs are of three types: the biological, the psychological and the social. The land, the Cree tell us, is fundamental to their culture. From the land the Attawapiskat First Nation derives one of its basic biological needs: the need for food and nourishment. Moose, goose and caribou, whitefish and berries are all harvested, and have been for countless generations. This was as true in 1990 as it was in 1901.

The land, an informant told me, "restores us." Another informant stated that the goose hunt was important because "people go away and are alone with the land and can think." And the land holds the ancestors. The land, in brief, provides the means for meeting psychological needs.

Finally, in the process of meeting the primary biological need of food, that is, in establishing the moose and caribou hunting partnerships, the land meets the third set of human needs: the social. The basic human need for companionship, for peer groups and for human warmth is met in part by the need to visit the land in search of food.

When the Cree state, then, that the land is of fundamental importance to them, it is not mere cliché or metaphor. It is simply the truth. The land is at the essence of Cree culture. The HBC may provide "store food" but it does not hold the final place of grandparents, nor does it create the kin link between brothers-in-law. The school or hospital may offer employment but, in Marxist terms, the worker is alienated from his product, whereas the hunter is part and parcel of the product. He is "of the land."

When I was told that fewer than 10 per cent of the people were using the land, I was somewhat skeptical. Surely more people were active than that. However, the extent to which the land is being used came as a surprise. In virtually every aspect of conceivable land use there is a significant number of active people. Those people with whom I spoke in September 1988, were mistaken. Access to the land and the resources it provides—physical, social and psychological—is still fundamentally important as we enter the 21st century.

CONTENT QUESTIONS

1. Outline what is happening with the contemporary goose hunt in terms of a) its importance relative to earlier times, and b) the role of kinship.
2. What kinship patterns are involved with the caribou hunt?
3. What factors have negatively affected fur trapping?
4. Other than hunting, trapping and fishing, how are the Attawapiskat Cree still drawing upon the resources of the land?

chapter nine

Continuities and Changes

LEARNING OBJECTIVES

After reading this chapter, students should be able to:

1. Explain why some Attawapiskat Cree believe that they do not use the land.

2. Describe the various ways that the Cree have resisted encapsulation.

3. Identify four major changes that trapping has undergone in the last 100 years in Attawapiskat.

4. Assess the impact of Western technology on Cree land use.

5. Distinguish between culture change and assimilation.

In order to analyze 20th century Attawapiskat land use and tenure, we must understand the Cree relationship to the State, the Church and the fur companies. These institutions, intentionally or not, started a process of subjugation of Aboriginal people: the government by political and legal control (including replacing indigenous Cree political systems with the elected chief and council), the Church by replacing Cree theology with Christianity and the fur companies by attempting to wield total economic control. This subjugation was put into force through the White society's complex political machinery, greater technological and economic resources and inherent belief that what they were doing was right for the numerically greater White society to the south and, ultimately, for the Cree. What they began was a process of encapsulation that was directed towards engulfing the economic, political, religious and social practices of the encapsulated group.

There are inherent dangers in examining the process of encapsulation, notably that of confusing normal social and cultural change with perceived conformity to the dominant group. For example, archaeologists have confirmed the existence of vast trade networks from the Gulf of Mexico to northern Ontario prior to the arrival of Europeans. Similarly, Henry Hudson's first contact with northern Native Canadians in 1611 was with a solitary Cree hunter seeking to trade with him. What this indicates, then, is the existence of trade among Native societies that long pre-dated European arrival. Therefore, when the Cree in James Bay (and Natives elsewhere) became involved in the fur trade, the concept of trade was not new to them. Nor were they initially encapsulated by it. Rather, it involved patterns of exchanges of valued goods for both Europeans and Natives. Without an awareness of these pre-contact trade systems, however, the inexperienced anthropologist or historian might assume that the Native population was swept up in this vast commercial conglomerate. Such a stance, of course, denies Native history and culture. What must be noted, though, is that pre-contact trade was undertaken among groups that shared a common understanding of the nature and meaning of trade. In the historic period, Europeans brought with them their notions of trade for profit and the accumulation of wealth—values not shared by Natives operating within the context of reciprocity.

For the Attawapiskat First Nation, trade with Europeans first began with the establishment of the post at Fort Albany. Thus, in the beginning, it was trade at a distance, with the Attawapiskat Cree largely restricting themselves to periodic trips to Albany for the sole purpose of trade. As the 20th century dawned, though, a post was established at Attawapiskat. With the post, it soon became apparent that Euro-Canadian interest in the Mushkegowuk region was not to be restricted to furs. The trader would not be the sole Euro-Canadian in Attawapiskat. The missionary, the government, the medical and educational professionals—all had interest in the Attawapiskat Cree, and sought to modify one or more aspects of their being: their economic system, their religion, their culture their pharmacology. Encapsulation is a many tentacled beast.

There is yet another consideration. The Cree, by virtue of being prime actors in the fur industry, were inevitably tied to the outside world. Shifts in the world fur market had direct impact upon the Cree hunter in James Bay. "Go out and trap," he was told, "the market is good and we want your furs." The market, though, was volatile. When times were bad the White trader—as much a part of his culture as the Cree hunter is of his—did not feel he could afford to be generous. "Go out and trap," he told the hunters, "if you want supplies." However, the land had never been excessively bountiful. Furs were scarce. Families starved at the post and in the bush. The hunter bore the brunt of market fluctuations thousands of kilometres away.

The messages conveyed by the trader and missionary were conflicting. The missionary had his own agenda. He was doing his best to convince the Cree not to go out on the land but to stay near the post so that he might educate the hunter and his family in the ways of Christianity, Euro-education and agriculture (yes, agriculture on James Bay). To his credit, however, the missionary will be remembered as doing his utmost to feed the Cree during periods of starvation.

The final step in this process of encapsulation was the most formal: the legitimization of White control. Bureaucrats arrived and essentially told the Cree to give up the land or else. The decision had already been made hundreds of kilometres away in Ottawa to take the land. In one of the last remaining Victorian attitudes towards Natives—that they are childlike and incapable of making rational decisions—the government had made the decision for them. The land would be surrendered by treaty.

With such power, of course, other government decisions were made unilaterally and without consultation. The registered trapline system was implemented irrespective, and often in ignorance, of the problems and conflicts it might create among those upon whom it was imposed. Power and authority do not need to listen to subordinates.

With all of this, have the Cree been encapsulated? Conversations with some local people would lead us to believe that they have. Some of the Attawapiskat First Nation appear to have bought the White society's notion that Aboriginal people have lost their Nativeness. Some non-Natives in the community voice the same position. As noted at the outset, some local people believe that fewer than 10 per cent of the population still use the land. As is apparent, this estimate is considerably off the mark. Why does this perception exist? Four basic explanations seem reasonable. First, while the structure of land use has changed, the traditional perception of land use has not. To some people, unless a hunter is in the bush for 50 or so weeks a year, he is not using the land. Thus, the week-long moose, goose and caribou hunting trips do not qualify as using the land. One young man suggested to me that he did not use the land because he and his wife "live like White folks." As it turned out, he was an ardent goose hunter and fisherman. Second, in a similar manner, in the eyes of some people, part-time trappers or those who trap for shorter periods of time are not using the land. Third, one cannot deny a century of acculturation. For decades, White influences have suggested that the bush was dangerous, and that a sedentary life around the village was more desirable than a hunting and trapping culture. The fourth reason is simply the fact that much of the land use that is done is routine: cutting firewood, fishing and snaring, for example. These are mundane activities in comparison with moose and caribou hunting. If you don't hunt big game, your perception of these mundane activities might be that they do not qualify as legitimate land use.

In contrast to Brody's (1981) finding then, that the Beaver (Dene) wanted to believe that people still hunted and used the land, the Attawapiskat people tend, in many cases, to be unaware of the degree of use that still exists. Nonetheless, when the various forms of land use are itemized, such as hunting, firewood gathering and berry picking, the reality of the extent of use is driven home. Similarly, the importance of these activities, beyond their role in subsistence, is apparent. Virtually all respondents indicated that they would continue to hunt geese, pick berries and so on.

Honigmann made the following observation regarding the Attawapiskat Cree as they were in 1961:

> Though the Cree could objectively sort out some elements of their culture as "White" or "Indian", they valued the one no more consistently than the other. They did not feel themselves becoming Whites or Canadians. They felt, rather, "that they [were] living in a world to which things are somehow added; a growing world to which they were able to adapt as their fathers did to theirs" (Nonas 1963) (Honigmann, 1981:226,227).

I can say with certainty that the Cree in 1990 still did not see themselves as "becoming White" (despite the contention of one young male). Indeed, I got the impression that there is a strong and growing sense of one's identity as being Cree. I saw this identification being particularly reinforced when I spoke with people, especially older people, regarding their hunting and trapping. It is in these activities that the differences between White and Cree interests in the land are sharply drawn. The relationship between the Cree and their land is highly personal and intimate. Thus, when legislation is enacted or enforced—such as the Migratory Birds Convention Act, the registered trapline system or the establishment of Polar Bear Park—there is a certain amount of questioning and resentment: How can White legislators from the south know and appreciate the land as well as we do when we were born and raised here? Furthermore, White interests in the land are not personal or cultural or even clearly defined. In the eyes of the Cree, White interests in their land are vague at best and they are definitely perceived as being potentially harmful to Cree interests.

The argument here then, does not assume a loss of Nativeness. If we want to have Natives living in traditional conical lodges, wearing leather and fur clothing and travelling exclusively by snowshoes during the winter, then we might argue that encapsulation is complete. We do not find that today in Attawapiskat, although there are snowshoes being made and used, tents are taken into the bush and caribou and moose hide mitts, gloves and moccasins abound.

However, a fundamental tenet of culture is that it is *dynamic*. Cultures change in both their material and non-material aspects. Just as Euro-Canadians have adopted snowshoes, canoes and kayaks (all of Native origin) for recreational purposes, so too have the Cree adopted outboard motors, snowmobiles and chainsaws to facilitate life in the bush.

This is the essence of the argument. Technology has changed. Social structures have been altered. New strategies have been adopted for coping. However, in terms of their relationships to the land, the basic integrity of Attawapiskat culture has remained intact. We must not confuse normal cultural and social change with perceived encapsulation. Nor must we confuse structural modification with structural replacement.

Throughout the first 50 years of the Attawapiskat post fur trade, there was adaptation to the new Euro-Canadian incursions. This included incorporation of some aspects of material and non-material Euro-Canadian culture and integration into the fur trade economy. However, hunting for trade did not come at the expense of hunting for subsistence. Indeed, there are many references in the HBC journals to traders encouraging the Cree (often without success) to give up their quest for country food in favour of furs. And, when times were hard, trade in country food supplemented trade in furs. Similarly, times of hardship meant social reorganization: downsizing the hunting group, and redefining and expanding traditional age and sex roles. These changes, however, did not alter the basic fundamental importance of the family. Adaptive change, not elimination or replacement, occurred. Honigmann's observations, as noted above, still applied in 1990. The Attawapiskat Cree are still adapting to White incursions.

In the area of traditional notions of tenure, the changes were perhaps more radical. The depletion of fur-bearers, and the "chronic shortage of big game," resulted in a shifting from the traditional family held territories to a notion of "hunting anywhere." This latter was likely encouraged by Euro-Canadians in their quest for more furs. But the Cree, who moderated the idea with their own notions of propriety and conduct, modified even this. Later, when the government sought to regulate the traplines, the Cree would simply try, and then abandon, this unworkable system and adhere to their own practicable systems of use. Such are not the actions of encapsulated people.

It is often asserted that the introduction of technology precedes the breakdown of traditional cultures. Such was not the case in Attawapiskat. Indeed, the introduction of Euro-Canadian technology in the latter half of the 20th century enhanced land use and actively promoted a diversification of land use options. Two-way radios, snowmobiles, outboard motors, all-terrain vehicles all facilitated the pursuit of hunting, trapping and fishing. It is not surprising, then, to find subsistence hunting increasing in the 1950s and beyond while trapping remained constant.

With White incursions in the form of schools, hospitals and stores, a number of options became open to the Attawapiskat people. Men could work at stores and trap part-time. Women could work at wage labour and their husbands trap full-time. Both could work at wage labour. In terms of major changes over the 90-year span, it is those that occurred in trapping that are perhaps the most noticeable. Four are noted here. First, there is considerably more diversity in terms of how much time people spend on trapping excursions. While there are still some trappers who stay in the bush for most of the winter (if not most of the year), there are considerably more who only go out for days or weeks at a time, returning to town. There are even more who make day trips to check on their traps. These changes reflect a number of factors: the permanent housing in the community, the interest in keeping children in school, the incredible flexibility made available by snowmobiles, the economics of trapping and the redefinition of territories. Since the intense localization of people around the community, increasingly more people have opted to trap closer to Attawapiskat.

A second major change is that because people do often trap close to town, there are more people who trap without partners. Although this is not yet the norm, it is yet another option available because of the proximity of many traplines and the availability of snowmobiles.

A third major change relates to how much time is spent trapping. Because of its high cost, trapping is, in some instances, a part-time occupation. For some people, the cost precludes pursuing trapping full-time for a dubious financial compensation. However ironic, those who work full-time elsewhere can better afford to trap on a part-time basis because they can afford the initial financial outlay for equipment. This is reflected in the nearly one-quarter of all trappers who work full-time at other jobs.

Also reflective of the high financial cost and dubious rewards of trapping is the fourth major change in the Attawapiskat fur industry, that is, the increasing specialization of trappers. Declining financial returns, escalating financial costs and uncertain animal populations have served to make a number of Attawapiskat trappers selective in what they trap. Typically, marten, beaver and muskrat (two species that generally promise fair prices, and one species that is easily caught in large numbers) are the target species. In light of recent developments, this pattern will likely continue.

Hunting for trade has also meant the adoption of new strategies that are consistent with traditional use. Beginning in the early part of the century when trappers began dealing in country food and cutting logs for wages, and continuing through to the establishment of goose camps, the Cree have sought to create income generating opportunities that do not imperil the environment or adversely affect traditional institutions such as the family.

Income generating land use activities created by the Cree have been successful largely because they have allowed the Cree to remain in control. Outsiders did not impose these activities. The Cree themselves conceived, nurtured and sustained them. These include the goose and fishing camps, firewood sales, sleigh sales and the trade in traditional arts and handicrafts.

There are perhaps two remarkable things about the hunt for subsistence. One is that people still hunt for their food at all. Second there still exists a very strong kin basis to the hunts. Anthropologists who work in the Subarctic may not find the first point that surprising, although non-anthropologists probably do. After all, since the mid 19th century non-Native Canadians have been told that Natives are "dying out" as "a culture."

The Attawapiskat Cree still do hunt for the bulk of their protein, and this pattern shows no signs of diminishing. The goose hunt remains vitally important, both as a means of supplying food and as a training ground for young boys in hunting and bush skills. Proportionally, there are probably more geese being taken today than in earlier years. Continuity is maintained as men seek out those spots where their fathers or fathers-in-law before them hunted. In this way, the land mediates the kinship ties between generations.

Caribou and moose are being killed at a constant, if not increasing, rate. The percentage of moose and caribou hunters has not decreased since Thompson and Hutchison's 1980s study, and the number of animals being harvested remains high. Further, following Cree practice for countless generations, the meat is distributed among community members. This distribution, as well as the formation and maintenance of crucial hunting partners, serves to nurture and sustain the all important kinship ties.

Throughout the last century, then, while the White society was seeking encapsulation, there was a simultaneous resistance on the part of the Cree. This is evidenced in everyday and major acts such as the following four: the practice of seeking trade at different posts when the HBC refused credit, an unwillingness to focus energies on the hunt for trade when hunting for subsistence was a priority (although not in the trader's eyes), a decade-long fight for a recognized reserve on the coast, and a perennial battle with the authorities over subsistence hunting, most notably the goose hunt. As recently as 1987, the newspapers carried accounts of the Cree hunters' battle to hunt geese for subsistence purposes (see *The Globe and Mail*, November 6, 1987). Region-wide concerns over proposed damming have also brought the Attawapiskat First Nation together, and closer to other Mushkegowuk First Nations to resist further White subjugation.

Other initiatives in Attawapiskat also demonstrate disengagement, although not necessarily related to the land. These include the presence of a Native police force on reserve, local control of education and, most recently, local control of the justice system beyond policing.

The process of encapsulation in Attawapiskat was one of increasingly formalized and restrictive actions on the part of Euro-Canadians. The fur trading companies and missionaries linked the Cree with larger White commercial and religious institutions, but these relationships were not, in any true sense, codified. Treaty 9 and the registered trapline system were inextricable links with the Canadian government and these were formal and codified. If politics is played out like a game, as Bailey suggests, then the Euro-Canadians set the rules by which the game would be played and the State sought to control the actions of the Cree.

The Cree, however, responded with their own forms of resistance to this intended encapsulation. These responses would become increasingly formal and sophisticated, paralleling the actions of the State. From the early days of making conscious decisions to trade with one trader over another, to the submitting of petitions in more recent years, the Cree would not merely give in to State demands.

However, the Attawapiskat people are very aware of the fact that change occurs, and part of this change involves continued and increased contact with White society. To this end, the economic initiatives that a number of them have been involved in necessitate, and indeed, invite, White participation. These include the selling of handicrafts, the goose camps and other proposed tourist developments. All of these involve continued use of the land, but on their terms. While there exists a dependency upon the government, the Attawapiskat Cree have also retained a strong relationship to their land. Attempts at encapsulation continue to be met with resistance.

CONTENT QUESTIONS

1. What four reasons are given for the perception held by a good number of Attawapiskat people that a low percentage of people still use the land?

2. What two remarkable observations were noted concerning the hunt for subsistence?

3. What forms of Cree resistance to encapsulation are discussed?

Afterword

The research for *Only God Can Own The Land* was conducted during 1989/90. The results of the research and analysis were submitted as a Ph.D. dissertation in anthropology at McMaster University under the title *Attawapiskat Cree Land Tenure and Use, 1901–1989*.

Since the initial research in 1989/90 a number of harvest studies, primarily by the TASO group (Research Program for Technology Assessment in Subarctic Ontario), have been conducted in the Mushkegowuk region. These confirmed the continued reliance upon the land by the Cree. Results of the TASO group's studies have been published in *Arctic* and as TASO Reports.

In 1993, I travelled to Attawapiskat to make a documentary film about the goose hunt. The goal was to explain to non-Natives how economically and culturally important the hunt is to the Cree. The film, *Attawapiskat Goose Hunt*, was completed in 1994 and shown at a number of academic conferences and film workshops. It has also been used in anthropology classes. In 2000, the Aboriginal Peoples Television Network (APTN) bought exclusive three-year broadcast rights to the film.

Attawapiskat has seen a number of changes. The community is growing rapidly and today the on-reserve population is about 1800. Construction has begun for an arena that will also house a gymnasium and dance hall. The region has taken over the control of the hospital, and the community is hoping to eventually have a resident physician. Three kilometres from the community there is a treatment centre for substance abusers. It welcomes people from across the country. Education remains very important. The school offers not only primary and secondary classes, but has an active adult education program.

People still rely on the land. Subsistence hunting is as strong, if not stronger, than ever. Trapping, however, has diminished dramatically, in part because the bottom has largely fallen out of the fur market. However, a much greater threat looms. Medium and high grade diamonds have been found along the Attawapiskat River. DeBeers, the diamond giant, expects to have government approval for what they are calling "The Victor Project" by 2003. If all goes according to plan, construction of an open pit mine will begin in 2004 and will be operational by 2005. The project is expected to have a mine life of 15 years. In addition to the mine itself, part of the project involves the construction of a 120-kilometre road through the heart of Attawapiskat territory. In July 2002, the Chief and Council terminated a Memorandum of Understanding, seeking to put the project on hold while the community conducted an internal and independent review of the project. The basis of their argument is the guarantee of hunting, fishing and trapping rights under Treaty 9, which are protected under Section 35 of the Constitution Act, 1982.

The people of Attawapiskat continue to meet encapsulation with resistance. May they prosper.

Bryan Cummins
August 25, 2002

Glossary

acculturation: changes to one or both cultures as a result of intensive, close contact between societies.

affinity: being related by marriage, instead of blood.

assimilation: the adoption by a minority group of the language, general culture and ethnic identity of the dominant group.

balanced reciprocity: a mode of exchange in which the giving and receiving are fairly specific in terms of the value of the goods and the time of their delivery. This typically occurs among people of roughly equal status, but who are not close kin.

bilocality (bilocal residence):   a pattern in which a married couple lives with or near either spouse's parents.

bride service: a designated period of time after marriage in which the groom works for the bride's family.

Coasters: Cree who generally stayed and made their living close to the coast of James Bay.

country food: items such as game, fish and berries harvested from the bush and consumed.

cross-cousin marriage: marriage to mother's brother's or father's sister's children.

egalitarianism: the societal ideal whereby each individual within a society has equal access to the resources of that society and in which there is no distinction in terms of social status, economics or political power.

encapsulation: the process in which a dominant society, through greater political resources, larger size and more complex political roles, subsumes a subordinate society.

ideology: a collection of interdependent ideas (including values, beliefs, myths and traditions) that serves to defend, rationalize and legitimize behaviours and practices of the group that holds the ideology.

Inlanders: Cree who generally made their living and remained mostly inland from the coast, making periodic trips to trade at the coast trading posts.

land tenure: the social relationships that condition land use.

land use: the physical exploitation of land by people.

macroband: a socio-political group usually comprising 10 to 15 families that typically occupy a river drainage.

matrilocality (matrilocal residence):   a pattern in which a married couple lives with or near the wife's parents.

microband: a socio-political group usually comprising two to five families and linked by kinship ties.

Mushkegowuk askii (Swampy Cree land):   an Algonkian term referring to the muskeg dominated region of northwestern Ontario occupied by the seven Cree communities of Winisk/Peawanuck, Attawapiskat, Kashechewan, Fort Albany, Moose Factory, New Post, and MoCreebec).

muskeg: a term from the Algonkian language family that translates literally as "grassy bog" and that refers to the soft, spongy landscape typical of the Hudson Bay Lowlands.

neolocality (neolocal residence):   a pattern in which a married couple establishes its household away from both the husband's and the wife's relatives.

nuclear family: a family unit comprising husband, wife and dependent children.

patrilocality (patrilocal residence):   a pattern in which a married couple lives with or near the groom's parents.

physical boundaries: tangible or visually identifiable markers, either natural (e.g., rivers or mountains) or human made (e.g., fences) that serve to separate one society from another.

reciprocity: an economic system, common among hunting and gathering peoples, which involves an exchange of goods or favours of roughly equal value.

registered trapline system: a government imposed system whereby the government sought to regulate trapping by establishing territories and licensing trappers.

resistance: the attempt, at both the individual and group level, of a minority group to limit or nullify the impact by a more dominant group.

self-enclosure: a form of resistance that occurs when a subjugated society minimizes its use of State channels but does not deviate from State regulations.

shaman: a part-time magico-religious specialist usually found in non-Western societies who is particularly adept at trance, divination and curing. The shaman derives his or her power directly from the supernatural with which he or she is able to establish contact.

shamanism: is the belief in the power of individuals, such as shamans, to manipulate spiritual forces for human ends.

social boundaries: culturally derived delineations such as language, religion and kinship that condition attitudes and behaviour concerning who belongs to a group and who does not.

References

A. BOOKS, MONOGRAPHS, ARTICLES, MANUSCRIPTS

Anderson, J. W. 1937. "Beaver Sanctuary." *The Beaver* (June).

Asch, Michael. 1977. "The Dene Economy." In *Dene Nation—The Colony Within*. Mel Watkins, ed. Toronto: University of Toronto Press.

Bailey, F.G. 1969. *Strategems and Spoils: A Social Anthropology of Politics*. New York: Shocken Books.

Berger, Thomas R. 1977. *Northern Frontier Northern Homeland: The Report of the MacKenzie Valley Pipeline Inquiry Volume 2*. Ottawa: Supply and Services Canada.

Bishop, Charles and Toby Morantz, eds. 1986. "Who Owns the Beaver." *Anthropologica* 28:1–2.

Bodley, John H. 1982. *Victims of Progress*. 2nd ed. Palo Alto: Mayfield Publishing Company.

Bodley, John H. 1983. *Anthropology and Contemporary Human Problems*. 2nd ed. Palo Alto: Mayfield Publishing Company.

Brody, Hugh. 1981. *Maps and Dreams*. Markham: Penguin Books.

Brown, Jennifer. 1980. *Strangers in Blood: Fur Trade Company Families in Indian Country*. Vancouver: University of British Columbia Press.

Canada. 1951. *Agency Report on Game Used By Indians on Reserves for Food During Year Ending March 31, 1951*. Indian Affairs (Regional Office, North Bay).

Canada. 1952. *Agency Report on Game Used by Indians on Reserves for Food During Year Ending March 31, 1952*. Indian Affairs (Regional Office, North Bay).

Canada. 1980. *Linguistic and Cultural Affiliations of Canadian Indian Bands*. Ottawa: Indian and Northern Affairs Canada.

Cooper, John M. 1933. "Is the Algonquian Family Hunting Ground System Pre-Columbian?" *American Anthropologist* 41(1):66–90.

Driben, Paul and Robert S. Trudeau. 1983. *When Freedom is Lost—The Dark Side of the Relationship Between Government and the Fort Hope Band*. Toronto: University of Toronto Press.

Dunning, Robert. W. 1959. *Social and Economic Change Among The Northern Ojibwa*. Toronto: University of Toronto Press.

Feit, Harvey. 1985. "Legitimation and Autonomy in James Bay Cree Responses to Hydro-Electric Development." In *Indigenous Peoples and the Nation State*. Noel Dyck, ed. St. John's: Institute of Social and Economic Research.

Feit, Harvey. 1986. "Hunting and the Quest for Power: The James Bay Cree and Whitemen in the Twentieth Century." In *Native People: The Canadian Experience*. R. Bruce Morrison and C. Roderick Wilson, eds. Toronto: McClelland & Stewart.

Flannery, Regina and M. Elizabeth Chambers. 1986. "John M. Cooper's Investigation of Family Hunting Grounds, 1927–1934." *Anthropologica* 28 (1–2):108–126.

Gardner, James S. 1981. "General Environment." In *Handbook of North American Indians Volume 6: Subarctic*. June Helm, ed. Washington: Smithsonian Institution.

Hansen, Lise C. 1989. *Indian Trapping Territories and the Development of the Registered Trapline System in Ontario*. Ontario: Ontario Native Affairs Directorate.

Henriksen, Georg. 1973. *Hunters in the Barrens: The Naskapi on the Edge of the White Man's World*. St. John's: Institute for Social and Economic Research.

Hoffmann, Hans. 1957. *Assessment of Cultural Homogeneity Among the James Bay Cree*. Ph.D. Dissertation. Yale University.

Hoffmann, Hans. 1960. "Culture Change and Personality Modification Among the James Bay Cree." *Anthropological Papers of the University of Alaska* 9(2):81–91.

Honigmann, John J. 1949. "Incentives to Work in a Canadian Indian Community." *Human Organization* 8(4):23–28.

Honigmann, John J. 1953. "Social Organization of the Attawapiskat Cree Indians." *Anthropos* 48(5–6):809–816.

Honigmann, John J. 1956. "The Attawapiskat Swampy Cree: An Ethnographic Reconstruction." *Anthropological Papers of the University of Alaska* 5(1):23–82. College.

Honigmann, John J. 1957. "Interpersonal Relations and Ideology in a Northern Canadian Community." *Social Forces* 35(4):365–370.

Honigmann, John J. 1958. "Attawapiskat—Blend of Traditions." *Anthropologica* 6(57–67). Ottawa.

Honigmann, John J. 1961. *Foodways in a Muskeg Community*. Canada. Department of Indian and Northern Affairs, Northern Co-ordination and Research Centre, Publication 62(1). Reproduced with the permission of the Minister of Public Works and Government Services Canada, 2002.

Honigmann, John J. 1966. "Social Disintegration in Five Northern Canadian Communities." *Canadian Review of Sociology and Anthropology* 2(4):199–214.

Honigmann, John J. 1981. "West Main Cree." In *Handbook of North American Indians Volume 6: Subarctic*. June Helm, ed. Washington: Smithsonian Institution.

Humphries, David. Personal communication.

Hutchins, Peter W. "The Law Applying to the Trapping of Furbearers by Aboriginal Peoples in Canada: A Case of Double Jeopardy." Unpublished ms.

Jenness, Diamond. *The Indians of Canada*. Anthropological Series 15. National Museum of Canada Bulletin 65. Ottawa.

Kupferer, Harriet J. 1988. *Ancient Drums, Other Moccasins: Native North American Cultural Adaptation*. Englewood Cliffs, N.J.: Prentice-Hall.

Leacock, Eleanor. 1954. *The Montagnais "Hunting Territory" and the Fur Trade*. American Anthropology Association Memoirs, no. 78, Vol. 56. Pt. 2.

Lee, Richard B. 1979. *The !Kung San: Men, Women and Work in a Foraging Society*. New York: Cambridge University Press.

Liebow, Elliot, and John Trudeau. 1962. "A Preliminary Study of Acculturation Among the Cree Indians of Winisk, Ontario." *Arctic* 15(3):191–204.

Lips, J. E. 1937 "Public Opinion and Mutual Assistance Among the Montagnais-Naskapi." *American Anthropologist* 39.

Long, John. 1978a. *Treaty No. 9—The Indian Petitions 1889–1927*. Cobalt: Highway Book Shop.

Long, John. 1978b. *Treaty No. 9—The Negotiations 1901–1928*. Cobalt: Highway Book Shop.

Louttit, Joseph. 1990. Personal communication.

Louttit, Reg. 1990. Personal communication.

Lundsgaard, Henry P., ed. 1974. *Land Tenure in Oceania*. Association for Social Anthropology in Oceania Monograph No. 2. Honolulu: University Press of Hawaii.

Martin, Lana. Personal communication.

Morantz, Toby. 1986. "An Historical Perspective on "Family Hunting Territories." *Anthropologica* 28:1–2.

Morrison, James. *Treaty Nine (1905–1906): The James Bay Treaty* (Treaty Research Report) Ottawa: Treaties and Historical Research Centre, Department of Indian and Northern Affairs Canada, 1986, p. 32. Reproduced with the permission of the Minister of Public Works and Government Services Canada, 2002.

Native Studies Review Vol. 5(2).

Nonas, Richard. 1963. *The Ever-Winking Eye: An Account of the Cree Indians of Attawapiskat, James Bay, and the Limitations of the Ethnographic Method*. M.A. thesis, University of North Carolina: Chapel Hill.

Preston, Richard. 1990. *The Mushkegowuk Cree: An Aid to Research, History to the 1960's*. Unpublished ms.

Preston, Richard. n.d. *From Beaver Preserve Co-management to MNR Registered Traplines*. Unpublished ms.

Preston, Richard. Personal communication.

Prevett, J. P., H. G. Lumsden, and F. C. Johnson. 1983. "Waterfowl Kill by Cree Hunters of the Hudson Bay Lowland, Ontario." *Arctic* 36(2):185–192.

Purich, Donald. 1986. *Our Land—Native Rights in Canada*. Toronto: James Lorimer and Company.

Ray, Arthur and Donald Freeman. 1978. *Give Us Good Measure*. Toronto: University of Toronto Press.

Ray, Arthur J. 1990. *The Canadian Fur Trade in the Industrial Age*. Toronto: University of Toronto Press.

Rodman, William. 1987. *Legal and Political Anthropology*. Unpublished ms.

Rogers, Edward S. 1963. *The Hunting Group—Hunting Territory Complex Among the Mistassini Indians*. Anthropological Series 63, National Museum of Canada Bulletin 195, Ottawa.

Rogers, Edward S. 1969. "Band Organization Among the Indians of Eastern Subarctic Canada." In *Contributions to Anthropology: Band Societies*. David Damas, ed. Ottawa: National Museum of Canada Bulletin 228.

Rogers, Edward S. 1972. "The Mistassini Cree." In *Hunters and Gatherers Today*. M. G. Bicchieri, ed. New York: Holt, Rinehart and Winston.

Rogers, Edward S. 1973. *The Quest for Food and Furs: The Mistassini Cree 1953–1954*. Ottawa: National Museums of Canada Publications in Ethnology, No.5.

Rushforth, Scott. 1977. "Country Food." In *Dene Nation—The Colony Within*. Mel Watkins, ed. Toronto: University of Toronto Press.

Scott, Colin. 1986. "Hunting Territories, Hunting Bosses and Communal Production in Coastal James Bay Cree Hunting." *Anthropologica* 28:1–21.

Smith, Bryan. Personal communication.

Speck, Frank. 1927. "Family Hunting Territories of the Lake St. John Montagnais and Neighbouring Bands." *Anthropos* 22:387–403.

Speck, Frank. 1931. "Montagnais-Naskapi Bands and Early Eskimo Distribution in the Labrador Peninsula." *American Anthropologist* 33(4):557–600.

Speck, Frank and Loren C. Eisley. 1939. "The Significance of Hunting Territory Systems of the Algonkian in Social Theory." *American Anthropologist* 41(2):269–280.

Tanner, Adrian. 1979. *Bringing Home Animals: Religious Ideology and Mode of Production of Mistassini Cree Hunters*. St. John's: Institute of Social and Economic Research.

Thompson, John E. and William H. Hutchison. n.d. "Resource Use by Native and Non-Native Hunters of the Ontario Hudson Bay Lowlands." Ontario: Ministry of Natural Resources. Copyright: 2002, Queens Printer Ontario.

Trudeau, Jean. 1966. *Culture Change Among the Swampy Cree Indians of Winisk, Ontario*. Unpublished Ph.D. dissertation. Washington: Catholic University of America.

Turner, David H. and Paul Wertman. 1977. *Shamattawa: The Structure of Social Relations in a Northern Algonkian Band*. Ottawa: National Museums of Canada, Canadian Ethnology Service Paper, No. 36.

Valentine, John. Personal communication.

Van Kirk, Sylvia. 1980. *Many Tender Ties—Women in Fur Trade Society, 1670–1870*. Winnipeg: Watson & Dyer Publishing, Ltd.

Vezina, Father Rodrigue, O.M.I. 1978. "Historical Notes on the Village of Attawapiskat, James Bay, Ontario." Unpublished ms.

Watkins, Mel, ed. 1977. *Dene Nation—The Colony Within*. Toronto: University of Toronto Press.

B. ARCHIVAL REFERENCES

1. Hudson's Bay Company Archives, Provincial Archives of Manitoba

A.74/10

A.74/11

A.74/23

A.74/45

A.74/46

A.74/47

A.74.48

A.74/49

A.74/50

A.74/51

A.74/53

B.243/a/1

B.243/a/2

B.243/a/3

B.243/a/4

B.243/a/5

RG3/2/7

2. National Archives Canada

RG 10, Volume 6961, 486/20-2

RG 10, Volume 6962, 486/20-2

RG 10, Volume 6963, File 486/20-2

RG 10, Volume 8620 1/1-15-15

3. Indian and Northern Affairs Canada-Treaty And Historical Research Centre Archival Material

File 486/30-5-91

File 44/20-4

File 44/20-4 (F)

File 44/20-4 (D1)

File 44/20-4 (A)

File 44/20-4 (D3)

File 44/20-4 (F)

File 44/30-1

File 44/30-5

File 44/30-5 (A)

File 44/30-4 (R.7)

4. Ministry Of Natural Resources (Ontario) Archival Material

Fur Harvest (Attawapiskat) 1971/72

Fur Harvest (Attawapiskat) 1981/82

5. Other Archival Material

John M. Cooper Papers, B. 7-9, "Indian Affairs Department, Canada". Catholic University Archives, Washington, D.C.

Index